THEORIES
of
MASS
COMMUNICATION

THEORIES
of
MASS
COMMUNICATION
Third Edition

Melvin L. De Fleur
Sandra Ball-Rokeach
WASHINGTON STATE UNIVERSITY

DAVID McKAY COMPANY, INC.   NEW YORK

International Standard Book Number: 0–679–30293–X

Library of Congress Catalog Card Number: 74–112656

Manufactured in the United States of America

Designed by Angela Foote

Contents

Preface

In the United States the study of mass communication has emerged as a full-fledged academic discipline in its own right. It has followed the general pattern set earlier by such disciplines as anthropology, economics, psychology, and sociology. Such social sciences broke formally with philosophy during the last century. By the beginning of the present century they were established as new scholarly disciplines in much the same way as is now the case with mass communication.

Several characteristics mark such rites of passage. First, of course, comes the accumulation of a scholarly literature with concepts, theories, and research findings devoted to problems confronting the new field. Generally speaking, this body of writing receives less serious attention from related disciplines until the scientific method becomes the basic epistemological approach to the adjudication of truth claims. Once science—as opposed to intuitive speculation, criticism, and more literary approaches—becomes the procedure by which new knowledge is developed and judged, the field moves more rapidly toward disciplinary status.

Early in the game, major contributions to the development of concepts, approaches, and research data are likely to come from persons in related disciplines who enter the field as a convenient arena for testing ideas more central to their own theoretical concerns.

At some point, a sufficient number of books, articles, and research reports are available so that formal programs of instruction can be offered in the new field. Gradually, these split into more specialized concerns, and the groundwork has been prepared for formal degrees in the field.

As these trends continue, pioneering universities establish not only degree programs in the new field but also departments and schools whose faculty share the common concerns. One of the most critical points in the history of a field of study on the way to disciplinary status is the granting of the Ph.D. with direct specialization in its problems. The recipients of these doctorates, in turn, staff the growing departments and gradually replace those drawn from related disciplines.

Concurrently, high-quality refereed journals are established as an outlet for research reports and scientific exchange. These are often sponsored by newly formed professional associations whose goal is to foster development of the new discipline. Such organizations intensify scientific reporting and exchanges through their annual conventions where papers are presented.

The result of all this is that the academic community

finds in its midst a group of formally organized colleagues who have staked out a given intellectual territory as their own. Often, some of the sillier aspects of science follow when conflicts are generated over proprietary anxieties, conflicting territorial claims, and so on. Cooler heads generally prevail, however, and the new discipline is welcomed for the contribution it can make to increasing our understanding of the human condition.

These steps can easily be traced in the movement of all the social sciences from parental sources to independent disciplines. They can now be seen as well in the field of mass communication. Like the rest of the specialized areas in the scientific community, its boundaries remain somewhat unclear; and discussion continues over what problems, methods, theoretical frameworks, and approaches are the most fruitful. This, of course, is true of even the most established science.

The characteristics that this field has had in the past are no sure guide to its future. The methodological and theoretical underpinnings of the growing discipline were forged in the behavioral sciences. Important substantive contributions have come from the communication arts and the several fields of applied communication. These various sources have yielded an amazingly diverse set of trends, specialized interests, subareas, and directions. In fact, the heterogeneity of the field has sometimes proved to be an embarrassment of riches. No one has been sure at any given time, or can be sure at the present time, precisely what constitutes the study of mass communication.

To some this diversity may represent confusion, or the inability of students of communication to make up their minds what they should study. But lay critics often make shallow judgments. Because of their own lack of understanding of the broadly interdisciplinary background and sources of the field, some have concluded that mass communication is hopelessly vague and befuddled not only as to its own boundaries, but in general as an area of academic study and research.

Heterogeneity undoubtedly exists, but it is superficial thinking indeed to conclude that investigators of mass communication have been less capable in their research, or more indecisive in choosing directions and modes of inquiry than individuals who have studied some other phenomenon. The diversity characteristic of this area of study arises because of the fundamental nature of the communication process itself, and the tremendous importance that mass communication plays in modern society. Students of human nature, whatever their disciplinary identification or theoretical orientation, cannot study human behavior without recognizing at the outset that communication processes are as vital to human beings as are biological processes. The latter permit them to function as living creatures; the former permit them to function as *rational* creatures. The principles of human communication, not the principles of biological functioning, most sharply distinguish human beings from other living organisms.

Moreover, interpersonal communication processes have been long recognized as essential to the formation and functioning of human groups both large and small. The modern urban industrial society could not exist as a social system without mass communication. It has become a deeply established part of every major social institution—political, economic, religious, educational, and familial—as these sociocultural patterns have taken shape in the advanced societies of the world.

If the field of mass communication seems widely inclusive, then, or if there does not seem to be any sharp line of demarcation that separates it from other fields which study social behavior, it is because mass communication occupies such a central place in the attentions of many related disciplines. As a result, it has developed many trends, many interests, and many directions. To conclude that this important area of knowledge should make its boundaries more rigid or should concentrate upon a narrower set of problems is simply to ignore the importance of the communication process to such a wide variety of interests. One can only hope that in its new disciplinary status mass communication will retain the flexibility it has had in the past.

Yet, in spite of the need for diversity and the advisability of keeping the boundaries of the field open-ended, there is a growing need to begin some type of theoretical integration. This does not imply that the interests of many fields should not be represented; it simply suggests that certain persistent problems seem to lie at the *center* of almost everyone's interest. Further systematic study of these common problems can best proceed by pulling together the ideas, concepts, and accumulated findings that now exist into some organized framework. Such integration would have the merit of pointing to those problems that have been most often studied and of suggesting lines of inquiry that will bring a more balanced theoretical perspective into the field in the future.

The present book is only a start in that direction. It is a modest start for several reasons, aside from the limitations of its authors. The field of mass communication has seen few attempts at sophisticated theory building, even with respect to highly focused topics. And no overall theoretical perspective of any integrative nature has been put forth. Despite the old adage about who rushes in where angels fear to tread, it is toward this goal that the present work is directed.

The intention of this book is to see the mass media within the context of society—with a special focus on American media and American society. Insofar as this can be done at this point in the development of the discipline, the book attempts not only to set forth theoretical perspectives on specific bodies of research, but also to pull these together into an overall pattern. Thus, the work first reviews the several media from the standpoint of theories of social and cultural change. Such theories focus on the processes of cultural accumulation, invention, and diffusion of innovations. The arrival and growth of the American media can be interpreted within such a framework. Once established in society, the media began to be the objects of analysis and research. These efforts drew upon several different intellectual backgrounds, and they came up with rather different explanations of the mass communication process.

A second and equally important goal of the present work is a purely selfish one, namely, to provide students with a guide and overview of the field of mass communication. Thus far, most publications in this field have been either books of readings or research monographs. With some notable exceptions, authors have seldom attempted to provide students with broad theoretical perspectives.

To some readers this book may seem heavily concerned with some important problems, but concerned very little with other problems of equal importance. This may be the case, but it was done intentionally. For example, considerable attention has been given to the historical development of the media in American society for two reasons. First, a theoretical problem of deep significance is concerned with the ways in which a society influences and determines the kind of mass media it eventually winds up with. Tracing the historical development of the media in a given society, with proper attention to the social, cultural, economic, and political events that shaped their directions of growth at given times, provides a fruitful way to understand the media of that society as they exist at present and to forecast the directions they are likely to take in the future. This can provide a framework for later comparisons between societies. Second, historical analyses of the media themselves within a given society *on a comparative basis between media* have not been widely reported. This has been attempted in the present volume. As we noted, the media are cultural innovations; they spread through societies according to the same principles as other cultural innovations. Furthermore, they influence one another in that process. Adequate analyses of these societal and intermedia influences have not been generally available for students in communication courses. The first chapters of the present book were prepared to meet this need for our own students; we sincerely hope that they will prove useful for others.

The book tries once again to portray the process of human communication. Many authors have tried their hand at this perplexing task. What the present analysis tries to do is to bring together the many ideas on this subject that have been advanced by writers from a variety of disciplines and points of view. The semanticists, symbolic interactionists, students of comparative animal behavior, mathematical model builders, and learning psychologists have all made important contributions to understanding human communication. The present analysis tries to present a *relatively simple* perspective on such communication, one which also includes a place for *mass* communication.

Extensive effort has been made to analyze the background and theoretical sources of the *mass* as a major concept in the study of "mass" communication. Much of the earlier thinking about the media focused upon a particular interpretation of that term. The older theories that rested upon this concept are posed as a background and point of departure for more comtemporary analyses. Although those older theories are of little substantive significance in explaining the media as they are now studied by communication researchers, they are still the basic orientation of the public.

In treating the more contemporary theories of mass communication, the present work does not attempt to summarize and report in great depth on the vast number of empirical studies of the "effects" of mass communication that have accumulated in the literature. This is not its basic purpose. Most instructors in communication courses make this a major part of their presentations. Also, excellent summaries already exist (such as those of Larsen or the more recent one of Weiss). For these reasons, we saw little need to retrace this ground. This does not mean that the relevance and importance of empirical research is not fully appreciated. It is in fact the matrix out of which theoretical integration of the field of mass communication will be achieved. For present purposes, however, only those studies that played a more or less central role in the development of a particular theoretical statement are noted.

The discussion of the mass media as social systems is intended to explore the use of functional analysis as a conceptual tool for portraying the mass communication process in a systematic way. Functional analysis as used in the present work is more of a means of describing the media within a particular perspective than a theory as such. The validity of the asserted propositions that pose systematic relationships between the components of the system remain to be demonstrated empirically. Despite this, it is heuristically useful in that it can give the student an appreciation of the stability inherent in the complex set of human relationships that make up the mass media of communication operating within a particular society.

The third edition also includes a chapter on the media and violence. This is done not so much because this rapidly growing body of research adds much to our overall theoretical knowledge, but because the issue itself is of central concern to the American public. Many people in our society, and agencies such as Congress, HEW, and others, see a frightening specter of unwanted media influence on the mental health of our nation and the overt behavior of its citizens. This view perpetuates many traditions of the past when the media were attacked repeatedly as sources of society's ills. The present book should enable the student to view such public concerns within a more sophisticated perspective.

Also included are attempts to look ahead. With communications technology accumulating more rapidly than ever, new media—or at least major modifications of present media—are bound to come. If the thesis of such pioneers as

Charles H. Cooley and Harold Innis is valid, that alterations of a society's communication capabilities and technologies bring social changes in their wake, then we can anticipate some of the trends we have in store.

Finally, the third edition in its concluding chapter attempts to pull together into an overall pattern the place that various more specific theoretical efforts will occupy in an integrated theory of mass communication. Such an integrated theory will have to be based upon several categories of variables. It will include those that describe individual behavior, societal structure and functioning, and the institutional arrangements of media systems within that society. The Dependency Theory, as set forth briefly in the final chapter, provides a means of fitting these parts together into a single pattern. We are the first to realize that such an attempt at overall integration of mass communication theory can at this point of time only map rather vaguely the shape such a theory will take as our empirical base of understanding the media in all its aspects becomes increasingly more adequate. Nevertheless, with mass communication now established as an academic discipline, the pace of movement toward that goal is quickening. It is our hope that the skeleton of theoretical integration set forth in this volume will take on increasing muscle and sinew as research on mass communication continues.

We would like to acknowledge the contributions of the many pioneers and contemporary students in this field from whom we have learned so much and upon whose ideas we have freely drawn: Paul Lazarsfeld, Elihu Katz, Joseph Klapper, Bernard Berelson, Edwin Parker, Morris Janowitz, Herbert Blumer, Otto Larsen, Harold Lasswell, Carl Hovland, and Robert Merton are but a few. To the many researchers, essayists, and other writers from the many fields that have built up the body of information accumulated to date, we express our respect.

Melvin L. De Fleur
Sandra Ball-Rokeach

1

MEDIA
and
SOCIETY

The origins of human speech
are lost in the mists of prehistory, but our most informed
guesses suggest that our remote ancestors were communicating animals living in small bands millions of years ago. At
some point, they began to use simple tools and to evolve a
primitive division of labor based on specialization of tasks.
Even then, we assume that communication played a key part
in defining the roles that people were expected to play in that
pattern of social organization and in transmitting the accumulating lore of the group to the next generation. Early
human beings, in other words, were probably as dependent

1

on communication to maintain their social structure and to socialize the young as we are today.

Languages developed into increasingly complex systems of symbols during succeeding eons, with few fundamental innovations other than slow changes in general structure, grammatical complexity, and vocabulary size. During this purely oral period, the communication process was limited to the face-to-face situation. Accuracy in transmitting to large numbers was limited to the ability of human beings to remember details correctly. A single person might address a multitude, but only if that multitude was collected together in an acoustically favorable location. Aside from this, such individuals could neither extend their ideas effectively across space, nor preserve them accurately through time.

It was not until writing appeared, less than 250 generations ago, that the concept of communication *media* could even be defined. Societies in the oral stage had no media—unless one would wish to include the air through which sound waves passed from mouth to ear. Perhaps one could say that such forms as animal representations painted on cave walls, pottery decoration, or even tattoos on the human body represented communication with "media." But if such phenomena are included as examples of communication media, then one would also have to make a place for representational dances and stylized rituals. Human beings, in other words, have been using the graphic and plastic arts for symbolic and representational purposes since they acquired speech. But such *pre-media*, and such pictorial or stylized art forms, need to be distinguished from the kinds of symbols as substitutes for words, phrases, and ideas that are used for what we would classify as writing.

The development of writing, which occurred independently and at different times in several areas of the world, appears closely related to discoveries in astronomy. For example, the early Egyptians were faced with the need to predict the behavior of the Nile River. The valley of the Nile was the only arable land they could use for agriculture. The Nile overflowed its banks every year, flooding the agricultural plain with rich new soil. The Egyptians discovered that certain star movements tended to coincide with the period of the flood. Eventually, they developed a calendar that reconciled lunar months with the solar year. Symbols and procedures for making calculations were devised in order to make calendrical predictions. These became a source of royal and religious authority.

The same was true at a later time in Central America when the Maya began to discover elaborate relationships between the growing seasons and movements of the sun, the moon, and the stars. Over a long period of time, they made astronomical observations and began to be able to predict the arrival of the rainy season and the best times for planting, harvesting, and other events. They symbolized the months and days in an elaborate code, and this provided the first step toward the development of written language. At first, pictorial symbols were used mainly to decorate tombs, temples, and monuments. These depicted the great power and authority of mighty people or gods. Once established, however, the pictorial writing method was extended, simplified, and stylized. Out of this came hieroglyphic writing.

From about 4000 B.C., Egyptians were recording the names of kings, accounts of wars, political events, and religious doctrines. These were still mainly carvings or decorations on stone. The Maya, at the other side of the world, independently developed hieroglyphic writing shortly after the birth of Christ. Similar events had taken place in China at an earlier time.

In ancient societies, the knowledge and power implied by the ability to use media—to read and write—was jealously guarded by great rulers and high priests. Literacy was a source of great power and prestige. This principle is illustrated well in the accounts of Diego de Landa, the great missionary and sixteenth-century scholar of the Maya.

> In the high priest was the key of their learning, and it was to these matters that they dedicated themselves. They taught the computation of the years, months, days, the festivals and ceremonies, the administration of the sacraments, the fateful days and seasons, their methods of divination and their prophesies, their events and the cures for disease, and their antiquities and how to read and write with the letters and characters ... along with the drawings which illustrate the meaning of the writings.[1]

Much the same situation prevailed in other places where writing was invented. Ordinary people could not read; they did not know how to calculate time nor how to interpret the almanacs. Such skills were reserved for the elite.

TRANSCENDING DISTANCE AND TIME

The earliest forms of writing beyond mere pictorial representation of words and ideas were in the form of elaborate glyphs. As we have noted, in its beginning such writing was generally restricted to stone carvings on temples and other monuments. The great problem here was that these "documents" were not very portable. Stone as a medium had the capacity to endure through *time,* but could not be transported readily across *space.* As ancient societies became more sophisticated, they sought media by which writing could be more easily transported.

About twenty-five hundred years before Christ, the

1. Frey Diego de Landa, *Relación de las Cosas de Yucatan,* ed. with notes by A. M. Tozzer, *Papers of the Peabody Museum,* vol. 18 (Cambridge, Mass., 1941). Original written in 1566.

Egyptians discovered a method of making a kind of durable paper from papyrus. Compared to stone, papyrus was extremely light. Moreover, it was much easier to write on papyrus with brush and ink than it was to chisel glyphs laboriously on stone. Papyrus is found only in the Nile delta. Fresh green stems of the reed are cut and stripped, sliced into thick strips, laid parallel to one another, and pounded until they weld into a single mass which is then pressed out and dried. Long rolls of considerable length can be prepared by joining one sheet to another. The scribe used two types of ink (black and red) and a brush made from another kind of plant. The glyphs began to be *simplified* as scribes required smoother, easier forms for faster writing.

Among the Maya, a similar transformation of media took place. They had discovered that long strips of light-colored bark could be pulled from the ficus tree. Long, clean strips of this inner bark, six to eight inches wide and as long as twenty feet, were removed from the trees. The strip was soaked in water and beaten to make it both uniform in thickness and pliable. The bark was then folded into a long, pleated, and very neatly trimmed book with wooden end pages to enclose it like an accordian. Hieroglyphic writing was painted on both sides, often beautifully decorated. The conquistadors were astonished to find people in the New World who lived in elaborate stone dwellings complete with libraries and books. During the conquest, thousands of these books were burned by the Spanish military in an effort to reduce the power of the priests and leaders over their people. Only a few examples remain.

The most important point in this change from heavy stone to light and portable media is that it opened the possibility for a significant change in the social organization and culture of society. The acquisition of a communications technology based upon a light and portable medium, plus a system of written symbols that could be produced quickly and read by scribes, provided necessary conditions for great social and cultural changes.[2] The whole institutional structure was influenced. For example, in Egypt by 2000 B.C., papyrus was widely used to transmit written orders and to record information of various kinds. The central administration employed an army of scribes. Literacy was a valuable skill, providing a kind of door-opener to prosperity and social rank. Scribes became a privileged class under the control of the elite. Great changes in political and religious institutions took place as a result of the ability to write and record. Libraries opened. Religious doctrines and scriptures were recorded. Schools were established to teach scribes. Even the arts and sciences began to develop. Successful treatments for diseases could be written down. Observations of numerous features of nature and their interpretations could be recorded. The human mind was freed from the burdensome task of having to remember entire cultures and reproduce them in the minds and memories of every new generation. Ideas could be stored, accumulated, and drawn upon by subsequent generations. This was the great step forward provided by the ancient communication revolutions.

THE SOCIAL MEANING OF PRINTING

Other transformations took place when still newer media arrived. Paper began to replace papyrus and parchment in the Islamic world during the eighth century. It slowly diffused to Christian Europe. However, the spread of written communication beyond priests, political elites, scholars, and scribes did not take place until the invention of the printing press in the fifteenth century. Movable type and presses began to be used to turn out multiple copies of books that

2. An excellent discussion of media and change in ancient societies is found in Harold A. Innis, *Empire and Communications* (Toronto: University of Toronto Press, 1972); see esp. p. 14.

could be read by persons literate in their own language. The availability of these books spurred broader interest in literacy.

For the first time in Germany, for example, the Scriptures were available—from the press of Johannes Gutenberg—in a language other than Latin. No longer could the Roman Church carefully guard the holy writings through the use of an ancient language. The availability of the Scriptures to ordinary people in their own languages eventually led to challenges of the authority and interpretations of Rome. A new medium of communication, then, opened the way for protesting the existing religious and social structure. The rise of Protestantism led to further profound changes that have had their impact on Western society right up to the present day.

In the twentieth century, a great variety of new media have emerged within society. Our historical perspective would lead us to hypothesize that they would produce still further changes in society and in the lives of individuals. Indeed, this has been the case. Motion pictures, radio, the modern newspaper, magazines, and television bring the ordinary citizens deeply into the communication process. It is a challenging task to discover the contemporary implications of new media.[3]

The basic idea of a newspaper developed quite early on the European continent, in England, and in the new United States. The American colonial press was established for some years before the new nation was formed, distributing small papers and pamphlets to the educated elite. Their content was, as we shall see in chapter 2 in more detail, at a level of sophistication and taste beyond the capacities of the common citizen.[4] They did provide, however, the basic form around which to develop a new kind of newspaper aimed at

3. For an excellent analysis of such changes, see Daniel Lerner, *The Passing of Traditional Society* (New York: Free Press, 1958).
4. Edwin Emery, *The Press and America* (Englewood Cliffs, N.J.: Prentice-Hall, 1972).

the broad base of artisans, mechanics, and merchants who constituted the growing middle and working classes of the emerging urban-industrial society. When a means was found to finance a cheap paper for wide distribution, and the techniques were devised for rapid printing and distribution, the first true *mass* medium was born in the form of the penny press. These events occurred in the mid-1830s in the city of New York. The mass newspaper was a great success, and within a very few years it spread to many parts of the world. The third decade of the nineteenth century, then, saw the technology of rapid printing and the basic idea of a newspaper combined into the first true *mass* medium of communication.

Two points are important in these events. First, the mass newspaper, like the other media that followed it, was an invention that occurred only after a complex set of cultural elements had appeared and accumulated within the society. Second, like almost all inventions, it represented a combination of these elements in a social setting that permitted the acceptance and widespread adoption of the newspaper as a culture complex. As a technical device, it was consistent with, and perhaps even required by, other cultural institutions of the day. The relevant institutional structure of the society in terms of economic, political, and educational processes, as well as demographic and ecological patterns, provided a setting within which the particular combination of elements represented by the penny press could emerge and flourish.

With the appearance and acceptance of the mass press, the pace of human communicative activity began to increase sharply. By midcentury the telegraph became a reality. Although not a *mass* medium of communication, this device was again an important element in a technological accumulation that would eventually lead to mass electronic media. A few decades later, experiments were being carried out successfully that were prerequisite to motion pictures and to wireless telegraphy. With the dawn of the twentieth century, Western society was about to experience the development of techniques of communication that had been beyond the wildest flights of imagination a century earlier. During the first decade of the new century, motion pictures became a form of family entertainment. This was followed in the 1920s by the development of household radio and in the 1940s by the beginnings of home television. By the early 1950s, radio had reached saturation penetration in American homes, with additional sets widely dispersed in automobiles. There was multiple penetration in the form of bedroom and kitchen radios, and a growing number of transistorized miniature sets. The late 1950s and early 1960s saw television beginning to approach such saturation. By the 1970s it was virtually complete in the United States and progressing rapidly elsewhere. Mass communication had become one of the most significant and inescapable facts of modern life.

This brief sketch of major milestones in the ability of people to communicate shows two major facts. First, communication "revolutions" have been occurring throughout human history. Each new medium provided a means by which significant changes could be brought about in the organization of society and in the accumulation of culture. Second, the rise of mass media—the most recent communication revolution—has in large part occurred very recently. Many of its major events have taken place within the lifetimes of substantial segments of the American population. Many people alive today can recall a society without radio. For our oldest generation there were no motion pictures to see on Saturday nights during their youth. Each of these media added to the total daily availability of language-using opportunities for the average person. Thus, the accumulation of these devices within recent history has implied a dramatic increase in the pace of communicative behavior for the majority of people in Western society; a fundamental change, the impact of which remains to be fully assessed.

The entrance of the newspaper, the radio receiver, or the television set into the ordinary citizen's home represents a technological change that has greater significance for ordinary people than our largest accomplishments at the frontiers of science. With spacecraft streaking through space, we may lose sight of the fact that these achievements are remote from the routine daily activities of the majority of us. The television set, however, is a technological device that has an immediate and direct impact. The children of our society spend more than twenty hours a week, on the average, viewing its offerings. The television set and the other media at the very least are innovations around which human beings organize their lives in different patterns because of their presence.

Although communication research scholars have not reached a full understanding of the impact that these media are having upon the psychological, moral, economic, political, creative, cultural, or educational aspects of the ordinary individual's life, they have begun to accumulate a base of research findings that will increasingly aid in understanding these issues. The growth of the social sciences as disciplines employing quantitative procedures and the logic of science, like the development of the mass media themselves, has occurred principally within the present century. Within that brief span, a limited number of sociologists, psychologists, journalists, media specialists, and others have specialized in the dispassionate study of the role of the mass media within our society. As larger numbers of research specialists turn their attentions to this field, we may expect the generalizations growing out of such research to yield more complete understanding of the relationship between the mass media and the societies within which they operate. In large part, discussions as to that relationship have been carried on in the past within something other than a dispassionate and objective framework. As each of the major media of communication emerged in our society, it became the object of considerable controversy and debate. These debates began when the first issue of the penny press hit the streets of New York in 1834. They continue today with respect to the role of radio, paperback books, television, comic books, magazines, and films in relation to a variety of issues.

One of the major tasks of students of mass communication in assessing this latest communication revolution, and the controversies it has caused, is to accumulate scientific findings concerning the impact of the media on their audiences. We must replace emotional speculation with valid evidence as a basis for public discussion about mass communication. The different media have variously been charged with responsibility for (1) lowering the public's cultural tastes, (2) increasing rates of delinquency, (3) contributing to general moral deterioration, (4) lulling the masses into political superficiality, and (5) suppressing creativity. This is a damning list, and if the apparently innocent devices in our living rooms are actually guilty of such monstrous influences, they should, of course, be viewed with alarm. The problem is that advocates of opposite points of view tell us that our newspapers, radios, television sets, and the like, are not insidious devices for evil, but are in fact our faithful servants or even saviors in that they are (1) exposing sin and corruption, (2) acting as guardians of precious free speech, (3) bringing at least some culture to millions, (4) providing harmless daily entertainment for the tired masses of the urban industrial labor force, (5) informing us of the world's events, and (6) making more bountiful our standard of living by their unrelenting insistence that we purchase and consume products to stimulate our economic institution. If such claims are true, to reject such benefactors or even to suggest that their content is uninspiring seems an act of flagrant ingratitude. Until reliable research findings can present a convincing case that the media either are or are not *causally* related to the claims of their critics (or champions), these controversies will continue to rage.

A second task for the student of communication is to identify the basic nature of the communicative act. A general theory of human communication (mass or otherwise) remains to be worked out. Many promising leads are available from general semantics, social psychology, the study of learning, and so forth. As yet, however, no comprehensive theory has been advanced that incorporates the many isolated but well-validated propositions available from such disciplines into a systematic explanation of human communication in general. The place of mass communication within such a conceptual scheme, of course, will remain a continuing problem until such a theoretical framework has been developed.

Another major task for those who specialize in the scientific study of the media is to provide adequate data with which to evaluate the consequences of operating mass communication systems under varying conditions of ownership or control. That is, within differing political structures, economic systems, and historical-cultural settings, the structure of the mass media themselves can be expected to take different forms. The production, distribution, and consumption of mass media content is sharply influenced by questions such as whether or not the society is a free-enterprise democracy, an outright totalitarian dictatorship, or something in between. Societies where mass communication systems operate under conditions of ownership and control quite different from those of the United States can provide a basis for comparative research. Similarly, studies of the historical development of particular media in particular societies offer possibilities of inducing generalizations about the way in which the various forms of the mass media have developed under different sociocultural conditions.

The assessment of the meaning of the most recent communication revolution, then, centers around three broad but fundamental questions:

1. What has been the impact of societies on their mass media? What have been the political, economic, or

cultural conditions which have led them to operate in their present form?

2. How does mass communication take place? Is mass communication a separate phenomenon from other types of communication? Does it differ in principle or only in detail from more direct interpersonal communication?

3. What has been the impact of the mass media upon society? What influences have they had on the psychological processes, overt behaviors, or cultures of the people among whom they have flourished?

For several reasons, it is to the third question that the majority of mass communication research has in the past been addressed. The first question, although of central significance, has not captured much of the attention of research specialists and scholars. To some degree, the same is true of the second question. It appears likely, since the storm of criticism and controversy surrounding the media has been phrased largely in terms of the third of these fundamental questions, that communication researchers have been guided in their investigations less by theoretical significance than by the dictates of popular interest. Whatever the reasons for this lack of balance between these three issues, the first and second questions have received considerably less scholarly attention than the third. In several of the chapters that follow, special attention is given to discussions of ways in which the social and cultural conditions in the United States have had a role in shaping our mass media. An attempt is also made to pull together what we now know about the nature of the communicative act. In addition, considerable attention is given to the third question.

What of the future? Can we assume that the final forms of mass communication have already been invented and adopted? If the past is even the crudest guide to the future, the answer must be an emphatic *no!* No industry seemed more secure and no medium seemed more ubiquitous than radio during the late 1930s and the 1940s. The same was true of the powerful motion-picture industry. Before the advent of television, these two media appeared as unassailable. But when television diffused widely during the 1950s both of these older media experienced declining audiences and severe economic problems. In decades to come, within our own lifetimes, the development of communication technology will continue at an increasing pace. The sociological principle that a society's rate of invention increases geometrically as its technological culture base increases arithmetically indicates that our present television sets, transistorized portable radios, and superspectacular movies will soon seem as obsolete as the Model T Ford. While the exact forms of the new media to come cannot be predicted, the conclusion that they will inevitably arrive seems inescapable. Although only the dim outlines of some of these changes can be seen now, we can confidently say that there will be more communication revolutions to come.

2
SOCIETY
and the
MASS PRESS

The first of the basic questions posed for analysis in the previous chapter is the most logical starting point for a contemporary assessment of the current communication revolution. We may begin, then, by asking what has been the impact of the American society as a social and cultural system on the development of its mass media of communication? The mass media as they exist today in our particular society have a somewhat unique structure of control, a particular set of institutionalized norms relating them to their audiences and readers, and characteristic forms of content. They have worked out specific types of financial support and clearly defined relationships to other important social institutions such as government. They have all experienced in greater or lesser degree a somewhat repetitive set of problems associated with conflicts between their goals and the goals, aspirations, and hopes of those whose cultural tastes and educational backgrounds are substantially higher than those of the common citizen. Finally, their developmental patterns, in terms of their quantitative spread as innovations through the society and in terms of general problems encountered during their institutionalization as culture complexes, have been rather similar from one medium to another.

Each of the media was, from the point of view of the ordinary family, a new device that could be adopted or rejected as a form of technology within the home or at least as an innovation requiring the family to adopt new modes of behavior. The sociological principles governing the adoption of innovation by individuals and families are becoming increasingly understood. While the mass media today are intimately involved in the stimulation of innovative behavior, they can also be viewed as innovations themselves. A study of their adoption patterns as well as the social and cultural variables related to their spread can reveal some of the ways in which a society can significantly influence and shape its mass media.

We need not go far back in history to talk about a society without mass media. For more than half a century after the original thirteen colonies had declared their independence from England, there was no true mass press to bring news to the average person. There were limited-circulation newspapers, to be sure, but these tended to differ sharply in their content, cost, audience, method of distribution, and size of circulation from the later mass readership papers. Motion pictures and broadcasting (both radio and television) have long technical histories; but as devices playing a part in the communication behavior of the average family, they are innovations of the present century.

A full understanding of how our various media came into being at the particular times they did requires considerably more than a mere listing of inventions of technical apparatus along with a few dates and names. The historical study of the mass media within any societal context, for the purpose of establishing recurrent patterns that have appeared during their growth, requires that attention be focused upon the three important questions: (1) What technological elements or other cultural traits accumulated in what pattern to be combined into new culture complexes such as the mass newspaper, film, radio, or television industry? (2) What were the social and cultural conditions of the society within which this accumulation took place and how did these conditions create a climate favorable for the emergence and widespread adoption of the innovation? (3) What have been the patterns of diffusion of the innovations through the society, and what sociological conditions have been related to their rates and patterns of growth?

Obviously, all complex questions of this kind cannot adequately be answered within two or three chapters of one small book. Such issues require the extended attention of investigators with different perspectives from the various social sciences and scholars devoted to the study of each particular communication medium as well. Our task, then, is to sketch briefly the highlights of these historical developments in an attempt to illustrate, within the context of the American society, the impact a society can have in shaping its mass media. We will summarize very briefly some of the major events and social forces that have been associated with the development of each of the larger media of communication within the United States. Beginning with the press, newspapers, motion pictures, radio, and television will be discussed within the framework of the three questions noted above.

THE MASS PRESS

The basic culture traits that were later to be combined into a mass newspaper extend far back into history. The modern newspaper is a combination of elements from many societies and from many periods of time. Even before the birth of Christ the Romans posted newssheets called *acta diurna* in public places. The Chinese and Koreans were using movable type and paper for printing several centuries before these appeared in Europe. In the sixteenth century, well after printing had come to Europe, the Venetian government printed a small newssheet which could be purchased for a *gazeta* (a small coin). The use of the word "gazette" to refer to newspapers has survived to this day. Something closer to our modern idea of a newspaper appeared in the early 1600s in Germany. Scholars of the history of journalism suggest that many features of the modern newspaper, such as the editorial, sports articles, illustrations, political columns, and even comics were used in one place or another long before the true mass press came into being.

Printing was introduced to England in the late 1400s, but it was not until 1621, nearly a century and a half later, that early forerunners of the newspaper began to appear. These were called *corantos*. Their content focused on foreign intelligence, and they were not published regularly as was the case with actual newspapers that came later. From the beginning, the publication of corantos was strongly regulated by the goverment. The seventeenth century in general was one of close regulation, or attempted close regulation, of all forms of printing. One of the interesting patterns discernible in the history of the press is that in societies with strong central governments, an unregulated press tended to grow only very slowly. In areas where centralized authority was weak, the press tended to develop under less control and to advance more rapidly. In a general way the greater the extent to which a form of government is actually dependent upon favorable public opinion, the more likely it is to support a free press. Where the common people play significant roles in the determination of their own political destiny, the distribution of news and political opinions is an important process. Strong monarchies, or societies with other forms of highly centralized power, do not require active public discussion of issues about which every citizen must reach an informed decision.

The long struggle to establish the important principle of freedom of the press was fought during a period when the older feudal monarchies were beginning to decline, and new concepts of political democracy were on the rise. Such considerations immediately suggest that one of the most significant changes in Western society, favoring the development of some form of mass communication, was the changing political institution that eventually vested voting power in the majority of citizens. This long and complex change established traditions of journalism which from the very beginning made the newspaper an arena of public debate, partisan protest, and political comment. By the time the other major media emerged, this political transformation had been substantially achieved and neither motion pictures nor the broadcast media, in the United States at least, have developed the deep interest in politics that has long characterized the press. These variables and factors have obviously been related in different patterns in other countries.

During the period before the seeds of the American and French revolutions began germinating, the whole fabric of Western society was undergoing change. The Dark Ages had given way to the Renaissance, and the ancient feudal society with its rigid stratification pattern was slowly being replaced by a new social structure within which a strong middle class would be a key element. These changes were inseparable from the growth of commercialism that eventually culminated in the industrial revolution itself. This commercialism was to be dependent upon improvement in the availability of various kinds of communication media. Techniques were sorely needed to coordinate manufacturing, shipping, production of raw materials, financial transactions, and the exploitation of markets.

Rapid, long-distance media would be slow in coming. Meanwhile, the rising middle class itself began to constitute an *audience,* not only for the latest information about commercial transactions, but also for political expression, essays, and popular literary fare. In England, these needs were met by such skilled writers and journalists as Addison, Steele, Samuel Johnson, and Daniel Defoe. In the American colonies a middle class with commercial interests developed rapidly. New England was a land of ships, seaports, and trade of all kinds. During the first part of the eighteenth century a number of small newspapers were published. Many were financial failures, but some survived over a period of years. Their circulations were never large, usually well under a thousand. By the time the Declaration of Independence was written, there were about thirty-five of these small and crudely printed newspapers in the thirteen colonies. For the most part, their publishers eked out a precarious existence by selling their newspapers on a subscription basis (they were relatively expensive) and by carrying a few commercial announcements. If the publisher happened to be a postmaster, or could land a government printing contract to help out, the financial risk was not so great.

The colonial press, as these papers are collectively called, was edited and published by people who were not great literary figures with the exception of notable American colonial journalists such as the remarkable Benjamin Franklin. They were still using basically the same printing technology that had been used by Gutenberg three centuries earlier. They did not have a mass audience with widespread reading skills. There were large concentrated urban centers that could serve as markets, and they lacked an adequate basis upon which to finance a mass press. However, a complex array of culture traits had accumulated in the society, including elementary printing technology, private ownership of newspapers, and, as was mentioned, the principle of freedom of the press.

Before a true mass press could develop, a series of sweeping social changes was necessary in Western society. The changing political roles of the common citizen have already been mentioned. Also noted was the growth of commercialism, which led to changing patterns of social stratification and the rise of the middle class. To these can be added the necessary development of printing and paper technology, which increased its tempo with the mechanical advances of the early industrial revolution. Finally, when mass public education became a reality with the establishment of the first statewide public school system (in Massachusetts) during the 1830s, the stage was set for a combination of these many elements into a newspaper for the common people.

A number of printers and publishers had experimented with the idea of a cheap newspaper that could be sold not by yearly subscription but by the single copy to the urban masses. Various approaches to this problem were tried both in England and in the United States, but without success. It remained for an obscure New York printer, Benjamin H. Day, to find a successful formula. His little paper, the *New York Sun,* began modestly enough on September 3, 1833, with the motto "It shines for ALL." All subsequent events proved, it did indeed shine for all. Day had begun a new era in journalism that within a few years would revolutionize newspaper publishing.

The *Sun* emphasized local news, human interest stories, and even sensational reports of shocking events. For example, to add spice to the content, Day hired a reporter who wrote articles in a humorous style concerning the cases brought daily before the local police court. This titillating content found a ready audience among the newly literate working classes. It also found many critics among more traditional people in the city. The paper was sold in single copies for a penny in the streets by enterprising newsboys. These boys soon established regular routes of customers; and circulation rose to 2000 in only two months. The breezy style and vigorous promotion of the paper shot this figure up to 5000 in four months and to 8000 in six months. The astonishing success of this controversial paper had the rest of the newspaper publishers in an uproar. By this time the steam engine had been coupled to the new rotary press. The famous Hoe cylinder press was available in the United States, along with abundant supplies of cheap wood-pulp newsprint. The technical problems of producing and distributing huge numbers of newspapers on a daily basis had largely been solved, and the emergence of the mass press was an accomplished fact.

The *Sun* attracted its impressive circulation primarily by appealing to new readers who had not previously been reached by a newspaper. One of the most important features of Day's penny paper, and of those that followed it, was the redefinition of "news" to fit the tastes, interests, and reading skills of this less-educated level of society. Up to that time, "news" generally meant reports on social or political events of genuine importance, or of other happenings that were of widespread significance. Benjamin Day, however, filled his paper with news of another sort—accounts of crimes, stories of sin, catastrophe, and disaster—news the people in the street found exciting, entertaining, or amusing. His staff even invented an elaborate hoax, concerning new "scientific discoveries" of life on the moon. When the hoax was exposed by another paper, his readers took it in good humor because it had been fun to read about. The paper was vulgar, cheap, and sensational; it was aimed directly at the newly literate masses who were beginning to participate in the spreading industrial revolution. There was some serious material in the paper to be sure, but its editorials and reports of political and economic complexities were much more superficial than in the earlier partisan papers written for more politically sophisticated readers. By 1837, the *Sun* was distributing 30,000 copies daily, more than the combined total of all New York daily papers when the penny paper was first brought out.

Imitators of Day had started rival papers almost immediately. The penny press was a financial success because it had great appeal for advertisers. In fact, advertising revenues were its only real support; the penny for which it was sold could scarcely pay for the raw newsprint. But goods and services for mass consumption could be successfully advertised through the penny press. These advertisements reached huge numbers of potential customers much more successfully than those appearing in the preceding limited-circulation newspapers. Patent medicines, "for man and beast," were one such mass-use product that played a prominent part in supporting the new penny papers. Early department stores also took readily to the newspaper as a means for publicizing their wares.

For such advertisers, size of circulation was thought to be a good index of the amount of profit one could anticipate. The newspaper that could place an advertising message before tens of thousands attracted the advertising dollar. This simple principle set into motion rugged competition between rival papers for new readers. This had important implications for the development of the popular press during the latter half of the nineteenth century, and indeed had implications for mass media that would not even be invented until a full century later! The foundations of an important institutionalized pattern of social relationships, which linked advertiser, media operators, and audience into a functional system for the production of particular types of mass communicated content, were worked out in the early years of the development of the mass press.

Meanwhile, Benjamin Day's most colorful and successful competitor was James Gordon Bennett, who founded a newspaper empire on only $500 in a barren office in a cellar. Bennett, a shrewd and tough Scot, started the *Herald* in New York. He flouted the conservative moral norms of the time and published flaming news accounts of murder trials, rape, sin, and depravity. At the same time, he reported effectively on politics, financial matters, and even on the social affairs of high society. This variety of content gave his *Herald* a wide appeal and made it a strong financial success. Bennett himself made many enemies with his forceful and often scandalous newspaper articles. For example, in 1836 he wrote:

> Books have had their day—the theatres have had their day—the temple of religion has had its day. A newspaper can be made to take the lead in all of these in the great movements of human thought and of human civilization. A newspaper can send more souls to Heaven, and save more from Hell, than all the churches or chapels in New York—besides making money at the same time.[1]

Although Bennett's startling prediction did not come true, the newspaper was about to begin its spread through the American society and to start playing an increasingly important part in its daily affairs.

THE PERIOD OF RAPID DIFFUSION

Although the mass newspaper arrived in the 1830s, it was still limited in terms of news gathering, printing technology, and distribution. Before it could diffuse widely into the homes of every American city, a number of important problems remained to be solved. The decades just preceding the Civil War were filled with important mechanical, scientific, and technical developments that were to make it possible for the infant mass newspaper to grow into a giant. Railroads were built between the principal cities in the eastern part of the nation. The steamboat arrived as a major transportation link after about 1840. The telegraph grew increasingly useful as a means for rapid transmission of news from the scenes of important events to editorial offices. These developments substantially increased the newspaper's appeal to its readers and increased the number of people to whom newspapers could be distributed.

1. Eric Barnouw, *Mass Communication* (New York: Rinehart, 1956), p. 7.

More and more, newspapers began to seek out the new
The role of reporter grew more complex and specialized as
papers added foreign correspondents and special news gatherers of various kinds. Reporters were sent to the scenes
of battles; others were permanently stationed in Washing-
tion, D.C., to cover political events. The "surveillance" function of the press became well established.[2]

The rising demand for fresh news was met by newly
formed cooperative news-gathering agencies, which made
use of the telegraph wires. These agencies sent stories to
papers in many parts of the country with which they had
contractual arrangements. Through such agreements, the
staff of a paper near an event could cover the story for many
papers elsewhere, thereby greatly reducing the cost of news
gathering. These advances brought the newspaper to the
smaller cities and towns and even to the newly established
cities in the West.

Printing technology was making rapid strides, moving
toward ever-increasing automation. Revolving presses, with
print cast in a solid lead stereotype, became capable of rolling
out ten and even twenty thousand sheets an hour.

The Civil War brought maturity of a sort to the newspaper as it reinforced the concept that the paper's principal
function is to gather, edit, and report the news. The older
concept of the paper as primarily an organ of partisan political opinion had faded considerably. The post-Civil War
papers increasingly clarified their roles as locators, assem-
blers, and purveyors of the news. This is not to suggest that
newspapers become either uninterested or nonpartisan with
respect to politics—quite the opposite. Individual editors
and publishers often used their newspapers to champion
causes of one kind or another and to wage "crusades" against
political opponents. But at the same time, they were all heavily involved in straightforward reporting of the news.

2. For an excellent summary of functions of mass communication today,
including "surveillance," see Charles R. Wright, *Mass Communication: A Sociological Perspective* (New York: Random House, 1959), pp. 17–23.

Papers continued to gain in popularity. In 1850 there were about two copies of a daily newspaper purchased in the United States for every ten families. The rate of growth of newspaper circulations increased steadily, but not spectacularly, until the 1880s. During the two decades 1890–1910, however, the rate of newspaper circulation per household rose sharply. This rapid growth actually continued until about the time of World War I, and then tended to level off during the 1920s. But, the last decade of the nineteenth century is one of special significance in the growth of the press because it was the beginning of a new kind of journalism. While this new journalism did not become permanently established, it left its mark on the American newspaper. Let us look in greater detail at this development because it is of importance for understanding patterns in the development of later mass media as well.

YELLOW JOURNALISM

While the newspaper was growing up, the second half of the nineteenth century was for American society a period of rapid change, upheaval, and transition. It was an era characterized simultaneously by an expanding frontier, a devastating Civil War and its aftermath, the arrival of wave after wave of immigrants, a pronounced rural to urban movement, and an increasingly rapid transition to an industrial society. Any one of these changes could have fundamentally altered the basic social organization of the society. Their combined effect was even more deeply felt. New norms replaced old; firmly established mores were cast aside; a traditional way of life gave way to a new type of social order. If ever a society was in a state of cultural upheaval and transition, it was American society during the five-decade period of the last half of the nineteenth century.

This was the social context within which the mass press spread and matured. Against this background of cultural conflict and anomie, the new medium had to devise and institutionalize the basic codes that would regulate its responsibilities to the public it served, and would place limits upon the kind of content it contained. With the normative structure of the society itself in a state of turmoil, it is not surprising that the mass press was able to work out its "canons of journalism" only after a rather stormy period of adolescence.

One of the most dramatic episodes in the development of the press was the period of "yellow journalism." By the 1880s, the newspaper had achieved wide adoption by American households, and further astronomical increases in circulation was increasingly difficult to stimulate. At the same time, the press was firmly established financially as long as the number of newspapers sold could be kept at a maximum. Within this competitive context, brutal struggles for additional readers developed between the leaders of giant rival papers. In New York, in particular, William Randolph Hearst and Joseph Pulitzer fought by any means available to expand their circulation figures. These were, of course, the key to increased advertising revenues and profits. Various features, devices, gimmicks, styles, and experiments were tried by each side to make its paper more appealing to the mass of readers. Newspapers today contain many of the devices that were actually products of the rivalries of the 1890s. (One of these was color comics. An early comic character was called the "Yellow Kid," from which "yellow journalism" is said to derive its name.)

As the competition intensified into open conflict, the papers turned more and more to any sensationalistic device that would attract additional readers, no matter how shallow and blatant. In the early 1890s yellow journalism burst full blown upon the American public:

> ...the yellow journalists...choked up the news channels upon which the common man depended,

with a callous disregard for journalistic ethics and responsibility. Theirs was a shrieking, gaudy, sensation-loving, devil-may-care kind of journalism which lured the reader by any possible means. It seized upon the techniques of writing, illustrating and printing which were the prides of the new journalism and turned them to perverted uses. It made the high drama of life a cheap melodrama, and it twisted the facts of each day into whatever form seemed best suited to produce sales for the howling newsboy. Worst of all, instead of giving its readers effective leadership, it offered a palliative of sin, sex and violence.[3]

Yellow journalism offended a sufficient number of groups and individuals so that a storm of criticism gradually made clear to the operators of the mass press that they had exceeded the limits which the society, and particularly representatives of the norm-bearing institutions, would tolerate. Intellectuals in general and the literati in particular were deeply wounded. The great new means of communication, which held forth the tantalizing potential of mass cultural and moral uplift, had in their eyes turned out to be a monstrous influence for societal degeneration.

Leaders in religion, education, law, and government increasingly voiced strong protests. The press lords were faced with the threat of losing public confidence, and the even more chilling possibility of regulation imposed from without. These considerations led a number of major publishers to begin to put their own houses in order. Gradually, the press became less sensational and more responsible. A set of codes and norms defining its limits and responsibilities gradually became increasingly clear. Professional associations of editors and publishers established canons of journalism intended to guide their members. While the mass press today varies substantially in its degree of adherence to such codes,

3. Edwin Emery and H. L. Smith, *The Press and America* (New York: Prentice-Hall, 1954), pp. 415–16.

the excesses of yellow journalism appear to be a thing of the past. Out of these experiences of the newspaper came a number of institutionalized principles which in one way or another have helped clarify the roles, responsibilities, and policies of media that followed. The way in which this has been the case will be made clear in later sections.

QUANTITATIVE DIFFUSION PATTERN OF THE MASS PRESS

Data on newspaper circulations are given in table 1. These figures report both circulations of newspapers and the growth of the number of households for the period 1850–1973. Rates of newspaper circulation *per household* are given in the last column of the table. The pattern which these rates form over time is shown in figure 1. Rates of daily newspaper circulation per household follow an S-shaped "curve of diffusion" that is more or less typical of growth patterns followed by a variety of cultural innovations as these are adopted by a given population.[4] This particular innovation had been accepted by only a small proportion of the population up to about 1870. A number of factors (e.g., limited education, transportation, and printing facilities) played a part in keeping the number of "early adopters" small. Between 1880 and 1890, however, the newspaper swept rapidly through the American population to a point of near saturation by the end of the century. Improved press technology, better transportation, and spreading literacy were significant actors in this sudden change. By 1910, at the eve of World War I, there was more than one newspaper circulated for every household. Thus, during the first decade of the

4. See, for example, H. Earl Pemberton, "The Curve of Culture Diffusion Rate," *American Sociological Review* 1, no. 4 (August 1936): 547–56; Stuart C. Dodd, "Diffusion Is Predictable: Testing Probability Models for Laws of Interaction," *American Sociological Review* 20, no. 4 (August 1955): 392–401; Everett M. Rogers, *Diffusion of Innovations* (New York: Free Press of Glencoe, 1962), pp. 152–59.

TABLE 1
THE GROWTH OF DAILY NEWSPAPERS IN THE UNITED STATES
(1850–1973)

Year	Total Circulation of Daily Newspapers Excluding Sunday (in thousands)	Total Number of Households (in thousands)	Circulation per Household
1850	758	3,598	.21
1860	1,478	5,211	.28
1870	2,602	7,579	.34
1880	3,566	9,946	.36
1890	8,387	12,690	.66
1900	15,102	15,992	.94
1910	24,212	17,806	1.36
1920	27,791	20,697	1.34
1930	39,589	29,905	1.32
1940	41,132	34,855	1.18
1950	53,829	43,468	1.24
1955	56,147	47,788	1.17
1960	58,882	52,610	1.12
1965	60,358	57,251	1.05
1966	61,379	58,092	1.06
1967	61,561	58,845	1.05
1968	62,535	60,444	1.03
1969	62,060	61,805	1.00
1970	62,108	62,875	.99
1971	62,231	64,374	.97
1972	62,510	66,676	.94
1973	63,147	68,251	.93

SOURCES: U.S. Bureau of Census, *Historical Statistics of the United States, Colonial Times to 1957* (Washington, D.C., 1960), Series R 176, p. 500; Series R 169, p. 500; Series 255, p. 16; Series A 242–44.

U.S. Bureau of Census, *Historical Statistics of the United States, Continuation to 1962 and Revisions* (Washington, D.C., 1965), Series R 170, p. 69.

U.S. Bureau of Census, *Statistical Abstract of the United States* (Washington, D.C., 1973), p. 53 and p. 503.

U.S. Bureau of Census, *Current Population Reports: Population Characteristics,* Series P 20, no. 166 (4 August 1967), p. 4.

NOTE: All figures after 1960 include Alaska and Hawaii. Some figures have been revised from previous editions because of revisions in source materials.

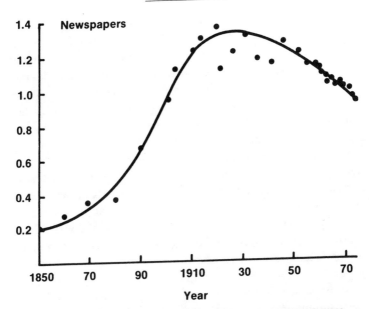

FIGURE 1. THE CUMULATIVE DIFFUSION CURVE FOR DAILY
NEWSPAPERS; SUBSCRIPTIONS PER HOUSEHOLD IN THE
UNITED STATES (1850–1973).

century, newspapers approached their peak in the American
society.

Increases in circulation slowed after 1910. The apparent
high point in the American newspaper occurred in about
1920, just following World War I. Since that time, the
medium has suffered a steady and very noticeable decline.
Even further improvements in the technology of news
gathering, printing, distribution, and literacy have not
slowed this downward trend. Even though more newspapers
are sold today in an absolute sense, they have not kept pace
with increases in the number of American households.

What has been the basis of this decline? An adequate
theory of the relationship between a society and its mass
media should be able to account for such a social change as

well as for media growth. In other words, an analysis of the invention, adoption, and institutionalization of a cultural item such as the newspaper, and the organizational complex which produces it, would be incomplete without consideration of variables that can lead to its *obsolescence*. As far as the newspaper is concerned, the factors that have led to its decline are not difficult to suggest. Other media forms, meeting needs in the population similar to those met by newspapers, began to appear in the society during the 1920s. Radio developed as a household medium during that decade. Shortly afterward (during the 1930s) weekly news magazines began to gain mass acceptance. Even the film played a part. By the late 1940s and during the 1950s, of course, television swept through the American society. To a greater or lesser extent, each of these *functional alternatives* to the newspaper has eaten into the circulation of the daily press. Each, in some sense or other, provides news, information, or entertainment in a way that once was the exclusive province of the newspaper.

But what of the newspaper's future? It will probably survive with some further decline. Few changes in literacy or other factors related to potential increases in readership are probable in the immediate future. By the same token, research on the kinds of satisfactions and gratifications provided for readers by the daily newspaper indicates that it is deeply woven into the daily lives of ordinary people. It provides certain unique services and gratifications. When the newspaper does not come, it is sorely missed. It apparently plays a role in our communication system that alternatives are unlikely to displace, at least for the present.[5] Thus, while newer media, and possibly others to come, pose a challenge to the newspaper, it remains as an institutionalized culture

5. The following two research studies bear directly on this point: Bernard Berelson, "What Missing the Newspaper Means," in *Communications Research, 1948–1949*, ed. P. F. Lazarsfeld and F. N. Stanton (New York: Harper & Brothers, 1949), pp. 111–29; Penn Kimball, "People Without Papers," *Public Opinion Quarterly* 23, no. 3 (Fall 1959): 389–98.

complex and as one of our fundamental modes of mass communication.

Our brief look at the newspaper has indicated in broad outline the accumulation of technological elements and other traits that were combined to form the early mass press. It has also indicated a number of social and cultural conditions that helped shape its financial basis, its relationship to our political institution, and the variables that help determine its content. Finally, we have provided a sociological perspective on the way in which the daily newspaper was adopted as a cultural innovation, as well as the prospects for its survival as part of the American system of mass communication.

3

SOCIOCULTURAL INFLUENCES on the DEVELOPMENT of MOTION PICTURES

The historical antecedents of the motion picture extend backward in time at least as far as those of the mass press. The development of its technological base, however, followed quite different paths and was a result of quite different social forces than those which characterized the background of the newspaper. The technological culture traits that were eventually combined in the development of the projected motion picture were invented and refined as by-products of several somewhat unrelated developments in science. The major contributors to the fundamental technology upon which motion pictures depend were for the most part persons of science who made their discoveries or developed their apparatus while searching for solutions to specific scientific problems. There were exceptions, of course, but generally the people who were to become the founders of the motion picture had little interest in the development of a medium by which people could be entertained. They were far more interested in discovering such things as the physical principles of light refraction, the neurological basis of human vision, or the way in which the illusion of motion was perceived. Throughout the long history of invention and development there were also indications of great potential popular interest in a medium of entertainment based upon the projection of shadow images. At least, the nonscientific friends of many of the inventors were continuously fascinated by the strange devices and effects these people produced.

THE INSTITUTIONAL FRAMEWORK

We may contrast sharply the development of the motion picture, as it occurred within the institutional framework of science, with that of the newspaper, which was traced out in rough outline in the previous chapter. We saw that the history of the mass press was very closely related to important developments within the *economic* and *political* institutions of Western society. Commercialism and political partisanship were characteristics clearly associated with early forms of newspapers as well as the more mature press. When a viable financial structure was found for a mass press in the democratic capitalistic societies, this structure was based firmly upon commercial advertising. And, even though the newspaper redefined its relationship to political affairs more than once, the press continued to regard political activities as one of its major areas of responsibility, at least in reporting and analyzing if not in actual proselytizing. The motion picture, on the other hand, has never been more than marginally related to the presentation of commercial advertising content in a direct sense. And, although movies occasionally deal with politically or socially significant themes, they have not often been used (in American society at least) for the open advocacy of political ideologies. A complete understanding of the impact of society upon its communication media requires that we understand why, in the United States, motion pictures became a major communication medium devoted principally to entertainment rather than edification or persuasion, and why paid admissions as opposed to advertising or government subsidy provided their most important means of financial support. The present discussion cannot fully provide answers to these questions. It can show, however, within the context of American society, how political, social, and economic forces played a role in the formation of the motion picture as a system of mass communication. Comparative analyses of other societies, where the structure of the political institution and the functioning of the economic system have followed different patterns, would indicate why the form and content of the entire system of motion pictures varies from country to country.

THE ACCUMULATION OF TECHNOLOGY

The early history of the motion picture is more accurately the story of developments related to three scientific-technical problems that required solution before an apparatus for the projection of motion pictures could be even be envisioned. We need to consider these three problems, and some of the technical devices that eventually led to their solution. The story of these devices and solutions is, however, inseparable from that of the human beings who achieved them, but the accomplishments of these people are intimately related to the social and cultural context within which they achieved their success.

The first of the major problems referred to above was the development of a means for showing shadow images with the use of an *illuminated projector* that passed light through a transparency to cast an image on a reflecting screen in a darkened room.

The list of elements making up this complex is obviously extensive. Basic to the technology of such projection is some understanding of the principles of optics. The use of mirrors and lenses is involved, including concave mirrors for the focusing of light from an artificial source so as to pass through a lens in suitable intensity. Of these various traits, the lens is probably the oldest. Adequate records exist showing that by the time of the Greeks, the "burning glass" was known by scientists.[1] Archimedes (born 287 B.C.), for example, attempted to construct a large lens, which was purported to have the power to set a ship on fire some distance away by focusing the rays of the sun. Whether this was actually accomplished or not is debatable, but the principle was understood. The field of optics was advanced further by the work of the Arab philosopher and scientist Alhazen (born A.D. 965) who worked out some of the first explanations of refraction and reflection with mirrors and lenses. The pace in invention and cultural accumulation was agonizingly slow in this beginning period. By the time of Roger Bacon (born 1214), scientists and philosophers had done little more than discover various ways to use mirrors in periscopelike devices to reflect images in such ways that the ordinary folk of the time were mystified.

One of the more important elements from this early period of invention and discovery was the *camera obscura* (literally "dark room"). The basic idea is that of the pinhole camera,

---

1. Martin Quigley, Jr., *Magic Shadows: The Story of the Origin of Motion Pictures* (Washington, D.C.: Georgetown University Press, 1948), pp. 18–20.

within which a weak, upside-down, and reversed image of an external scene can be oserved on a wall opposite a small hole in a lightproof rectangular chamber.[2] This phenomenon had undoubtedly been observed very early in human experience, but the rules and principles of its operation were not systematically investigated until the time of Leonardo da Vinci (born 1452).[3] Leonardo worked in a small room sealed from light and into which light rays coming from a scene outside were allowed to enter through a hole about the size of a pencil. The image formed on the opposite wall could be clearly recognized as the outside scene in full color, although weak and sometimes blurred. With the suitable addition of a lens for focusing and a mirror to reverse the image, the camera obscura became a useful device for artists who were concerned with the problems of perspective and color in the painting of landscapes. The camera obscura caught the attention of a number of scientists as well as artists, and it was used to observe eclipses of the sun. This avoided the damage to the eyes that resulted from direct observation, even through darkened glass.

The camera obscura fell into the hands of magicians, charlatans, and others who preyed upon the ignorance of people of the period and who claimed magical powers for themselves on the basis of the effects they were able to produce. Scientists and experimenters were constantly harassed with the problem of magic and witchcraft being associated with their work. Attempts were made from time to time to publicize the "secrets" of these wonders to dispel such charges. This was true not only in the area of optics, but in all branches of science. One of the most interesting of the early attempts to popularize science was a book by Giambattista della Porta or Giovanni Battista della Porta (born

2. Helmut Gernsheim and Alison Gernsheim, *The History of Photography From the Earliest Use of the Camera Obscura in the Eleventh Century Up to 1914* (London: Oxford University Press, 1955). See esp. chap. 1, "The History of the Camera Obscura," pp. 1–19.

3. Quigley, *Magic Shadows*, pp. 29–35.

about 1535). In the seventeenth "book" (chapter) of his famous work, *Natural Magick*, translated and published in English in 1658, della Porta discoursed on the matter "Of Strange Glasses" (lenses and mirrors).[4] After discussing the mechanics of the camera obscura, he went on to describe how the device could be used to present plays and other amusements:

> *How in a Chamber you may see Hunting, Battles of Enemies, and other delusions.*
>
> ...nothing can be more pleasant for great men, and Scholars, and ingenious persons to behold; That in a dark Chamber by white sheets objected, one may see as clearly and perspicuously, as if they were before his eyes, Huntings, Banquets, Armies of Enemies, Plays and all things else that one desireth. Let there be over against that chamber, where you desire to represent these things, some spacious Plain, where the Sun can freely shine: Upon that you shall set Trees in Order, also Woods, Mountains, Rivers, and Animals that are really so, or are made by Art, of Wood, or some other matter. You must frame little children in them, as we use to bring them in when Comedies are Acted: and you must counterfeit Stags, Bores, Rhinocerets, Elephants, Lions, and what other creatures you please: Then by degrees they must appear, as coming out of their dens, upon the Plain: The Hunter he must come with his hunting Pole, Nets, Arrows, and other necessaries, that may represent hunting: Let there be Horns, Cornets, Trumpets sounded: those that are in the Chamber shall see Trees, Animals, Hunters Faces, and all the rest so plainly that they cannot tell whether they be true or delusions: Swords drawn will glitter at the hole, that they will make people almost afraid. I have often

4. A reproduction of this famous work has recently been made available. See John Baptista Porta, *Natural Magick*, ed. Derek J. Price (New York: Smithsonian Institute for Basic Books, 1957).

shewed this kind of Spectacle to my friends, who much admired it, and took pleasure to see such a deceit.[5]

Although della Porta was a scientist, it is clear he also had considerable interest in using various devices and effects to astonish his friends. The moving images of the camera obscura were a source of delight and amusement for the wealthy and prominent of Europe for some time to come. All through the historical development of the technological devices which were prerequisites to the modern motion picture, we see the continuous fascination and awe with which the projected image was regarded by the nonscientist.

The camera obscura, of course, produced its image from light reflected from objects in bright sunlight. A step of some importance lay in substituting artificial light for the sun and in passing this light through a transparency instead of depending upon reflected light. The illuminated projector that could throw images on a screen, using precisely the principles involved in the modern slide projector, became a reality through the work of Athanasius Kircher (born 1601).[6] Kircher was a German Jesuit whose learning and scientific discoveries earned him a place at the Collegio Romano, where with the encouragement of Pope Urban VIII and other ecclesiastical authorities he pursued mathematical and scientific investigations. Kircher was able to demonstrate in a dramatic showing before a distinguished audience the crude projector which he developed and the dim images it produced with the use of hand-painted transparent slides. Kircher became the object of ugly accusations and gossip as a result of his work. He was accused of being in league with the devil and of practicing the black art of necromancy (conjuring up the spirits of the dead for nefarious purposes). The principles upon which his ghostlike projected images were called forth were not well understood, or were deliberately mis-

5. Ibid., pp. 364–65.
6. Quigley, *Magic Shadows*, pp. 48–61.

understood by his enemies, even among the most highly educated people of the time.

Kircher went on to refine his apparatus. He, too, had a flair for the dramatic and he arranged ways in which stories could be told, illustrated with projected slide images. A number of later inventors added refinements to the "magic lantern" and still others exploited its use as a means for entertainment. The solution to the first basic technical problem of the motion picture was thus complete by about 1645.

The second of the major problems requiring solution was to discover the way in which the human being perceived the *illusion of continuous motion.* Unlike the problem of the projector, this involved a relatively large number of elements. Complex discoveries in the theory of human vision and human perception had to be worked out. Essentially, the problem was to discover how a rapid series of drawings, or other figures, could be presented to the human eye in such a way that the afterimages and the visual lag occurring within the neural-perceptual processes would cause the figures to be consciously experienced as a single figure in smooth motion.

In the early 1800s children in London and Paris were playing with a device called the Thaumatrope. It was a small disc about the diameter of a teacup mounted on a shaft. It had a figure on the front and another on the reverse side. By twirling the device with the aid of short strings or threads, various illusions could be created. Several forms of the toy were prepared with amusing figures of one kind or another. There has been some controversy about the origin of this device, but it is generally attributed to a London physician, Dr. John Paris (born 1785). It was described and discussed by David Brewster, the student of the polarization of light and the inventor of the kaleidoscope, in one of his scientific works. The toy is not of particular significance in itself except insofar as it depended upon the phenomenon of visual lag and suggested that an illusion of motion might be produced by rapid presentation of slightly changed figures in sequence.

One of the great students of the so-called persistence of vision or visual lag was the Belgian scientist Joseph Plateau (born 1801).[7] Early in his career, he became interested in various aspects of vision and particularly the way in which the human being perceives motion and color.

Plateau's doctoral thesis from the University of Liege outlined the problems of vision that had to be considered in producing the illusion of motion in the human perceiver. First, each individual figure, drawing, or picture in a rapidly presented series had to remain stationary for a brief but sufficient amount of time for the neural-perceptual process to apprehend it clearly. The eye does not operate absolutely instantaneously. It takes a certain amount of exposure time for a given scene to register an impression. The rapidly whirling blade of a fan seems to "disappear" because of this feature of the human eye. The second point is also a time factor. An impression once registered within the neural-perceptive mechanisms of vision does not stop registering at the instantaneous moment the stimulus itself is withdrawn. There is a substantial lag as the impression lingers briefly. The simplest demonstration of this principle can be made with a common "sparkler" such as children use on the Fourth of July. If this bright light is moved quickly in a figure-eight pattern in the dark, the individual "sees" a complete figure eight, and not simply a rapidly moving dot of light. This is what is meant by visual lag.

With these principles in mind, Plateau worked out a rather cumbersome apparatus of belts, cranks, pulleys, disks, and shutters that enabled him to create a simple illusion of movement, based upon the rapid successive presentation of a drawing. He refined this to a large disk, around whose circumference was arranged a series of drawings, each of which was slightly varied so that the same basic figure advanced to a slightly different position from one drawing to the next. When suitably shown to a subject a moving figure was perceived. This machine was called the Phenakistiscope or Fanta-

7. Ibid., pp. 85–97.

scope. It was the first true motion-picture device. A system had thus been invented, based upon known principles of vision, that permitted a human observer to perceive an illusion of smooth and continuous motion from serially presented still figures. Professor Plateau pursued his quest for the principles of vision to the point where he experimented on himself by testing the effect of prolonged staring at the most powerful light he could think of—the sun. As a result of such experimentation, he became permanently and tragically blind, and much of his important work had to be done after his sight had gone completely. The irony of a blind scientist establishing the visual principles of the motion picture is paralleled only by the tragedy of the deaf Beethoven, who wrote some of the world's great symphonic music after his hearing totally failed, and Edison's invention of the phonograph when he himself was deaf. Joseph Plateau moved the accumulation of technology a great step closer to the day when the motion picture would be used as a cheap form of entertainment for the amusement of the masses.

Only the last of the three important technical problems needed to be solved before the culture complex of the motion picture as a form of mass communication could be synthesized out of these elements. The technology of *photography* in general, and of taking rapid sequence photographs of objects in motion in particular, remained as prerequisites to the motion picture.

The scientific struggle to achieve a workable photographic process is in itself a story of tremendous difficulties, great complexity, and deep fascination. It depended upon developments within the growing science of chemistry and in particular upon that part of the science concerned with chemical changes in substances produced by the action of light. The development of photography also involves the already familiar camera obscura. When sufficiently reduced in size, provided with a lens and a removable reflecting surface coated with a light-sensitive chemical, it became the camera with which we today capture the inverted images of scenes reflected within. In so doing we are still utilizing principles known in the time of da Vinci. The problem, then, was not the camera itself, but the film. What chemical processes and techniques could be used in order to fix the image of the camera obscura? Even here knowledge was well advanced by the beginning of the nineteenth century. In the early 1700s it had been shown experimentally that there were particular chemical compounds, such as various salts of silver, that were rapidly altered by exposure to light. This realization permitted speculation about the possibility of capturing the image of the camera obscura. It was not until the third decade of the nineteenth century, however, that the mechanical and chemical techniques for preparing, exposing, developing, and fixing an actual picture from the camera obscura were worked out.

Solutions to this problem were in fact reached by at least three separate individuals. Each worked without knowledge of the other; each employed a somewhat different approach; and each announced his discoveries at almost the same time (between January and March of 1839). Louis Daguerre in France, William Talbot in England, and John Herschel, also of England, all succeeded in producing photographs based upon the same general chemical principles, but upon rather different specific mechanical techniques.[8] The Daguerre process produced a sharp image of exquisite detail on a polished plate of copper that had been coated with silver metal and exposed to iodine fumes (to form silver iodide). Light striking this plate when correctly exposed in the camera caused the silver iodide to be drastically altered where bright light struck, but to remain relatively unaffected where light of less intensity fell on the plate. The resulting *daguerreotype* produced an excellent picture with sharpness and clarity. There were no negatives; only one picture could be obtained at a time. The processes of Talbot and Herschel employed paper treated with similar light-sensitive chemicals and pro-

8. Josef M. Eder, *History of Photography* (New York: Columbia University Press, 1945), pp. 209–45, 263–64, 316–21.

duced negatives, from which it was necessary to make a second (positive) print. Although the latter procedure proved in time to be by far the most useful, it was in its early form very crude, cumbersome, and unreliable. Furthermore, the pictures produced on the paper of the time lacked the precision of the daguerreotype. For this reason, the daguerreotype was an instant success, and the name of Louis Daguerre became very well known. In a world which had never seen a photograph, the daguerreotype seemed an almost incredible accomplishment. Such pictures were, in fact, when carefully produced, the equal of the finest and most carefully made photographs of today. The use of a polished metal plate of silver gave them a great brilliance and sharpness. They were less "grainy" and showed more detail than even a very good modern paper print. Some indication of the world's astonishment and delight with this new product of science can be gained from the following account, written in 1839 by the editor of a popular American magazine, who had just seen a display of the new daguerreotypes:

> We have seen the views taken in Paris by the "Daguerreotype" and have no hesitation in avowing that they are the most remarkable objects of curiosity and admiration, in the arts, that we ever beheld. Their exquisite perfection almost transcends the bounds of sober belief. Let us endeavor to convey to the reader an impression of their character. Let him suppose himself standing in the middle of Broadway, with a looking glass held perpendicularly in his hand, in which is reflected the street, with all that therein is, for two or three miles, taking in the haziest distance. Then let him take the glass into the house, and find the impression of the entire view, in the softest light and shade, vividly retained upon its surface. This is the "Daguerreotype"![9]

9. Robert Taft, *Photography and the American Scene* (New York: Macmillan, 1938), p. 3.

The acceptance of the Daguerre photographic process was immediate and enthusiastic. Improvements in technique were quickly made so that portraits were possible in indoor "salons." Rigid iron head clamps were used, and light was reflected from overhead skylights. The first daguerreotypes were made in the United States in 1839, the same year that the process was announced in Paris by various scientists and enthusiasts, among whom was Samuel F. B. Morse. While Morse is best remembered for his work with the telegraph, he was actually a portrait painter of some distinction. He was also a professor in the arts of design at the University of the City of New York. The daguerreotype was closely related to both these interests. He was immediately enthusiastic about the new art, and he actually visited Daguerre in France in 1839. Morse became an active daguerreotypist in New York, and is said to have supported himself financially by making portraits and by training students in the process, while awaiting recognition and financial support from the U.S. government for his telegraph.

The production of portraits provided an immediate link between the art of daguerreotypy and the art of making money. Here was a new kind of profession, requiring a relatively brief period of technical training, a small outlay for equipment, and the potential of financial success. The 1840s were in the United States a period of economic depression. A number of enterprising young people were looking about for an opportunity to enter into some venture whereby they could make a living without investing large capital and without having to undergo extensive university professional training. The occupational role of daguerreotypist was almost made to order. There were villages, towns, and cities all over the settled part of the United States that had not yet seen the new process. The cost of having one's portrait made, especially in the smaller sizes, was not prohibitively expensive. A family of average means could easily afford it. Daguerreotype equipment was loaded on wagons, flatboats, oxcarts, and mules. The photographer's art spread out over the country. In all the major cities, daguerreotype salons were established, and business was exceedingly brisk. Quality of work varied greatly. The roving daguerreotypist with poor training and little skill turned out a dreadful product, paying attention neither to graceful poses nor to technical precision in the production of the plates. Some combined the photographic art with other occupational pursuits. A given individual might be a combination blacksmith, cobbler, watch repairer, dentist, and daguerreotypist. It was possible to have one's boots resoled, watch oiled, teeth pulled, horse shod, and portrait made—all at one stop, all in a "package deal" so to speak.[10]

At the other extreme were the beautiful and luxurious salons that developed in the principal population centers. Mathew Brady gained an international reputation as a fine portrait artist in Washington, D.C., long before the beginning of the Civil War.[11] Stretched between these two extremes were establishments large and small that were producing over *three million portraits a year* in the 1850s![12]

The insatiable demand for portraits was undoubtedly related to a number of characteristics of the times. The United States was a society on the move. People were no sooner settled on one frontier than another opened up farther on. The males often left their families in more settled areas until they could be brought out to reasonably favorable accommodations. The movements of population associated with the various gold rushes, land rushes, oil booms, and other events separated men from their wives, and children from their parents. Along the Atlantic seaboard, the Yankees were a maritime people, with menfolk often "gone awhaling" or engaged in world commerce and shipping. The vast upheaval and movement of persons during the Civil War gave portrait photographers a decisive boost. Portraits were a way of reducing the pain of the separations in some small

10. Ibid., p. 48.
11. Ibid., pp. 55–62.
12. Ibid., p. 76.

measure. In some degree, they even breached the great gulf between the living and the dead. They were prized reminders of significant primary-group ties.

The product of the portrait artist also had a deep tradition as a status symbol. To be able to display portrait paintings of assorted ancestors testified to a family's place in time. It was a society where aristocratic birth or family background was decreasingly related to power and wealth. Still, there was a pronounced cultural lag which permitted such symbols to suggest high social position. Achieved criteria were becoming objectively more and more important, but ascribed criteria had not lost their significance. In the early period of the industrial revolution, some members of the newly rich are even said to have hired portrait painters to manufacture for them a set of distinguished ancestors. For the less wealthy, and for the growing middle and working classes, the silver iodide plate of the daguerreotypist provided a mass-consumption substitute for the more distinguished canvas of the portrait artist.

Some indication of the rapid adoption of this innovation can be gained by a study of the growth of the occupational classification of "photographer." Table 2 indicates the number of photographers in the United States per 100,000 population for the years 1840 to 1930. These data show the rapid diffusion of photography as a cultural innovation. This occurred in the four decades 1850–1890. By the last decade of the nineteenth century, there is little doubt that the average American was widely familiar with photographs. The transition between a still photograph and one that gave the illusion of motion was not an impossible step for the imagination of the ordinary citizen.

The technology of photography became increasingly sophisticated; it also became more and more important as part of the growing industrial complexes of society. Factories for the manufacture of photographic chemicals, photographic equipment, and photographic plates were developed. Among these, the name of George Eastman is perhaps the

TABLE 2
THE GROWTH OF THE OCCUPATION OF PHOTOGRAPHER
IN THE UNITED STATES (1840–1930)

Year	Size of Population (in thousands)	Number of Photographers	Photographers Per 100,000
1840	17,000	0	0
1850	23,000	938	4
1860	31,000	3,154	10
1870	39,000	7,558	19
1880	50,000	9,990	20
1890	63,000	20,040	32
1900	76,000	27,029	36
1910	92,000	31,775	35
1920	106,000	34,259	32
1930	123,000	39,529	32

SOURCE: U.S. Bureau of Census, *Population Census of the United States* (for the decennial years 1840, 50, ... 1930, Washington, D.C.).

most widely known. The first daguerreotype photography had given way to other techniques. The ambrotype grew in popularity and then quickly declined. The tintype was widely used during the Civil War, but was discontinued with the perfection of newer technology. Wet-plate processes, with light-sensitive chemicals suspended in a thin collodion film on glass, were widely used for many years. It was the dry plate, however, that permitted preparation in advance of glass photographic plates. This led to their commercial manufacture, distribution, and sale. The miniature camera and the amateur camera were popularized when this technology became available. George Eastman went into the business of manufacturing such photographic plates in the year 1880. From a modest enterprise started on a capital of three thousand dollars, he built a business that thirty-four years later could pay five million dollars for exclusive rights to the patented process of making flexible photographic plates on nitrocellulose film.

The development of flexible film actually occurred in several places at the same time.[13] One type of film was developed in France in the early 1880s. One of Eastman's chemists applied for a patent in the United States at about the same time. Still another patent was applied for in 1889, by the Reverend Hannibal Goodwin, an obscure clergyman. These films were all based upon more or less the same process, with minor variations from one to the other. However, several years of extremely complex litigation ensued, during which the patent office reviewed and re-reviewed the various claims. The patent was finally awarded to Goodwin, but in the meantime, Eastman had been manufacturing flexible film for almost a decade. This roll film was designed for his "foolproof" camera that could be used by the novice (the famous Kodak). With the availability of this flexible film, the development of the motion picture was a step nearer. Edison had produced the light bulb, and the technology of electricity was widely understood. The study of objects in motion had progressed with the use of instantaneous still photography. As we have seen, the principle of projection had long been common knowledge. The neurophysiology of visual lag had been worked out to an adequate extent. It remained only for these various elements to be combined into a workable projected motion picture. The camera obscura and the magic lantern were about to be combined in ways that would have astonished Kircher, della Porta, and da Vinci.

It was Thomas Alva Edison who achieved this combination, but hundreds of others in various parts of the world also contributed.[14] From Edison's laboratory came the motion-picture camera, and a motion-picture projector. It was early in the last decade of the nineteenth century.

Edison lacked confidence in the financial feasibility of the commercial projection of motion pictures on the ground they would be a novelty and the public would soon lose interest. His conception of the way to exploit his device com-

13. Ibid., pp. 384–404.
14. Quigley, *Magic Shadows*, see esp. chaps. 15 and 16.

mercially was to develop a machine that could be used by only one person at a time, paying a fee to view a few moments of photographed motion. His peep show Kinetoscope was scheduled for premiere at the Chicago World's Fair of 1893, but it was not ready in time. It was in fact the following year, 1894, when the Kinetoscope was placed on public exhibition for the first time. An enterprising exhibitor opened up a "Kinetoscope Parlor" with ten of the machines right on Broadway in New York. But the limitations of the Kinetoscope were severe, and the possibilities for a more complete exploitation of the magic lantern of movement were seen by a number of people both in the United States and in Europe. While Edison made the most significant contribution to the actual emergence of the motion picture by achieving the basic technological combination, it remained for more adventurous souls to try to perfect the technique and to turn it into a process for the mass entertainment of the multitude.

In the final years of the century, literally dozens of people were clamoring for patents in as many countries. They were looking for financial backing and for recognition of a variety of motion-picture cameras or motion-picture projectors. From England, France, Germany, and the United States came conflicting claims and reports that these devices had been invented, improved, modified, or perfected. It was in fact a period of high excitement, intense activity, and inventive ferment. Showmen such as Emile Reynaud in Paris were exhibiting projected motion-picture stories, based upon the principle of animated drawings, with great success. It took no vast stretch of imagination to see that the commercial exhibiting of projected motion pictures could be a considerable financial success.

In 1895 an establishment was opened in Paris, called the Cinematographe. For a single franc patrons were admitted to a "salon" where they could view a few very brief films. The exhibition became so popular within a few days that it attracted thousands of viewers, and was operated on a standing room only basis.

The Cinematographe was soon exhibited in New York, and the system was widely imitated. In the meantime, in England, the motion-picture camera was focused on such events as the Derby of 1896, and the exhibition of these projected films caused a sensation. These and other attempts at public showings stimulated further interest in the idea of projected motion pictures for entertainment of the public. It was clear that there were fortunes to be made in the motion-picture business.

By this time, Edison had become convinced. He combined efforts with a young American inventor named Thomas Armat, who had obtained certain patents involved in the improvement of the projector. Together they manufactured the Vitascope, or Armat-Edison projector, which was used in the most successful of the early efforts to exhibit motion pictures to the public.

With the dawn of the twentieth century, then, all the technological problems had been solved. The motion-picture theater had been more than two thousand years in the making, but it was now ready to take its place as the second of the major mass media of communication and to play its role in a growing communication revolution.

THE EARLY MOTION PICTURES: CONTENT AND AUDIENCE

From the outset, motion pictures were concerned with content of low cultural taste and intellectual level. Even the very first moving pictures in the Edison Kinetoscope parlors exhibited such inspiring works as *Fatima and Her Danse du Ventre*, which was the sensation of the Chicago World's Fair in 1896. Naive and slapstick comics were popular. A view of a mischievous boy squirting a hose on a dignified dowager or even pornography (within the limits of the era), such as the brief *How Bridget Served the Salad Undressed*, were received with enthusiasm by the patrons of the penny arcades in which the Kinetoscopes were installed.[15] These first films, with their boxing matches, low comedy, and shimmy dancers, can be contrasted with the efforts of the first printers. Gutenberg's first product represented the most significant and important ideas of his time. Books in the early period were works of philosophy, science, art, or politics. The motion picture concerned itself in its early period with the trivial and inconsequential. The content mattered little to anyone; it was the novelty of movement that was the important factor. The film's first audiences stared with open mouths at any picture that moved. But even among the habitués of the penny arcades, an important principle quickly began to manifest itself. Such films as *Beavers at Play* or *The Surf at Dover* brought in fewer pennies than the brief but exciting *Danse du Ventre,* or the titillating *What the Bootblack Saw.* Efforts toward the filming of more serious or artistic subjects were not received with enthusiasm. Film content aimed at more elementary gratifications brought in the money. From the first, then, systematic relationships between audience tastes and the financial structure of the infant "industry" governed the production of film content. Audiences were selective in what they would pay to see, and because of this producers were selective in what they produced.

It would be tempting to analyze the characteristics of the clientele of the penny arcades, which were to say the least not located in the more discriminating sections of the urban centers. One might be tempted to draw the inference that it was their low level of cultural taste that left a permanent stamp of mediocrity upon the film. The problem was that the film moved out of the penny arcade very quickly, but it did not noticeably rise in the seriousness or in the artistic taste of its content. The film went from the arcade to the vaudeville house, where it was exhibited as a scientific novelty following the major acts. Again, the tastes of the burlesque theater governed the content of the films.

15. Richard Griffith and Arthur Mayor, *The Movies* (New York: Simon and Schuster, 1957), pp. 1–8.

In about the year 1900, a number of enterprising arcade owners, former circus operators, medicine showmen, ex-pitchmen, barkers, etc., began to rent unused stores, to equip them cheaply with benches or chairs, and to project films with secondhand equipment. Their working capital was meager, their repertoire atrocious, their establishment dismal, but above all it was cheap. For only a nickel the audience member could watch an assortment of exciting short pictures, ranging from *Life of An American Fireman* to *Dream of a Rarebit Fiend*. These were either trick movies of brief length or exciting little sequences of dramatic events such as the firemen responding to a call. Various names were used but the term "nickelodeon" caught on as a popular way of referring to these enterprises. The most important things about them were that they were popular with people at the bottom of the social structure, and they made money. Then nickelodeons began to clean up their interiors and dress up outside. Many opened up in principal cities in the country. The first decade of the twentieth century, then, saw a new form of communication begin to spread. The film was about to become a true mass medium.[16]

The content of the films soon changed markedly. They became longer and more sophisticated technically. They did not rise far in taste or seriousness. Such fare as *The Great Train Robbery* was just about what the nickelodeon audience wanted to see in 1903. Films with stories became the norm in a very short time. These places of entertainment thrived in their most prosperous form in the same areas of the metropolis where the penny arcades were located. As the motion picture was establishing itself, its audience tended to be heavily weighted with poor immigrants, drifters, and the anonymous residents of the city's zones of transition The most significant groups in numbers were by far the immigrants. The first ten years of the 1900s was a period of unprecedented immigration, unequaled in more contemporary times. People from many cultures were pouring into the

16. Ibid., p. 19.

United States from eastern and southern Europe. By the millions they established ethnic neighborhoods within the ecological and social structure of the city. Immigration laws were not strict by today's standards, and many of these new citizens were illiterate, even in their own language. A large proportion had no knowledge of English whatsoever. Substantial numbers were agricultural peasants in their own land. For these humble people, surrounded by a bewildering and complex industrial society which they had not yet begun to understand, the primitive movie was a source of solace and entertainment. The plots were simple; the stylized acting needed no knowledge of the language in order to understand the idea. Today's viewer is amused at the stereotyped facial expressions and the gross body movements of the actors in early films. Such techniques become more understandable when it is realized that the audience had only occasional subtitles with which to follow the plot in a verbal sense. Even many of the English-speaking members of the audience could read only with difficulty, if at all, and a great many of the foreign-born knew not a word.

The immigrants, then, along with rustic Americans newly arrived in the big city were the most important audience types toward whom the early nickelodeon movies were aimed. With slapstick and burlesque they even poked fun at such people themselves and made them laugh at their own plight. The country bumpkin and the immigrant were often seen in films. The cop, the crook, the pretty girl, the jealous husband, the boss—this was about the total range of personalities that appeared in the movies. It was enough. Their antics were easily understood. In intensified form, such stereotyping and slapstick led to such content as the Keystone Cops and the pie-throwing scenes.

By the second decade, however, the nickelodeon had spread far beyond the urban centers. It had started to become a form of family entertainment. Enthusiastic operators were demanding more complicated fare. Movie companies had mushroomed to fill the demand for films. This booming entertainment medium was well on its way. The "star" system came; movies discovered the classics; more flexible techniques of photography were developed. The films grew longer to the feature length we are now accustomed to. This increase in technical competence was due in part to the growing enthusiasm of motion-picture audiences. The dreary nickelodeons had given way by the beginning of the 1920s to much larger and more elaborate picture palaces. Some were so luxuriously decorated they almost appeared to be temples of worship for the new gods and goddesses of the screen. Such stars were receiving the adoration of millions of shop girls and factory hands. They were also receiving astronomical salaries which made Hollywood synonymous with ostentatious consumption of wealth.

The Great War had given the American film industry an unprecedented boost. The production of motion pictures in the studios of Europe had ceased after 1914, but the demand for films had become tremendous and worldwide. This placed U.S. films in the export market with an advantage, which was retained for years. The silent film, with written subtitles easily changed to any language, was made by directors and producers who were themselves immigrants from other countries. It was a particularly flexible product for export to foreign countries. Almost inexhaustible markets were opened up when the more remote regions of the world began showing films with subtitles in Urdu, Hindi, Chinese, Arabic, or whatever local language was required. If the local audience was not literate in its own language, a "storyteller" was employed to explain to the native audience what was transpiring in the film as it progressed. Any relationship between these versions and the original intent of the film's designers was purely coincidental. The political position of the United States in World War I, then, had the most significant impact upon the American motion picture as a mass medium. It made the medium one of world significance.

The events of the Great War also point up other ways in which a society can have an impact upon its media. When the war broke out in Europe, the American public increasingly began to focus its public opinions in two opposite directions. The pacifists wanted to stay out of the European war and to avoid engaging in any military expansion that might eventually lead the country into participation in the war. Those in favor of preparedness felt that the United States would more than likely have to enter the war at some point, and it might as well make military preparations to make the task easier if the need arose. These were issues of great importance during the years just before the United States declared war on Germany. When war came a large bloc of the American public still retained attitudes, opinions, and sentiments unsuitable for total commitment and participation in the war effort. To reduce these "unhealthy" pacifist feelings, George Creel, chief of the Committee on Public Information (the official U.S. agency for domestic propaganda), mobilized motion pictures as part of an all-out effort to "sell the war to the American public." This thrust upon motion pictures a propaganda role they had not played before, at least in the United States.[17] Motion pictures had been simply a form of entertainment. They had not seriously engaged in persuasion for political partisanship, moral uplift, social responsibility, or cultural betterment. In general, they had *followed* public tastes and attitudes, rather than *led* them. In the minds of some, experiences of the war opened up new possibilities and objectives for the film as a medium of persuasion. Actually, the motion picture in its form as a medium of entertainment has never become a consistent vehicle for effective political or social comment. While Hollywood has cooperated during wartime and has occasionally produced a film with a social "message," these are considered departures from the norm. The position of the film in this respect is distinct from that of the newspaper, which has consistently assumed that it has the responsibility to instruct us politically.

During the last part of the 1920s the sound track came

17. Ibid., pp. 113–19.

to the film. By this time the motion-picture theater was a permanently established and respectable place of entertainment for American families. As a business the production, distribution, and exhibition of motion pictures was firmly entrenched in the American economy, and as a cultural innovation it had become deeply institutionalized into our weekly routines. Accurate records of motion-picture attendance are available on a national basis beginning with 1922. By that time, the film was so popular that the number of paid admissions in an average week in the United States already exceeded 40 million!

The adoption of the motion picture as a cultural innovation for mass use was both swift and extensive. The United States was literally transformed into a nation of moviegoers between 1900 and 1930. Table 3 shows both average weekly attendance from 1922 to 1973 and the number of households during the same period. Although attendance data are not available from 1900 to 1921, it appears most likely that this early period of movies followed the estimated trend as shown in figure 2.

Perhaps the most significant aspect of the adoption pattern for the film is its *variability*. This is particularly apparent in the middle section of the curve, when attendance figures fluctuated wildly. These were the Great Depression years; hard times in the early 1930s had a sharp impact on moviegoing. Admissions dropped by more than 30 percent between 1930 and 1932. However, the late 1930s and the decade of the 1940s were the Golden Years for the film. Even so, functional alternatives were becoming increasingly available. As these grew in number and popularity, their impact on motion-picture attendance was to be little short of disastrous. Clearly, the rapid rise of television, beginning at the end of the 1940s and continuing through the next decade, had the deepest possible impact on the mass use of the motion picture. Even though the society as a whole was moving toward unprecedented economic affluence, average weekly

TABLE 3
THE GROWTH OF MOTION-PICTURE ATTENDANCE IN THE UNITED STATES (1922–73)

Year	Average Weekly Movie Attendance (in thousands)	Total Number of Households (in thousands)	Weekly Attendance per Household
1922	40,000	25,687	1.56
1924	46,000	26,941	1.71
1926	50,000	28,101	1.78
1928	65,000	29,124	2.23
1930	90,000	30,000	3.00
1932	60,000	30,439	1.97
1934	70,000	31,306	2.24
1936	88,000	32,454	2.71
1938	85,000	33,683	2.52
1940	80,000	35,000	2.29
1942	85,000	36,445	2.33
1944	85,000	37,115	2.29
1946	90,000	37,900	2.37
1948	90,000	40,523	2.22
1950	60,000	43,468	1.38
1954	49,000	46,893	1.04
1958	40,000	50,402	.79
1960	28,000	52,610	.53
1965	21,000	57,251	.37
1970	15,000	62,875	.24
1971	14,000	64,374	.22
1972	15,000	66,676	.22
1973	16,000	68,251	.23

SOURCES: U.S. Bureau of Census, *Historical Statistics of the United States, Colonial Times to 1957* (Washington, D.C., 1960), Series H 522, p. 225; Series A 242–44, p. 15.

U.S. Bureau of Census, *Historical Statistics of the United States, Continuation to 1962 and Revisions* (Washington, D.C., 1965), Series H 522, p. 35.

U.S. Bureau of Census, *Statistical Abstract of the United States* (Washington, D.C., 1968), tables 11 and 302, pp. 12, 208 (1973); tables 53, 347, 349, pp. 41, 211, 212.

U.S. Bureau of Census, *Current Population Reports: Population Characteristics*, Series P-20, No. 166 (24 August 1967), pp. 1, 4.

NOTE: Figures do not include Alaska and Hawaii. Some figures have been revised from previous editions because of revisions in source materials.

FIGURE 2. THE CUMULATIVE DIFFUSION CURVE FOR MOTION PICTURES; AVERAGE WEEKLY ATTENDANCE PER HOUSEHOLD IN THE UNITED STATES (1900–1973).

attendance per household dropped from 2.37 in 1946 to only .79 in 1958. This drop has continued to the remarkably low rate of .23 in 1973.

The movie industry struggled mightily to slow the rate of decline. As competition with television increased, numerous experiments were tried. At one point, moviegoers were issued special glasses so that they could see the picture in three dimensions. Screens widened—to almost unbelievable proportions in some cases. Special sound effects, with speakers in various parts of the theater, were tried. These gimmicks did not help much; the decline continued. Perhaps more significantly, the older moral standards governing film content all but collapsed. At an earlier time, motion pictures shown to American audiences were about as racy as the proverbial Sunday school picnic. Solid, middle-class America didn't need to be titillated with taboo themes to get them to pay at the box office. Today, unless a movie promises a blood-bath or frank sex portrayals, it may not be a big moneymaker. Much legal maneuvering and litigation has accompanied this change, and the issues of "freedom of speech" versus "ob-scenity" have been widely discussed in connection with mo-tion picture portrayals. Currently, public officials and others are sharply criticizing film violence as well as explicit sex.

Whatever the eventual significance of these issues within the context of the motion picture, it seems reasonably clear that the real pressure for change has been an economic one. The most logical projection for the future would be that the decline will continue, and that the movie theater as we now know it will eventually disappear. This does not mean that films will no longer be made. Television provides an insati-able demand for even the dullest films—as any viewer of the Late Late Show will testify. Thus, while the industry may survive, or even prosper, the behavioral forms of its con-sumers appear likely to continue their present trend. The strong shift of interest of the American public from the movie screen downtown to the television screen at home is likely to continue as color television achieves saturation, and as TV moves toward codes concerning content which will probably eventually resemble those of contemporary movies.

The conditions and factors related to the abandonment of a given behavioral form within a social system have largely been neglected in the recent surge of interest in the innova-tion process. Obsolescence is a natural counterpart of inno-vation, and a necessary feature of an adequate theory of social change. There are undoubtedly systematic principles that govern the way in which a given item, trait, or culture com-plex is abandoned by a population. We no longer make much use of quill pens, detachable collars, automobile cranks, the Townsend Plan, and the chaperoned party for young adults. These forms undoubtedly followed some reverse pattern of declining usage, symmetrical in form to the usual S-curve of adoption. In spite of the obvious significance of such obsolescence patterns for understanding social and cultural change, no systematic theory is available concerning the conditions under which they are generated.

In the case of the motion picture, the causes of obsolescence are not particularly obscure. The depression, the population shift to the suburbs, and, of course, the continued growth of the electronic media have cut deeply into paid attendance. To these fairly obvious factors could be added the increasing congestion of central business districts where most theaters are located and the burden of mounting labor costs, which has resulted in continuous box-office increases and a correspondingly smaller number of consumers.

Overall, our analysis has shown the long and complex accumulation of culture traits and technological innovations that were necessary conditions for the emergence of the film as a medium of mass communication. It has indicated the many social and cultural conditions, such as wars, populations shifts, and changes in the economic institution that were significantly related to the eventual widespread adoption and probable impending obsolescence of motion pictures as a behavioral innovation on the part of the American population.

The impact of a society on a communication medium could not be more clear than in the case of the motion picture. As a technology, and as as industry, it will undoubtedly continue to occupy a place in our social system. However, there are considerable doubts concerning its survival in the form in which it was originally adopted by our population.

4

The
SOCIAL CONTEXT
of the
BROADCAST
MEDIA

In tracing the principal ways in which society has influenced the broadcast media, three somewhat distinct issues require clarification. First, there are the numerous and complex social factors that established the need and consequent search for an instantaneous medium of communication that could leap across oceans and span continents. Second, there is the chain of scientific and technical achievements that accumulated as one invention led to another when various means of fulfilling the need were sought. Finally, there are the events that resulted in the translation of commercial wireless-telegraphy and radiotelephone technology into a mass medium with which to broadcast programs to the home receivers of entire nations. We might add, of course, the growth of television out of radio as still another issue; but as will be made clear, the newer medium not only shared a common history with radio but it inherited its financial basis, traditions, structure of control, and even much of its talent.

THE NEED FOR RAPID COMMUNICATION

People's need for a reliable means of communicating rapidly over long distances increased relentlessly as their society grew in complexity. As long as their social activities were confined to a small band, which moved about together or stayed close to a fixed village, the range of the human voice, or at most the distance a strong runner could cover without rest, proved sufficient as a means for handling their communication problems. But as complex social organizations were invented for military, commercial, and governmental purposes, such groups were continuously faced with the problem of coordinating their activities without a really reliable method of transmitting information quickly over long distances.

Human ingenuity is vast, and people of every age have shown a remarkable ability to take the technology of their time and apply it in some fresh way to the solution of practical problems. So it was with long-distance communication. Our earliest records tell of military commanders who signaled information at night from the tops of hills with the use of torches arranged in previously agreed upon patterns or crude codes.

The word *telegraph* itself comes from the Greeks fully three hundred years before Christ. Its two component words imply "at a distance" and "to write." In the Greek, Persian, and Roman civilizations social organization in military affairs, government, and commerce had far outstripped communication technology, and the inability to coordinate complex activities was a frequent source of great difficulty. Armies were defeated, navies were sunk, governments collapsed, and fortunes were lost (literally), all for the want of a word.

But an impressive array of technical gadgets were invented and pressed into service over the intervening centuries to find a solution to this cultural lag. Even primitive people, needing to communicate but sorely handicapped by their crude technology, were able to burn out the inside of a log and stretch the skin of an animal over one end to form a drum. With this they could conquer surprising distances using coded sounds. Smoke signals are another familiar example; carrier pigeons are still another (used right up into the twentieth century). Flashing mirrors, lantern signals, cannon shots, and fire beacons were all used in the struggle to surmount distance and time. But these early communication techniques were severely limited. Most were terribly cumbersome and distressingly unreliable. Many depended upon good weather, and the others could handle only very simple messages.

In more recent times, many interesting communication systems were invented. All were in some way dependent upon line-of-sight vision between communicator and receiver. However, by relaying a message along a series of stations, complex messages could be sent over surprisingly long distances. During the height of Napoleon's power in France, that country actually had a total of 224 semaphore stations which spanned over a thousand miles in all.[1] This type of system was the most elaborate and widely used of all of the line-of-sight communication devices. An outgrowth of a simple idea developed by three French schoolchildren for sending messages to each other, it depended upon positioning a pair of large wooden arms on top of a tower in such a way

1. Gleason L. Archer, *History of Radio to 1926* (New York: American Historical Society, 1938).

that given configurations represented the letters of the alphabet in agreed-upon patterns. The signals could be read and interpreted by a receiving operator in another tower several miles away. This operator in turn sent the message along to the next station, etc. It was expensive and cumbersome, but the system was in use in a number of European countries right up to the time that the electrical telegraph replaced it. The semaphore still has some limited applications, especially aboard naval vessels maintaining radio silence.

As Western society came into the nineteenth century, the need for a means of communication that would quickly transverse even the oceans themselves began to become critical. The tempo of commercial intercourse between nations had increased greatly with the advent of the industrial revolution. Great Britain was developing a colonial empire so vast and far-flung that it would be able to boast with impunity that it was one upon which the sun never set. Britannia ruled not only the waves but also a substantial portion of the world's land surface and a sizable segment of the world's population. Other nations, too, were building mighty navies and great merchant fleets. They were consolidating new political systems, developing colonial markets, and exploiting new sources of raw materials. Along with all of this came fundamental changes in the very organizational nature of Western society. These changes have been discussed by social scientists in various terms such as complex organic evolution analogies, the movement from Gemeinschaft to Gesellschaft, the change from mechanical to organic solidarity, and the trend from a sacred to a secular society (to mention only a few). There can be little doubt that a communication medium such as the electrical telegraph was sorely needed in the face of growing societal complexity and could have been put to immediate, practical, and important use long before it was finally available.

The dream of an instantaneous telegraph based upon

magnetic principles had been around in one form or another for a long time. Giovanni della Porta, the author of *Natural Magick,* had discussed a very special kind of lodestone (a type of iron ore with magnetic properties).[2] If two similar compasses were to be fashioned by using this mineral to magnetize their needles, it was said they would be locked together by some mysterious force so that if the needle of one were forced to point in a given direction, the other would then instantly and automatically move to the same orientation, regardless of intervening space. With an alphabet fixed around the circumference of the compass, the telegraphic possibilities which such a system might provide were obvious. But sadly, search as they might, scientists, philosophers, and learned people were never able to find quite the right variety of lodestone needed to construct such a marvelous *sympathetic telegraph.* Like the philosopher's stone, the Golden Fleece, and the fountain of youth, it remained forever beyond their grasp.

THE BASIC THEORY OF ELECTRICITY

But while the legendary lodestone failed to provide the means for a telegraph, the scientific laboratory eventually would yield devices that would transcend the hopes and dreams of all the ancient wise ones. The development of an adequate understanding of electricity came during the nineteenth century as part of the great surge of accomplishment in the physical sciences. Radio itself was a by-product of a long, continuous, and basic inquiry into the nature of electrical energy.

The theorizing and research that led to this communication medium occupied the lifetimes of large numbers of sci-

2. John Baptista Porta, *Natural Magick,* ed. Derek J. Price (New York: Smithsonian Institute for Basic Books, 1957).

entific workers, only a few of whom ever achieved popular recognition, financial success, or even lasting scientific honors. The list of problems these people solved is simply staggering. Today's teen-agers who tune in to their favorite program of popular music while lying on the beach and the factory workers who prop up their feet at night and view their favorite ball team in action are acting in ways dependent upon the end products of centuries of brilliant scientific advances, the solution of which absorbed some of the most creative imaginations and most tireless workers of the last two centuries. These pioneers grappled with an endless list of conceptual, theoretical, and mechanical-technical problems whose solutions permitted today's systems of broadcasting.

The problems needing solution before radio could become a reality included the basic theory of electricity and elementary circuitry, including generating, conducting, and measuring electric currents. Also included were the theories of electromagnetic fields, coils, and the electromagnetic radiation and detection of high frequency oscillations. Another series of problems centered around the alteration of currents, such as rectification and amplification. The diode and triode electron tubes were required to couple voice transmission to the dot-and-dash wireless telegraph. Finally, for television, an offspring of radio, the problems associated with broadcasting patterns of light and shadow and receiving these on a viewing screen had to be solved. The light-sensitive photoelectron tube in the heart of the television camera was a substantial advance, as was the kinescope-receiving picture tube. The latter two opened the way for commercial television.

The principles by which sound or light are converted to electromagnetic waves that can be broadcast through space, to be received and converted back into sound or light, involve the most basic of the physical sciences. Some of these principles govern the nature of matter itself.

The key to radio transmission and reception and to television is the *electron*. In oversimplified terms, the electron is conceptualized by physicists as an infinitesimally small *particle* that has the electrical characteristic of being negatively charged. Electrons, of course, are one major type of particle that make up *atoms*, but there are other kinds such as protons and related types that constitute the *nucleus* of a given atom. These tiny nuclear particles have positive electric charges that exactly match the negative electrical charges of the atom's electrons. It is this balance of electrical forces that holds the particles together in a given atom.

Each atom of the elements has a different number of electrons and other particles, making up its overall structure. The heavier a given element is, the more electrons it has in its atoms, and vice versa. An atom of a given element is a tightly organized structure of particles that are electrically balanced against each other in a tiny system. Some elements, however, have atoms whose outer electrons for various reasons are less solidly attached to their structures.

For some elements (like copper and many other metals), electrons can be temporarily picked off or added to the outer parts of these systems by chemical or electromagnetic processes, thus throwing the atom into a temporary electrical imbalance. When this happens, the atom attracts an electron from its neighbor to replace the one lost. Or if it has too many it passes one on to its neighbor. Then the neighbor reacts similarly with *its* neighbor, and so on. If the element is a good "conductor" of electricity, and is arranged in a long thin wire, the result will be a "flow of electrical current" along that wire. Nothing really "flows," of course, but the successive electrical imbalances in the atoms of the wires making up an electrical circuit can be thought of in this way. Storage batteries, generators, fuel cells, and many other devices are capable of producing these electrical imbalances at the end of a wire. This disequilibrium creates an energy source in the form of an electrical charge at the other end.

From this comes our familiar host of applications of the resulting energy. It is used to create magnetic fields, heat, light, and other effects such as radio and television. If the foregoing seems complex, it is an indication to the reader of the difficulties that were overcome as part of the accumulation of ideas and technology prior to the invention of radio.

THE DEVELOPMENT OF ELECTRICAL TECHNOLOGY

All during the period from the Greeks up to the latter part of the eighteenth century, experimenters had marveled at the phenomenon of electricity. Static electricity was easily produced by friction, and with that principle in mind, experimenters built larger and larger devices for generating charges. The Greeks rubbed an amber rod on a piece of cloth and generated weak electrostatic induction currents capable of attracting a light pith ball suspended on the end of a thread. Centuries later, European scientists of the 1700s had elaborated the mechanics of this process to a point where they could generate awesome charges of static electricity with ponderous friction machines. Huge rotating disks with cloth pads to pick up the electrical charges were constructed. They astounded their friends by letting these charges smash between two metal points in lightninglike fashion up to a distance of several feet. Such machines were capable of attracting bits of thread or other objects from as much as thirty feet away. But actually, they were still using the same principle that had fascinated the Greeks, and they really did not understand why it all worked! While they must have been having a great deal of fun with their dramatic devices, they had not been able to solve the critical problem of *storing* electricity so that it could be used when and where it was needed.

Several people seem to have found a crude solution to this problem at about the same time. A jar half filled with water and corked with a wire down through the middle of the cork can "store" a charge of electricity. One end of the wire must dip into the water and the other end must be temporarily attached to the business end of a friction machine that is generating static electricity. An unsuspecting soul who later grasps the wire coming out of the jar will receive a bone-jarring shock if a large enough static charge has been fed into the storage jar. Called a Leyden jar (after the place where it seems most likely to have been invented), this device was used by Benjamin Franklin in his well-known experiment with the kite. He succeeded in charging up a Leyden jar with a kite flown into an electrical storm. One end of the (wire) kite string is said to have been attached to a key dipped into the water. The experiment demonstrated that the electricity of lightning and the electricity of the laboratory are the same. Why Mr. Franklin was not instantly electrocuted remains a mystery. It definitely is not advisable to attempt to repeat this interesting experiment. The storage battery of Alessandro Volta eventually replaced the Leyden jar, and more adequate devices for generating electrical currents were under development by Faraday and others.

A key element in the inexorable movement of technology toward the electrical telegraph was the development of the electromagnet. By the 1830s, the various technical traits prerequisite to an electrical telegraph were available within the scientific culture. It remained only to put them together in the required pattern. The idea of the sympathetic telegraph had tantalized people for centuries. The need for such a communication device was critical, and the technological base had accumulated to a point where no fundamental problem remained to be solved.

Several people at about the same time seem to have hit upon one scheme or another that would constitute a workable telegraph. But it was the American Samuel F. B. Morse whose patents and system prevailed. Morse, the portrait painter, was not a scientist, and in his naiveté he seems to have blundered onto solutions for making a workable telegraph that scientists had overlooked as unlikely possibilities. He had set up a workshop in one of the buildings of the University of the City of New York, where he served as professor of literature and the arts of design. He tinkered with numerous gadgets and frequently sought the advice of several of his somewhat skeptical scientific friends. He eventually worked out a telegraph system that permitted him to transmit messages through ten miles of wire strung around and around in his workshop.

Morse immediately applied for a government grant to enable him to perfect the device (which he had promptly patented). After a great deal of fumbling, hesitation, and delay, the federal government eventually financed a telegraph line between Washington, D.C., and Baltimore, Maryland. The historical message "What hath God wrought?" flashed between the two cities on May 24, 1844, and the world entered into the era of instantaneous electric communication.

After an initial period of hardship, hesitation, and financial loss, the electric telegraph was gradually accepted by business, the military, and other groups; and the thin wires soon led to most major centers of population. The federal government, which had financed the original long-distance line, threw away its opportunity to control the patents and relinquished all its rights. They became the property of private corporations, with Morse as a major stockholder, and the development of this medium was left to private enterprise. It is clear now that the failure of the government to maintain itself in the telegraph business *set a precedent* that would be followed in the United States, where private ownership of the media of public communication constitutes a central condition in determining the type of content which the audiences of the broadcast media now enjoy. It was this seemingly unimportant turn of events that forged an important link in the chain of development of the mass media in this country. As the telephone came, then the wireless telegraph, the wireless telephone, and eventually home broadcasting, the federal government was never again a serious contender for controlling rights to these media (although on one occasion it obtained and relinquished control of radio). This was certainly not the case in other countries.

After conquering tremendous financial and technical problems, cables were laid across the Atlantic Ocean by Cyrus W. Field, and on July 27, 1866, a message crossed the great sea with incredible speed. Within a very short time, networks of cables were laid under the oceans to the principal population areas of the world. By 1876, Alexander Bell and his brilliant assistant had succeeded in transmitting the human voice over electrical wires, and the pace of cultural accumulation in the area of communication technology was increasing swiftly. Soon the huge cultural lag between communication technology and complexity of social organization would begin to close. From the telegraph and the telephone it was only a short and very natural step to elimination of the wires to achieve a wireless telegraph and eventually a wireless telephone.

ELECTROMAGNETIC RADIATION AND THE WIRELESS TELEGRAPH

While the development of the telegraph had been occurring, scientists like Volta, Ampère, Henry, Faraday, Maxwell, and Hertz were continuously working to understand the basic nature of electricity. The growth of increasingly sophisticated theory permitted an ever more elaborate technology for generating, storing, measuring, transmitting, modifying, and variously harnessing electrical power. Along about the time of the American Civil War, James Maxwell in Scotland had worked out a mathematical theory of mysterious electromagnetic waves which were supposed to travel at the speed of light. By 1888, a young German, Heinrich Hertz, had demonstrated the actual existence of these waves and built a laboratory apparatus for generating them and detecting them. The scientific world became intensely interested in this phenomenon, and experiments with the Hertzian waves were being carried on in laboratories in many countries.

In the early 1890s, Guglielmo Marconi, who was then only twenty years old, became acquainted with these experimental studies of Hertzian waves and the apparatus used to generate and detect them. He reasoned logically that if their distance could be extended beyond the few hundred feet of the laboratory devices, signals in code might be transmitted with them in a kind of telegraph without wires. He promptly purchased an apparatus and began experimenting with it, sending its signals across the garden on his parents' estate. Although not a scientist, he was an imaginative tinkerer, and he succeeded in modifying the laboratory device and strengthening it to a point where he could send dot-and-dash messages up to about a mile. His apparatus had become the first wireless telegraph.

Marconi's work was never intended to advance basic science. His experiments had immediate practical and commercial goals rather than theoretical or scientific ones. He hurried to England in 1897 to patent his wireless telegraph. It was essentially a system of fairly common laboratory devices built on a very large scale for sending and receiving the Hertzian waves in the dots and dashes of Morse's telegraph code.

> There was a well-defined raising of eyebrows among the scientists when they learned that their laboratory gear had found its way into the patent office. Only a few, notably Crookes, Sir Oliver Lodge, and

Ernest Rutherford, had given any thought at all to its practical use.[3]

Marconi soon built larger and larger devices that reached out over longer distances. Eventually even the Atlantic was spanned. Although Marconi's work may not have advanced basic science noticeably, it did represent a most significant step in the development of radio as an instantaneous medium of long-range communication. It brought the end product of more than a century of scientific research out of the laboratory and into the hands of groups who desperately needed a device with which to communicate rapidly over long distances.

"Marconi had come to England from Italy because he believed that England with her large mercantile marine, would prove the more profitable market for the discoveries he had made."[4] The wireless was by no means a mass medium at this time. By the end of the first decade of the new century, it was in the hands of commercial, military, and governmental groups for the transmission of confidential information. It was especially suitable for use on ships, which could carry its heavy and bulky apparatus. The general public knew of the wireless telegraph only through what they occasionally read in the newspaper. The thought that they would ever have one in their homes or that it would begin to alter their family's daily routines surely never entered their heads.

FROM WIRELESS TELEGRAPH TO RADIOTELEPHONE

When radio had proved itself capable of performing the task Marconi and others had envisioned, powerful economic re-

3. Monroe Upton, *Electronics for Everyone* (2nd rev. ed.; New York: American Library Association, 1962), p. 137.

4. S. G. Sturmey, *The Economic Development of Radio* (London: Gerald Duckworth, 1958), p. 17.

sources were brought to bear upon its development. The British and American Marconi companies soon had strong rivals. The naval establishments of powerful countries lost little time in adopting the wireless. Shipping firms found at last a practical means of keeping in contact with vessels at sea. Inevitably, ships with wireless apparatus found themselves colliding with icebergs or otherwise in difficulties. Dramatic messages of distress brought other ships similarly equipped to the rescue. These events attracted great popular attention. Meanwhile, radio technology continued to develop. Involved legal battles were fought over invention after invention during the time that radio's pioneers were improving the reliability, power, distance, and clarity of wireless messages. International conferences attempted to work out rules governing the transmission and receiving of messages. Hundreds of shore stations were built along coastlines by commercial, marine, and official naval interests. In the years just before World War I, wireless telegraphy was a widely used, commercially sound technique that had substantially begun to close the great cultural lag between communication technology and the development of complex and far-flung social organization. But no one had yet thought of the device as a medium of communication for the ordinary member of society.

The transmission of the human voice by wireless was the next step, and a number of inventors and scientists were working on the idea. It was not really such a tremendously difficult problem. The existing dot-and-dash wireless system had been developed in such a way that it was technically capable of receiving such broadcasts if they could be properly incorporated into the radiated signal. It was on Christmas Eve 1906 that wireless operators on ships up and down the Atlantic sea-lanes off the coast of the United States first heard a human being speak to them through their earphones. They could scarcely believe their ears!

Reginald A. Fessenden had prepared an apparatus that permitted the broadcasting of infinitely more complex signals than those of the simple tone of the dot and dash. He had also constructed a very powerful transmitter to use in his experiments. Several persons spoke over the wireless on that eventful evening; one made a speech, one read a poem, and one even played the violin. The radiotelephone had become a reality.

In spite of Fessenden's early success with radiotelephony, it was to be many years before Americans had regularly scheduled radio programs to listen to in their own homes. Yet, there was a growing popular interest in radio. In that same year, 1906, it was discovered that several mineral substances were capable of detecting radio transmissions when used in an extremely simple circuit. A very inexpensive "crystal set" radio receiver could be built by almost anyone with elementary mechanical skills. The cost of the parts was insignificant. This meant that people all over the country, even youngsters, could listen in on the code signals in the air. Once the code was learned, the sport had great appeal, and they never knew when they might eavesdrop upon an agonized signal of distress from some vessel sinking in mid-ocean.

> Thus at the very period when it was important that the general public be educated to the possibilities of radio the efficient crystal detector came along to boost the industry. The Morse code had great appeal to boys and young men, but when music and spoken words might occasionally be picked up out of the ether there arose a veritable army of enthusiasts for the new science. Boys love to tinker, to experiment with chemistry or mechanics, and here was the opportunity of the ages.[5]

The first decade of the new century brought many refinements, improvements, and significant new ideas. One of these was to revolutionize radio broadcasting and was even to provide the basis of an entire electronics industry that

5. Archer, *History of Radio*, p. 91.

would follow. Its inventor, Lee De Forest, called it an *audion*; in the technical jargon of early radio it was called a *valve*; today we would call it a *vacuum tube*. Only recently has it been displaced by the transistor, a device which performs approximately the same task. De Forest's audion was the key element in electronic amplifiers that could enlarge both broadcast and received radio signals. After refinement, it permitted the human voice to be transmitted to all parts of the globe. Radio receivers became far more reliable and the clarity of reception improved. Refinement followed refinement. The heterodyne circuit and superheterodyne circuit significantly improved reception. Radio equipment, which was once so huge and heavy that only ships could easily transport it, now became increasingly light and portable. In fact, during World War I, radiotelephones were successfully mounted in airplanes for the purpose of informing gun batteries on the ground of the accuracy of their fire.

In some ways, one of the most crippling of the social conditions surrounding the early development of radio was the concept of private ownership and the profit motive. Every minor and major invention was immediately patented in the United States, in Britain, and in other countries as well. It became nearly impossible to make needed improvements in radio components or to market equipment thus improved without falling into bitter court entanglements over patent claims. In fact, all the major pioneers in radio, from Marconi on, frequently found themselves battling each other in court. Lee De Forest, one of the principal inventors of major radio components, was actually arrested and charged with fraud. The problem was, of course, that there were fortunes to be made in wireless, and the competition to tie up important inventions for exploitation was intense.

At the same time, it is also true that millions of dollars were expended by private individuals and syndicates to aid inventors in improving their ideas to the point where they could be turned into marketable devices. In the final analysis, this financial support for research may have compensated

for the many problems that the concepts of private ownership, corporate profit, and commercial exploitation brought
to radio.

World War I brought urgent military needs for the improvement of radio systems. It brought not only new organization, manpower, and funds to bear upon unsolved
technical problems, but it had another important effect. All
patent litigation and restrictions were temporarily suspended
for the duration of the war. The federal government was in
complete control of the infant industry, and this brought
new cooperative efforts to the task of technical advance-
ment which would have taken much longer in peacetime.

THE RADIO MUSIC BOX

A young radio engineer by the name of David Sarnoff had
advanced rapidly in the ranks of the American Marconi
Company. He had achieved considerable public attention
during the sinking of the ill-famed *Titanic* when it was ripped
by an iceberg in mid-Atlantic. David Sarnoff remained at
his telegraph key in a radio station in New York City decoding messages from the disaster scene. For three days and
three nights he kept a horrified public apace of developments concerning the tragic incident. He later moved up
from this post to more important positions in the company.
In 1916, Sarnoff sent a memorandum to his superiors. This
now-famous memorandum in a sense did for radio what
Benjamin Day did for the press almost a century earlier. It
showed an economically profitable way by which radio could
be used as a medium of mass communication for ordinary
families. While the company did not immediately follow
Sarnoff's advice, he successfully predicted the major outlines of radio as a mass medium. He wrote:

> I have in mind a plan of development which would
> make radio a "household utility" in the same sense

as the piano or phonograph. The idea is to bring music into the house by wireless.

While this has been tried in the past by wires, it has been a failure because wires do not lend themselves to this scheme. With radio, however, it would be entirely feasible. For example—a radio telephone transmitter having a range of say 25 to 50 miles can be installed at a fixed point where instrumental or vocal music or both are produced.... The receiver can be designed in the form of a simple "Radio Music Box" and arranged for several different wave lengths, which should be changeable with the throwing of a single switch or pressing of a single button.

The "Radio Music Box" can be supplied with amplifying tubes and a loudspeaking telephone, all of which can be neatly mounted in one box. The box can be placed on a table in the parlor or living room, the switch set accordingly and the transmitted music received....

The same principle can be extended to numerous other fields as, for example, receiving lectures at home which can be made perfectly audible; also events of national importance can be simultaneously announced and received. Baseball scores can be transmitted in the air by the use of one set installed at the Polo Grounds. The same would be true of other cities. This proposition would be especially interesting to farmers and others living in outlying districts removed from the cities. By the purchase of a "Radio Music Box" they could enjoy concerts, lectures, music, recitals, etc. While I have indicated a few of the most probable fields of usefulness for such a device yet there are numerous other fields to which the principle can be extended.[6]

If Sarnoff had added the singing commercial and the soap opera, his description of radio as it would develop into a system of mass communication would have been almost

6. Ibid., pp. 112–13.

perfect. Within ten years he was to see radio grow into a medium for household use, following almost to the letter the outline that he had dictated. David Sarnoff's suggested application of existing radio technology to this imaginative, new, and practical usage ranks as an insight with that of Marconi's idea of taking existing laboratory devices and using them as a wireless telegraph. Sarnoff himself played a major role in bringing about this transformation; he became in a short time the manager of a new corporation in the radio field and was able to help make his dream become a reality.

Feeble attempts to perpetuate governmental control over radio at the close of the Great War were crushed by outcries by private interests. Just as the federal government had allowed control of the telegraph to fall into the hands of private persons, it similarly handed over this important new medium of public communication to commercial interests. Radio was defined by this act as an *arena of business competition* as opposed to a public medium of communication to be operated by organizations of government. This decision was to have far-reaching effects and ramifications with which we live today. Other societies formulated different definitions concerning the control of broadcasting, and the systems of broadcasting that have developed in such countries as Great Britain, the Soviet Union, and others offer interesting contrasts with our own. That is not to say that they are better, only that they are very different due largely to historical decisions and events.

Once direct governmental control was eliminated, British and American commercial interests, which had prospered during the war, fought each other to gain control. The General Electric Company finally bought up the British shares of American Marconi and formed a new corporation with a patriotic name (apparently designed to dispel fears of foreign control). The new Radio Corporation of America (RCA) was able to consolidate a number of conflicting patent interests, and it gave control over wireless telegraphy and radio broadcasting in the United States to American stockholders. In 1919, David Sarnoff, who had forecast the "Radio Music Box," was appointed its first commercial manager.

COMMERCIAL BROADCASTING BEGINS

Shortly after World War I, the Westinghouse Company, a major American manufacturer of electrical equipment, attempted to move into the international wireless telegraph field. It was not particularly successful. This was due largely to the fact that its rival RCA owned most of the important patents. However, some of its directors were interested in the newer field of wireless telephony, and the company had done considerable research in this area. Dr. Frank Conrad was in charge of experiments with new and powerful transmitters of this type. In connection with this work, he not only built such a transmitter for experiments at the Westinghouse laboratory, but he constructed one at home over his garage so that he could continue his work in the evening. He licensed his home transmitter nearly a year later as station 8XK in April 1920. He started to broadcast signals during the evening hours as he worked with his apparatus in attempts to improve its design. He soon found that people in the area were listening in on their amateur receiving sets. This proved to be a boon at first, because their letters, cards, and phone calls gave him some indication of the range and clarity of his transmitter. Before long, however, his circle of amateur radio listeners began to become a problem. To create a continuous sound, he had started to play the victrola over the air. His listeners began to demand particular songs and would even call him at odd hours to ask him to play a favorite record. Dr. Conrad solved the problem by regularizing his broadcasts, and with the cooperation of a local phonograph dealer, he was able to present continuous music for a two-hour period two evenings a week. The number of listeners grew rapidly, and his family enthusiastically joined in the fun to become the first "disc jockeys."

All this activity increased the demand for receiving sets in the area, and it became increasingly clear that there might be money to be made in the manufacture of such sets for home use. The commercial possibilities of this did not escape the attention of officials of the Westinghouse Company. They decided to build a larger transmitter in East Pittsburgh for the purpose of stimulating the sale of home receivers of their own make and the sale of the components from which amateurs built such sets. It was in this way that Station KDKA, Pittsburgh, came into existence in the year 1920.

Although David Sarnoff had forecast the radio music box several years earlier, it was the decision of Harry P. Davis, vice-president of the Westinghouse Electric and Manufacturing Company, which concretely gave birth to commercial household radio. He decided that a regular transmitting station, operated by the manufacturer of receivers, would create enough interest in the sale of sets to justify the expense of operating the station. Although this financial basis for broadcasting has long been replaced by the sale of air time for advertising, it was sufficiently practical at the time to get radio started as a medium for home use.

To stimulate interest in the new station and, of course, to promote the sale of receiving sets, it was announced that the transmitter would broadcast the results of the 1920 presidential election over the air. Bulletins were phoned to the station from a nearby newspaper, and the returns were broadcast during the evening of November 11 as they came in. An audience of between five hundred and a thousand people heard the word through the air that Warren G. Harding had been elected President of the United States. The event was a sensation; the dream of David Sarnoff had become a reality.

The Pittsburgh experiment was so successful that other stations were quickly launched. Transmitters began regular broadcasts in New York in 1921, followed by stations in Newark and other cities. Westinghouse soon had several competitors. The public's interest in radio had been growing. Its appetites for the new signals in the air had been whetted by the glamor and excitement of radio's brief history. The dramatic stories of rescues at sea, of daring flights over wild terrain with radiotelephones, and the struggles of giant corporations to gain control over wireless telegraphy had all contributed to this surging interest. When radio stations actually began to broadcast during regular periods with music and voices people could receive at home in their own cities, this latent interest suddenly burst into a full-blown craze. The public began to clamor for radio. By 1922, the manufacture of home receivers was lagging hopelessly behind the receipt of orders. New stations were being built at a staggering pace. In the last half of 1921 licenses were issued for 32 new stations, but in the first half of 1922, this number had risen to 254! Although there were still many problems to work out concerning its financial base, its content, and its technical functioning, radio as a mass medium was off to a flying start.

THE EARLY DAYS OF RADIO AS A MASS MEDIUM; THE PROBLEMS OF INTERFERENCE AND FINANCE

One of the earliest problems that household radio encountered was brought on because of its own popularity. There is a limited spectrum of frequencies available that are suitable for broadcasting. In the beginning, no attempts were made by either government or private groups to regulate the frequencies transmitters in a given area would use. The Radio Act of 1912 did not specify frequencies for privately operated broadcast stations. The Secretary of Commerce, who licensed all new transmitters, had selected two frequencies, 750 kilocycles and 833 kilocycles. All stations were assigned one or the other. As the number of transmitters operating grew quickly, there developed an annoying number of instances where two stations were operating near enough to each other so that the program of one would be imposed upon the sound of the other. This type of interference could not easily be controlled. Many stations worked out informal agreements to divide up available time. There was no legal authority that could assign different positions on the radio band for every station to use and could rigorously enforce such regulations. Obviously, such a problem could be handled only by some form of governmental agency, but there was no adequate provision by Congress or by the states for such a controlling body. The Department of Commerce issued licenses to operate transmitters, but did little else. Because of the lack of control over this technical problem, confusion began to mount.

In the meantime, radio was advancing at a tremendous pace. In 1922, station WJZ in Newark successfully broadcast the World Series. Stations began to broadcast opera, concerts, news, dance music, lectures, church services, and a great variety of events. Voluntary experiments were tried by having nearby stations broadcast on wavelengths at least twenty meters different from each other as a means of avoiding overlap. In spite of efforts to combat interference, the problem continued to grow.

Successful experimentation with networks was tried, and it was found that several stations linked by wires could simultaneously broadcast the same program. The rush to build new transmitters continued, and by 1923 stations were to be found in most major cities across the nation.

But two major problems continued to plague the medium. The technical problem of interference was already badly out of hand, but there was also the problem of paying for the broadcasts. While the larger electrical manufacturers could afford to finance their stations out of their profits on the sale of sets, this was a limited expedient at best, and it was no help at all to the owners of stations who were not electrical manufacturers.

By the end of 1923, some of the initial enthusiasm for constructing radio transmitters began to sag as the hard financial facts had to be faced. Thre was simply no profit as such, and only those with other financial resources were in positions to continue in operation.

> Now that a full year of nation-wide radio broadcasting had been completed the summer of 1923 afforded an opportunity to cast up the accounts, so to speak. This was indeed a disturbing experience, since the studio ledgers of every station disclosed entries almost entirely in the red ink. Fortunes had been squandered in the mad rush.... As early as December, 1922, the Department of Commerce reported the suspension of twenty stations for that month alone. With every succeeding month the casualty list had grown more appalling. Between March 19 and April 30, 1923, forty-two stations gave up their franchises. In the month of May there were 26 failures. June, 1923, saw fifty radio stations become silent. In July twenty-five franchises were surrendered. Thus in the period from March 19th to July 31st of this fateful year 143 radio stations went out of business.[7]

Unless some viable financial basis could be found, radio as a medium of communication to the American home was doomed.

But the public was not to be denied radio. The mid-1920s were years of prosperity for most Americans. The grim remembrances of the Great War were fading, and the nation was entering a period of industrial and financial growth. The new practice of installment buying was part of a great expansion of credit which was taking place in the entire economic structure. No one had any inkling of the eventual collapse

7. Ibid., p. 312.

that would begin in October of 1929. Installment buying made it easier for families of modest means to purchase consumer goods such as radio receivers. Radio listening was becoming increasingly popular, and pressure was being exerted on Secretary of Commerce Herbert Hoover to do something about the interference problem. He did work out a system for assigning different wavelengths to various broadcasting stations, but the attempt to implement it was not completely successful. People who owned sets capable of picking up only one major frequency did not like the idea. Also, there was no actual way of enforcing the assignments, and some transmitters simply ignored the plan. On the other hand, many of the major stations, which were engaged in regular broadcasting, tried to follow the secretary's assignments and did so with success.

The industry itself was exerting great pressure upon the Department of Commerce not only to regulate frequencies, but to limit the number of stations that could be licensed in a given area. The public, too, was becoming disenchanted with the cacophony that came out of their sets night after night. The problem of interference was getting unbearable. Ancient spark transmitters used for marine broadcasts, Morse code amateurs, powerful stations which broadcast regularly, and local fly-by-night operators were all blasting each other over the airwaves.

Four major conferences were held during the years 1922–1925 in Washington, D.C., to discuss the problems of broadcasting. The position of government was that it was up to the industry itself to clean up its own house. The newspapers had gotten along without government control. In fact they had fought it bitterly. The film industry was cleaning up its products. In a political system which stressed private initiative, it was felt by many government officials that federal control over broadcasting would be a dangerous precedent. In fact, Congress had repeatedly refused to consider bills on the subject. The only legislation in existence on radio was the old Radio Act of 1912, which was hopelessly out of date.

The problem was not an easy one to solve, even by government control. Since wireless telegraphy would also need regulation, the matter had international complications. In addition, there were the thousands of amateurs whose rights had to be protected. Not only were there more than 500 major stations operating on a regular basis, but there were approximately 1400 small stations of very low wattage that operated when their owners had the urge. Yet, to pick up this jumble of signals, Americans spent $136 million for receiving sets in 1923 alone.[8]

Secretary of Commerce Hoover struggled valiantly to find a solution. He tried limiting the power and hours of operation of some stations so that they could share a given frequency. By 1925, every spot on the frequency band was occupied, some by several stations. The broadcast band could not conveniently be extended without severely infringing upon other important kinds of radio and wireless operations. There were 175 additional stations clamoring for licenses that could not be accommodated.

In 1926, this arbitrary system collapsed. A federal court decided that the secretary of commerce had no legal basis to impose any restrictions on a station's power, hours of operation, or transmitting frequency. In that same year also, the attorney general issued the opinion that the only existing legislation, the Radio Act of 1912, really did not provide a legal basis for any of the regulations he had been using. Hoover simply had to abandon the entire attempt in disgust, and he issued a public statement that urged radio stations to regulate themselves. They were unable to do so.

In the face of the utter chaos that followed, President Coolidge asked Congress to enact appropriate legislation to regulate broadcasting, including provisions for adequate en-

8. Girard Chester, Garnet R. Garrison, and Edgar Willis, *Television and Radio* (3rd ed.; New York: Appleton-Century-Crofts, 1963), p. 24.

forcement. They did so in 1927. They first enunciated the important principle that *the airwaves belong to the people,* and that they can be used by private individuals only with the formal permission of government on a short-term license basis. Licenses were to be granted or revoked when it was in the public interest, convenience, or necessity to do so. All licenses of existing stations were automatically revoked; and the industry had to start all over by applying formally for a franchise to operate and by providing adequate statements and explanations as to why it would be in the public interest for them to do so.

The Radio Act of 1927 was to be a temporary solution. After a seven-year period of observation, trial, and some readjustments, a new and more permanent set of statutes was written and a Federal Communications Commission (FCC) was established to enforce the provisions. The Federal Communications Act of 1934 has since become, with appropriate amendment from time to time, the principal regulating instrument for the broadcast industry in the United States.

Meanwhile, the boisterous new industry continued to seek an adequate means of financial support. By the mid-1920s, broadcasters were still grappling with this problem. A committee of New York business people tried the experiment of soliciting funds directly from the listening audience for the purpose of hiring high-quality talent to perform over one of the larger stations in the area. While a trickle of funds came in, most listeners decided they would rather listen free to whatever happened to come their way than pay directly out of pocket to be assured of higher-quality programs. This response typifies the feelings of the majority even today. It also explains in part why the public eventually accepted advertising messages as a means of financing broadcasting. They would rather put up with somewhat objectionable commercials than pay directly for their entertainment.

Other schemes were proposed. David Sarnoff felt that wealthy philanthropists should endow radio stations just as they did universities, hospitals, or libraries. Others suggested charging a license fee for operating a home receiver, the proceeds of which were to be divided among broadcasters. Many felt that the industry itself would solve the problem. The larger manufacturers of receiving sets were said to have an obligation to provide something to hear on their products. It was thought that this would eventually result in a small number of networks, each operated by a different manufacturer or group of manufacturers, and that there would be few if any independent stations.

But while these debates were being carried on, advertising was quietly creeping in as a dependable source of revenue for radio broadcasts. In fact, as early as 1922, station WEAF had sold radio time for ten-minute talks on behalf of a Long Island real estate company that was selling lots. Then major companies began to sponsor programs. A department store paid for an hour-long musical program. A tobacco company sponsored a radio variety show. A candy company presented two comedians. The public was much drawn to these, and audiences wanted more. At first, these sponsors made no direct advertising appeal for their products. They simply mentioned their name as sponsor or titled the program after the name of their product. This form of subtle advertising found little criticism. The general goal of sponsoring such a program was to create goodwill among the audience.

The secretary of commerce was dead set against open huckstering on radio. He said, "it is inconceivable that we should allow so great a possibility for service, for news, for entertainment, and for vital commercial purposes to be drowned in advertising chatter."[9] Many other voices were added to this view. Responsible officials in government, leaders of the industry, and many groups of listeners concurred.

---

9. Alfred N. Goldsmith and Austin C. Lescarboura, *This Thing Called Broadcasting* (New York: Henry Holt, 1930), p. 279.

But in our society, such an idealistic position was doomed from the outset. With listeners more interested in "free" entertainment than quality programming; with government playing only a technical role, primarily to keep frequencies unscrambled; with ownership of the media in the hands of profit-seeking companies and corporations, the noble views of the secretary of commerce and his supporters were not consistent with the value system, the political structure, and the economic institution of the society within which the new medium was developing. The same socioeconomic forces that led newspapers to turn to selling space to advertisers so they could sell their products to a mass audience were to result in a parallel pattern for radio. The surrender to advertising was strongly resisted for some time, but inevitably it came. It was somewhat artificially held back briefly by the policies of the American Telephone and Telegraph Company, which controlled many patents, transmission lines, and radio equipment used by broadcasters. But even this opposition was relaxed, and the way was opened for the flood of commercial messages that are now so much a part of broadcasting in the United States.

At first, advertising was restrained and dignified. But soon it became increasingly direct and to the point. It would be incorrect to say the public welcomed advertising, but it is certainly true it welcomed what advertising revenues made possible. People were willing to hear the sponsor's pitch in order to be able to listen to their programs. One reason for this was that programs were quickly designed to have great popular appeal. Money from advertising made it possible to hire effective talent. Individual comedians, singers, and bands soon developed large and enthusiastic followings. Weekly drama programs became popular. Programs for children were developed; sports broadcasts drew large audiences. A great variety of content was designed to capture the interest of different large components of the population.

By the end of the decade, the major problems of radio as a mass medium of communication were solved. Almost everyone could buy reasonably priced and reliable receiving set on time payments. The broadcasters received generous profits from selling their time to advertisers; sponsors sold products effectively over the air to a mass market; and talent with great popular appeal captured the nightly attention of the public. In the background, the new federal legislation had brought order out of chaos with respect to the interference problem. Only the ominous event of the crash of 1929 threatened to muddy the picture. But as it turned out, this was to have little negative impact on the growth of radio.

THE GOLDEN AGE OF RADIO

Radio flowered during the 1930s and 1940s. These were very trying decades for the American society. The Great Depression and World War II were events that affected the destinies of every citizen, but they had little inhibiting effect on radio.

An overview of radio's growth in the American society can be obtained from table 4, which shows the number of receiving sets in operation for selected years. By the end of the 1930s there was slightly more than one set per household in the United States. This remarkable growth in the use of radio receivers had occurred in spite of ten years of economic depression following the stock market collapse of 1929. It should be emphasized for those who did not experience those tragic days that this was a period of great distress for American families. Millions of workers were unable to find employment and there were few public agencies to turn to for relief. The trauma of such conditions cannot be adequately appreciated without having been personally involved. It was a time when the people of the United States were gravely depressed in spirit as well as in an economic sense.

But in spite of the hardships of the times, radio seemed to thrive on the depression! Advertising revenues, instead

TABLE 4
THE GROWTH OF RADIO SET OWNERSHIP IN THE UNITED STATES
(1922–72)

Year	Total Number of Sets, Home and Auto (in thousands)	Total Number of Households (in thousands)	Sets per Household
1922	400	25,687	.015
1925	4,000	27,540	.145
1930	13,000	29,905	.434
1935	30,500	31,892	.956
1940	51,000	34,855	1.463
1945	56,000	37,503	1.493
1950	99,000	43,468	2.277
1955	120,000	47,788	2.511
1960	156,000	52,610	2.965
1965	227,000	57,251	3.964
1970	320,700	62,875	5.100
1971	336,000	64,374	5.219
1972	353,500	66,676	5.301

SOURCES: New York World Telegram Corporation, *The World Almanac, 1970* (New York, 1970).

U.S. Bureau of Census, *Historical Statistics of the United States, Colonial Times to 1957* (Washington, D.C., 1960), Series A 242–44, p. 15.

U.S. Bureau of Census, *Current Population Reports: Population Characteristics,* Series P 20, no. 106 (9 January 1961), p. 11; no. 119 (19 September 1962), p. 4; no. 166 (4 August 1967), p. 4.

National Association of Broadcasters, *Dimensions of Radio* (Washington, D.C., 1974).

NOTE: Figures after 1960 include Alaska and Hawaii. Some figures have been revised from previous editions because of revisions in source materials.

of drying up, grew at an ever increasing pace. The number of radio sets owned by Americans about doubled every five years. Families who had reached the limit of their financial resources would scrape together enough money to have their radio receiver repaired if it broke down. They might have to let the furniture go back to the finance company or to stall the landlord for the rent, but they hung grimly on to their radio sets.

Radio fit the needs of millions of hard-pressed people during that trying time. It had music to restore their sagging spirits, funny people to cheer them up, and dramatic news to divert their attention from their personal problems. Amateur nights, evening dramas, soap operas, Western adventures, and variety shows were all followed avidly by loyal listeners night after night. On a summer night people could walk down a street on the evening that a particularly popular comedian was on the air and hear the program uninterrupted through the open windows of every house they passed.

By the time the depression eased and the war was about to begin, radio was reaching every ear. In mid-1940, there were nearly one and a half sets per household in the United States. Radio had also become increasingly sophisticated in every sense. It was technically excellent. It was possible for direct broadcasts to be picked up and relayed to listeners in their homes from almost any point on the globe. News broadcasting had become a sophisticated art, and outstanding journalists had established themselves within this new medium. The press and radio had learned to live with one another after prolonged feuding, and radio had full access to the world's wire services.

During World War II, the radio industry made all its resources available to the federal government. War information messages, domestic propaganda, the selling of war bonds, campaigns to reduce the civilian usage of important materials, and many other vital services were performed. It should be noted that the manufacture of home receiving sets was completely curtailed during the war years. Figure 3, the cumulative diffusion curve for radio sets, shows that from 1940 to 1945 few new sets were acquired by American households. Special attention should be called, however, to the sharp rise in sales during the following five-year period, when the cumulative diffusion curve recovered from the retardation of the war years and resumed its regular pattern of growth.

FIGURE 3. THE CUMULATIVE DIFFUSION CURVE FOR RADIO; OWNERSHIP OF RECEIVING SETS PER HOUSEHOLD IN THE UNITED STATES (1922–72).

Of greater sociological significance are the postwar years when radio was faced with vigorous competition from television. If radio had retained its original format and content, it would have remained a direct competitor of the newer medium, which was apparently capable of gratifying the relevant needs of the mass audience in a more effective manner. At first, radio attempted to do this with the somewhat optimistic argument that over the years people had built up a deep loyalty to radio, which had served them so well, and they could not easily be lured away to a flashy new thing like television. The public turned out to be completely fickle, however, and as soon as families could afford television, they gleefully abandoned radio in favor of the tube.

To put it in sociological terms, radio had been satisying certain needs within the American society as a social system. When a more effective functional alternative became widely available, however, the earlier medium began to show signs of obsolescence.

Faced with the prospect of oblivion, radio was forced to find audience needs to satisfy that were not being effectively served by television. It successfully found such needs, and radio remodeled itself along new lines. During the 1930s, '40s, and even the early '50s, radio had successfully captured the attentions of the American family during the major evening hours. People turned to their radio to listen to the country's most popular entertainers. As television grew, it took over these entertainers along with the family's evening time. Radio was displaced from the living room and had to be content with the bedroom, the kitchen, the automobile, and the beach. Transistor technology, which opened up a huge market for miniature sets, helped keep radio from the type of postwar decline that occurred with motion-picture theaters as a result of television (figure 2).

At present, radio seems to have found a workable formula. It caters to its audience during times when television is inappropriate. People listen when they wake up in the morning, while they are working, driving, playing, etc. But when evening comes and they settle down in their living rooms, the radio dial is turned off in favor of the television set. Nevertheless, radio remains as one of the most massive of our mass media in terms of the ownership of sets. Table 4 shows that Americans now own more than five sets per household. Figure 3 suggests that the curve of diffusion for radio has not yet begun to level off; it has by no means reached its peak. The trend toward miniaturization will probably continue, and set ownership will soar even higher. Needless to say, the impressive number of sets owned by American families does not imply that they spend a corresponding amount of time in radio listening.

DEVELOPMENT OF THE TELEVISION INDUSTRY

The newest of the broadcast media inherited many of the traditions of radio. Several factors worked together to make its technological development and its diffusion through the American society a much more rapid and less chaotic process than was the case with its parent medium. The technology of television was really quite sophisticated before mass-manufactured sets were placed on the market for the public. There was no period comparable to the "crystal set" era in any widespread sense. The new medium did not have to work out a structure of control with the government. The FCC and its supporting legislation were simply taken over from radio. The financial basis of television was clear from the start. The public was completely accustomed to "commercials," and television promised to be even more effective as a vehicle for the sales pitch. No great problem was foreseen in attracting advertising money. There was no period of feuding with newspaper and wire-service interests. These arrangements were simply extended from established radio interests. The network idea was already popular from the older medium. An adequate coaxial-cable technology was available, and only the physical facilities needed to be constructed. The public was already completely familiar with the moving picture, and its transmission through broadcasting was not difficult for them to accept. For this reason, little public resistance to adoption of the new device was anticipated.

Actually, the television set quickly became a status symbol. In its early period of diffusion, families who could ill afford a set would sometimes scrimp on necessities to be able to buy one. The "easy payment plan," by now a deeply established American folkway, was widely used by families of modest means to acquire their sets. The urge to be identified as a set owner in the initial period of diffusion was so strong that in some cases families are said to have purchased and installed television antennae conspicuously on top of their dwellings long before they actually had sets to hook on. Stories of this type were widely circulated during the late 1940s. The definition of the television set as a luxury and as a status symbol led to occasional public outrage when it was discovered that people on public welfare or other forms of relief owned sets. Apparently the experiences of the depression years when radio sets were regarded as extremely comforting to people in trying economic circumstances had been forgotten.

Actually, television might have been a household medium even earlier had it not been for World War II. The electronic technology of television was worked out during the 1920s and '30s. By 1939, television broadcasts were being made in the United States. The World's Fair of that year featured demonstrations of this latest marvel of science, and President Roosevelt gave an address over the new communication medium. This particular broadcast was viewed by only a handful, because commercial manufacturers had not yet begun to mass-produce sets. In 1941, on the eve of World War II, the FCC approved home television, and the communication industry began to work out elaborate plans for its development. By this time there were nearly 5000 television sets (mostly in the New York area) in private hands, and several small stations were broadcasting regularly for two or three hours a day.

World War II interrupted any further development for the duration. In some ways this block to development may have accounted for the very rapid growth of television when the country returned to a peacetime economy. Electronics manufacturing techniques that aided in overcoming problems of television receiver production were developed during the war. Furthermore, the war completely ended the depression of the prewar period. In fact, with minor fluctuations the country entered a period of continuous economic growth, which was uninterrupted for more than two decades. The purchasing power of the average family rose to a point where television ownership was within the means of almost everyone.

THE FREEZE

With the bitter lessons of the interference chaos in the early days of radio before them, the government took a much more active role in controlling the broadcasting frequencies of television. By 1948 there were about seventy stations in operation and several million sets in use. Applications for new permits began to come in rapidly. Since television has only thirteen VHF channels for the whole nation, a rigorous means of control was needed to avoid interference. Fortunately, the television signal does not follow the curvature of the earth as does a radio signal. This means that two stations broadcasting on the same channel would not interfere with each other if there were sufficient distance between them. A master plan for the whole United States had to be worked out so television channels could be fairly allocated. There was also the need to study competing color systems to see what problems lay there. In addition, there were a substantial number of UHF channels on the spectrum, and these had to be allocated among competing interests. With these and other technical problems in mind, the FCC stopped granting new permits for television stations in 1948. Those stations in operation were permitted to continue, but time was needed to work out a master plan in detail so that as many problems as possible would be avoided when television reached its maturity. Actually, the stations already in operation (about seventy) were located in urban centers and were concentrated in the more eastern, and therefore more populated, sections of the country. Thus, the sale of sets could continue, even though no new stations were being built.

TABLE 5
THE GROWTH OF TELEVISION SET OWNERSHIP IN THE UNITED STATES (1946–72)

Year	Monochrome Sets in Use (in thousands)	Color Sets in Use (in thousands)	Total Number of Households (in thousands)
1946	8		37,900
1947	250		39,138
1948	1,000		40,523
1949	4,000		42,107
1950	10,600		43,468
1955	37,400		47,788
1960	56,900	200	52,610
1961	59,500	400	53,291
1962	61,900	800	54,652
1963	64,000	1,600	55,189
1964	65,800	3,000	55,996
1965	66,400	5,000	57,251
1966	66,100	9,700	58,092
1967	64,370	14,630	58,845
1968	62,900	20,100	60,444
1969	61,900	26,400	61,805
1970	61,400	31,300	62,875
1971	61,100	37,500	64,374
1972	60,600	45,400	66,676

SOURCES: U.S. Bureau of Census, *Historical Statistics of the United States, Colonial Times to 1957* (Washington, D.C., 1960), Series A 242-44, p. 15.

U.S. Bureau of Census, *Current Population Reports, Population Characteristics,* Series P 20, no. 106 (9 January 1961), p. 11; no. 119 (19 September 1962), p. 4; no. 166 (4 August 1967), p. 4.

New York World-Telegram Corporation, *The World Almanac, 1970* (New York, 1970).

Table 5 shows that in spite of this "freeze," which continued until 1952, the sale of sets rose steadily through the early 1950s. When the freeze was discontinued, a large number of applications for stations were received, and areas of the United States that had been without a television signal began to find television stations in their midst. These factors

TABLE 5 (Continued)

Year	Monochrome Sets per Household	Color Sets per Household	All Sets per Household
1946	.0002		
1947	.0063		
1948	.0246		
1949	.0949		
1950	.2438		
1955	.7826		
1960	1.0549	.0038	1.06
1961	1.0801	.0075	1.09
1962	1.1326	.0146	1.15
1963	1.1596	.0289	1.19
1964	1.1750	.0535	1.23
1965	1.1598	.0873	1.25
1966	1.1378	.1669	1.30
1967	1.0938	.2486	1.34
1968	1.0406	.3325	1.37
1969	1.0015	.4271	1.43
1970	.9765	.4978	1.47
1971	.9491	.5825	1.53
1972	.9088	.6809	1.59

National Association of Broadcasters, *Dimensions of Television* (Washington, D.C., 1974).

NOTE: All figures after 1960 include Alaska and Hawaii. Some figures have been revised from previous editions because of revisions in source materials.

stimulated the sale of sets, and figure 4 shows that the period 1950 to 1955 was one of very rapid diffusion. By 1960 the statistical average shows approximately one television set per household. As shown in table 5, a slower but steady rate of increase continued, so that in 1972 there were more than 1.5 sets per household. Figure 4 shows that the purchase rate for monochrome sets started to decline around 1965, brought about largely by reductions in the cost of a color television set. The diffusion rate of television will probably continue upward into the near future, but an increasing proportion of the television sets purchased will be color sets.

It is difficult to predict when the saturation point of television will be reached or when a functional alternative to conventional television will emerge. It is conceivable that ongoing technological developments might allow television to become truly portable so that it, like transisterized radio, could be used in a car, on the beach, or in numerous other environs outside the home. Or technological innovations, such as the video cassette, might emerge to compete effectively with conventional television. Or, even more probable, the conventional television set might take on new functions, such as serving as a receiver and transmitter for two-way cablevision or in a computer-based data processing system.

Another difficulty in forecasting the final outlines of television in the United States is the future role of subscription television. There is clearly a portion of the population who are dissatisfied with current popular fare on television and who are also sufficiently affluent to pay for better programs. "Pay" television has not been a popular idea with the general public. Many seem to see it as some kind of threat to the "free" television which they now enjoy. Similarly, educational television is a confusing issue. Many residents of a community without an educational television channel bitterly complain about it. However, when such a channel begins to operate in their city, many of those who formerly complained do not view it.

One of the most constant factors about our electronic mass media is their continuous change. The television set of today is a vastly different object from what people were viewing in the late 1940s. The sets that will be used in the decades to come will make present equipment appear quaint

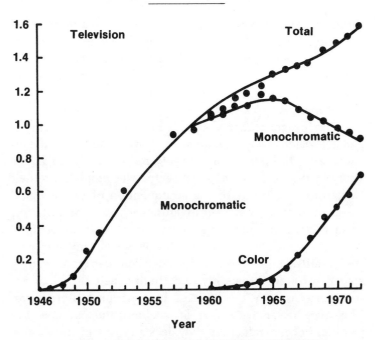

FIGURE 4. THE CUMULATIVE DIFFUSION CURVE FOR TELEVISION; OWNERSHIP OF RECEIVING SETS PER HOUSEHOLD IN THE UNITED STATES (1946–72).

and amusing. As electronic technology continues to advance, media that are beyond our imagination may become as commonplace in the future as a radio receiver or a television set is today.

As each of our mass media was invented and converted to a form suitable for use by American families, it was diffused more or less rapidly throughout the population. The longer adoption period of the newspaper stands in contrast to the swift diffusion of television. The decline of the newspaper reveals the impact of functional alternatives. The drastic reduction in motion-picture attendance indicates what happens when a new medium becomes capable of gratifying the entertainment needs of a society in a more effective way. Clearly, the older media are showing signs of obsolescence, while the newer electronic media have not yet reached their maximum points of diffusion. However, as even newer media are invented, different patterns of usage can be expected to emerge.

The foregoing chapters on the newspaper, the film, radio, and television have attempted to show some of the details concerning the impact of a society on its mass media. The study of the media within this perspective emphasizes their background in terms of the accumulation of technological culture traits. It notes their invention as new configurations of such traits. It follows their transformation from technical devices known only to a few to forms which can be used by the multitude. It traces their diffusion patterns as they spread through the society and studies their curves of obsolescence as they are replaced by functional alternatives. This type of analysis says little about the psychological processes of individuals as they decided to adopt the various media or as they were influenced by the absorption of media content. Such an analysis does stress the broad social, economic, political, demographic, and other changes that characterize the society during the development of each medium. Such factors as war, depression, affluence, immigration, urbanization, the spread of education, and the presence of given technological elements in the culture of a society can facilitate, inhibit, or otherwise affect the development and adoption of a given mass medium.

The spread of the media is a set of social events that offers important data to the student of social change as well as to those whose interest is more specifically in communication. No medium of mass communication exists in a social vacuum. It is linked inextricably to complex and changing cultural constraints. The older idea that the media are independent forces, shaping and molding the society as they wish, is simplistic and outmoded. The development of a given medium and what it presents to society are dependent not only upon the characteristics of the medium itself, but also upon the salient norms and values of the sociocultural system within which it operates. In other words, there are numerous and pervasive ways in which a society has a profound influence upon its media.

5

ELEMENTARY CHARACTERISTICS of the COMMUNICATIVE ACT

Having seen in some detail a number of ways in which a society has had an impact upon its media, we need now turn our attention to the second of the basic questions with which social scientists approach the assessment of the communication revolution, namely, how does communication take place? Answers to this question are particularly important. A realistic assessment of a phenomenon such as mass communication can scarcely be achieved if there remain a number of controversies and unsettled issues concerning its basic nature. Unfortunately, this is precisely the situation with respect not only to *mass* communication, but to other forms of human communication as well.

The communication process is utterly fundamental to all of our psychological and social processes. Without repetitively engaging in acts of communication with other people, none of us could possibly develop the human mental processes and human social nature that distinguish us from other forms of life. Without language systems and other important tools of communication, we could not carry on the thousands of organized group processes that we use to coordinate our societal activities and lead our intensely interdependent lives. Yet, in spite of the awesome importance of the communication process to every human being, every group, and every society, we know less about it than we do about the life cycle of the bat or the chemical composition of the sediment on the ocean floor.

Perhaps communication is too much a part of us even to study. It is so ubiquitous and pervasive that it seems like the air. You know it is there, but it is available and so common that it does not seem terribly important to worry much about it. But worry about it we must, if we are to know *homo sapiens* better. If we are to unravel such mysteries as the basis of personality formation, the nature of mental illness, the sources of human conflict, and the principles of social change (to mention only a few), a more complete understanding of human communication is of paramount importance. This does not imply that the sole source of human difficulty or human achievement lies in communication. It is simply to suggest that such a wide variety of human problems in some way begin with the communication process that its nature urgently needs to be understood more adequately.

In spite of the fact that knowledge about communication has not accumulated in a manner commensurate with the importance of the problem, there are available the findings and conclusions of several disciplines that can offer a basis for beginning the task of developing a theory of the nature of human communication. The field of general semantics has yielded important insights into the nature of language and symbolic processes. Social psychology, especially the branch that focuses on symbolic interaction, has developed important propositions concerning the individual and communication. Learning theory, as developed by experimental psychologists, offers a number of leads to understanding the acquisition, uses, and consequences of language. Other fields as well have made important contributions to an accumulating body of theory and research findings concerning different facets of communication. It is to these sources that we must turn in order to develop a theoretical analysis of the elementary characteristics of the communicative act. In the following sections, a number of propositions from a variety of fields are drawn together in an attempt to summarize not only the nature of communication, but also some of its consequences for individuals and groups. No pretense is made that the resulting conceptual schemes are either sophisticated or particularly new. They will serve the purpose, however, of indicating about where we are now in the development of a theory of interpersonal communication. As will be quite clear, we really have not gotten very far.

COMMUNICATION PROCESSES
IN NONHUMAN ORGANISMS

One way of analyzing human communication is to contrast it with nonhuman communication. This, of course, implies that nonhuman creatures actually have the ability to communicate with one another. There are many living creatures, some far below *homo sapiens* on the phylogenetic scale, that have the ability to influence one another. This is not to say that such forms of communication proceed on the basis of exactly the same principles as human communication. Nevertheless, what occurs between the so-called social insects as they carry out their highly organized group life or among a flock of migratory birds as they signal one another are forms of communication.

The social insects provide a convenient point of departure. Ants, bees, termites, and other insects exist together in colonies, often with an elaborate division of labor and a highly developed social organization by means of which they coordinate their activities and work toward their common goals.

> Termites, like bees and ants, are social insects living in colonies. Like bees and ants, they work together, performing special tasks for the good of the colony, but, unlike them, they live together continuously, instead of interruptedly, in the nests or burrows. This colonial habit has given rise to different kinds of individuals or castes fitted structurally to perform definite functions in the life of the colony: soldiers for defense; a king and queen for reproduction, often replaced or supplemented by the supplemental reproductives; and usually a special caste called workers for the collection of food, the care of the king, queen, soldiers and young, and for the construction of the nest, burrows, exits, tunnels, towers, and exploratory extensions of the burrows.[1]

To maintain this organization, to carry out and coordinate the tasks that different individuals perform, some method of interindividual exchange of influence is required. Insects of various types possess a variety of mechanisms by which they are able to influence each other's behavior. These mechanisms may be techniques for generating and receiving odors, sounds, tactile stimulation, or even visual stimuli. With the use of such techniques, fairly complex social activities can be coordinated as individual insects generate and receive stimuli from one another.

1. Charles A. Kofoid et al., eds., *Termites and Termite Control* (Berkeley: University of California Press, 1934), p. 8.

There is no reason to equate such behavior with the far more complex communication processes upon which human beings depend, but insect activities of this type can be recognized as a true form of communication—differing in principle from that of higher animal forms, but communication nevertheless. Insect communication is based exclusively upon inherited biological mechanisms. These can be very complex indeed, and many are as yet only poorly understood, but there is little doubt that whatever communication techniques an insect possesses were part of its genetic endowment. When appropriate stimuli are present in the environment, these communication techniques are triggered off automatically. The individual insect responds automatically to the communication signals of its own kind; this is not a process over which it has voluntary control.

> Termites instinctively communicate with one another on contact in the burrow by means of their long sensitive antennae, which play rapidly over the surface of their neighbors. Alarm is also communicated throughout the colony of stridulating movements of the soldiers, feebly imitated by other members of the colony. The hard heads of the alarmed soldiers are rattled against the resonant walls of the narrow burrows, producing sounds which may be heard by applying one's ear closely to the surface of an infested post or pole. Rapping the pole sharply with a hammer will call forth these sounds of alarm.[2]

Communication among insects is for present purposes more interesting for what it is *not* than for what it is. It is an inherited, instinctual form of behavior, undoubtedly an end product of eons of adaptive evolution by means of which these relatively simple creatures maintain the social organization essential to their survival. Such communication does not involve learning. The individual insect is perfectly able to perform the communicative acts even if it has been raised

2. Ibid., p. 11.

in isolation and then returned to the colony as an adult. We need postulate neither conscious processes on the part of the individual nor culture processes on the part of the colony. Once the biology of the insect becomes completely understood, the basis of the communicative act at this level of life will stand fully revealed. The assertion that insect communication does not involve learning, consciousness, or cultural processes implies that it is indeed an elementary form of communication compared to what occurs among animals higher on the phylogenetic continuum.

It is important to note, before leaving the communicating insects, that there is a close link between the structure of the individual organism and the communication process. In the case of the insects, this is an obvious and relatively simple relationship. *Biological* structure determines the kind of communicative acts such insects can perform. They can perform only those in their genetic repertoire, and they cannot help performing them upon receiving the appropriate stimuli. In other animal forms there are also important links between the communication process and individual structure. However, biological structure becomes somewhat less the rigid, limiting, and completely inflexible factor among higher animal forms than it is among bees, ants, termites, and other related insects. The learning process, at a minimum at the level of the insect, becomes increasingly important as one moves up the scale. The relationship between the organization of the individual and the communication process can still be said to exist, but it is not biological structure that is so important, but the *habit structure* the individual acquires as a product of learning.

To illustrate how communication takes place among animals higher on the evolutionary continuum than insects, but lower than humans, to show the relationship between this process and the habit organization of the individual, we may turn to the so-called pecking order among hens. This interesting phenomenon is simply the organization or pattern of dominance and submission that develops between the individual members of a newly formed flock of hens when they are kept for some time in the same pen or confined area. In any given pair, the dominant hen pecks the submissive one, but not vice versa. An elaborate hierarchy is eventually worked out, with a particular hen at the top, able to dominate all others, and with the more submissive hens near the bottom, dominated by those above. This particular type of social organization is widely found among animals, where patterns of dominance and submission are established and continuously reinforced by various techniques. The relationship between this process and the communicative act is that some form of communication is essential to maintain the social organization, once it has been worked out. Also, the position of the individual within this pattern is largely a product of communicative experiences within the structure. Thus, both social organization and individual organization of response patterns are closely linked to the communication process as it is carried on within such a setting.

We will show clearly that the individual's position in the pecking order, and the techniques for helping maintain it, are *learned* and not inherited. Yet, the pecking order is by no means completely independent of biological factors. Experiments have shown that hens injected with male hormones will be more aggressive and will fight their way up higher in the structure. Similarly, large doses of female hormones will make the hen more submissive and it will suffer a consequent loss of position. The pecking orders are also sexbound. That is, roosters peck one another but do not peck hens. Hens establish their own order and do not challenge the roosters. In a mixed flock there will be two such hierarchies. In short, such biological factors as hormone balance, sex category, strength, and of course general anatomical structure operate as prerequisite and limiting factors in helping determine the place of a given individual within the so-

FIGURE 5. FORMING THE PECKING ORDER AMONG CHICKENS.

The pecking-order position of a given chicken results from a series of individual combats among the members of a newly established flock. This drawing depicts two Rhode Island Red pullets fighting to determine dominance and submission. From A. M. Guhl, "The Social Order of Chickens," Scientific American *94, no. 2 (February 156): 42–47.*

cial structure that is eventually worked out. At the same time, the pecking order is not simply a product of inheritance, and it can be quickly forgotten:

> A chicken's memory is short. Hens that have been separated for two weeks or more will fight the battle for dominance all over again when they are brought together. If a strange bird enters an organized flock, it has to fight each of the residents to establish its status.[3]

But what does this all have to do with communication? The phenomenon of the pecking order, and indeed the act of

3. A. M. Guhl, "The Social Order of Chickens," *Scientific American* 94, no. 2 (February 1956): 43.

pecking itself, is a classic illustration of a particular *type* of communication, namely communication based upon the *natural sign*. To explain the implications of this assertion, consider the following simplified explanation of how the act of pecking becomes established and how it operates as a means of communication.

When adult chickens that have not previously been together are placed as a group into a pen, they engage in a series of combats by pairs. Each chicken will pair off against one opponent at a time, until eventually the order of dominance is established. A given pair may have to fight it out several times before the final outcome is clear and the dominance-submission issue is settled. Finally, the dominant chicken is able to signal to the submissive one its higher position by simply delivering a peck. The simple peck has in some way become a *substitute* for the elaborate series of acts that make up a complete beating given to another chicken. Similarly, the slight gesture of submission on the part of the recipient of the peck has become a substitute for the complete act of getting beaten by and eventually submitting to the more aggressive chicken. In some manner, these simplified and much truncated acts come to "stand for" the more dramatic, complicated, and extended series of behaviors associated with victory and defeat in combat.

Whenever a beginning portion of an act or series of acts, or some other portion or limited segment of the series, becomes capable of arousing the same internal responses that were previously aroused only by the entire act or series of acts, we are confronted with an example of a *gesture*. Just as the clenched fist shaken in the face of opponents arouses in them the response of a potential blow which could follow, or one which perhaps did once occur, the peck arouses for the chicken the inner response that was formerly aroused by its part of the combat. This substitution of a limited segment of the act for the whole complex act or series of acts is a natural product of learning for the chicken. The peck is a *natural*

sign for each of the chickens of the events of the more extended action series. Gestures are one type of natural sign
when they occur in this way among animals. Such gestures
really should not be confused with those used by human beings, and the example of the clenched fist was not directly
comparable. The reason for this is that we need not assume
that the chickens have any cognitive processes related to
the use of such signs. Although the peck as a means of communicating dominance and submission is a product of learning, it may be in every way nearly as automatic as is the ini-
tiation of a sound signal by an insect under appropriate
stimulus conditions or response to such a sound by another
insect. We need not assume that the dominant hen says to
itself, "I think I'll peck that other chicken to show who's
boss," or that the other chicken upon seeing the first chicken
advance says internally, "Oh-oh, here it comes again; I might
as well submit." The exchange of influence on each other's
behavior is simply a product of *learned responses* that have
emerged from the positive and negative reinforcements of
the combat situation.

The conclusion that pecks are learned sign substitutes
for more complex forms of behavior is well supported by an
additional characteristic of the dominance-submission behavior among chickens. Eventually, they even substitute a
simpler act for the peck itself:

> Once the peck order has been determined, pecking
> begins to decline in frequency as members of the
> hierarchy recognize their superiors; eventually a
> mere *raising or lowering of the head* [italics supplied] may
> be enough to signify dominance or submission
> respectively.[4]

Thus it is that the beginning phase of the pecking act
begins to serve as a natural sign for the entire act. This new
and much simplified gesture then becomes the means of com-

4. Ibid.

munication the flock uses to maintain and reinforce its social organization when it has become deeply institutionalized.

The communication patterns among chickens, like those among termites, are interesting primarily as a contrasting framework against which human communication can be compared. Termite communication and chicken communication illustrate how creatures very different from humans are able to influence and coordinate each other's conduct. While biological factors alone are sufficient to account for communication among the social insects, and biological factors plus reinforcement learning of individual habit patterns are enough to explain communication among more advanced forms of animal life, these factors cannot fully account for the incredible complexity of communication among human beings. But before discussing human communication in depth, several additional issues need clarification.

We noted that the communicative act among animals capable of learning is based upon the natural sign. The essence of a natural sign is that it is a new stimulus preceding another stimulus (capable of calling out some response) in time in such a way that after a limited number of occurrences of an appropriate sequence the new stimulus becomes capable of calling out the response, bypassing the original stimulus, and thus forming in the individual a new habit. There is no assumption that the individual organism learning to respond to a natural sign is capable of voluntarily initiating the sign itself. If the natural sign happens to be a gesture that is initiated by one organism and serves as a stimulus for another organism, it is assumed that the initiator simply makes the gesture as a normal response to whatever environmental stimuli are present to which its behavior has become linked through learning. Only when two organisms have individually developed a set of learned habit patterns that *happen to be coordinated*, so that a response from one can serve as a stimulus to the other, can communication of this type take place. However, this type of communication is common in nature. It is widely found among mammals, birds, fish, and other animals that normally travel or exist in some sort of band, flock, or grouping.

Communication of this type is automatic, requires no assumptions of consciousness or cognitive functioning on the part of either organism. Furthermore, there is no assumption that whatever movement or act is used as a signal is assigned *arbitrarily* as a substitute for the more extended series of acts (combat, flight, etc.). One of the chickens in our example could not arbitrarily decide to let a wiggle of the claw or a flip of the tail be the substitute stimulus signifying dominance or submission rather than the peck. Neither do they mutually agree in any sense that the appropriate response to a peck will be to make a minor submissive gesture on the part of those who have been defeated in combat. They are simply incapable of establishing any such *conventions* among them. The peck becomes a sign because it occurs quite naturally at the appropriate point in the chicken's repertoire. The same is true of the submissive gesture. In short, the relationship between the sign (substitute stimulus) and its referent (that for which it is a substitute) is neither arbitrary nor conventional. It is part of the specific habit structure of the individual. It may or may not have a parallel in the specific habit structure of other individuals with which the animal associates. If such counterpart stimulus-response relationships exist for two or more organisms, these constitute a basis for the communicative act—they permit mutual influence on conduct and even possible coordination of activities.

Coordination of activities can take place only if the responses each animal makes internally to the particular sign used in communication are mutually coordinated. Thus, if the truncated act of raising the head arouses in the dominant chicken the internal feeling of engaging in and winning a combat, and if the sight of this stimulus arouses in the submissive chicken the internal experience of having fought but been defeated, then there can be the coordinated mutual influence that we have identified as one type of communication. In a very restricted sense, the internal learned responses thus aroused in the animals can be called "meanings." We must note immediately, however, that each chicken in the exchange has a "meaning" which is unique to it, a product of its particular experience that is quite different from the internal meaning response of the other animal. That is, there is no *shared* meaning, no isomorphism, no identity of form between the structure of the internal responses aroused by the act for the dominant chicken as compared to the submissive one. (It is on this point in particular that substantial differences exist between communication occurring among animals and among human beings.)

The usage of the term "meaning," which is implied in the above analysis, may seem unusual to the reader accustomed to think of this term in more complex ways. However, defined in this way, the concept of meaning is simply the internal experiences animals have in connection with particular stimuli that impinge upon their perceptual processes. If stable habit patterns are connected with such stimuli in such a way that they arouse internal responses of the type that only the actual object or event originally aroused, this constitutes *sign behavior*. If the sign behaviors of two animals are coordinated adequately (as in the example of the chickens), then communication of a particular type can take place. We can, of course, never directly observe such inner experiences and must make inferences about them. Such inferred constructs are widely used in science.

Recent research on chimpanzees suggests that chimps may have language capacities which far exceed the natural signing behavior of chickens. The Gardners and Fouts, for example, have had some success in teaching Washoe, a chimpanzee, American sign language—the same language taught to many deaf people.[5] Having noted that most of the natural

5. Allen Gardner and Beatrice Gardner, "Teaching Sign Language to a Chimpanzee," *Science* 165 (August 1969): 664–72. Roger S. Fouts, "Use of Guidance in Teaching Sign Language to a Chimpanzee," *Journal of Comparative and Physiological Psychology* 80 (September 1972): 515–22.

signs chimps use in the wild involve the use of their hands, the Gardners concluded that it makes more sense to try and teach a gesturial language that builds on their natural sign behavior than to try and teach a vocal language which does not. The evidence must be considered tentative at this point, but it suggests that Washoe has acquired a vocabulary of approximately 160 signs including signs for objects, such as cat or flower, and signs for feelings, such as sorry and hurt. Washoe has learned to *generalize* signs such that she learned the sign for "open" in context of opening doors, but generalizes the sign to drawers and refrigerators. Washoe also learned to combine signs into simple sentences and even made up some of her own combinations such as "gimme tickle."

Premack has used classical conditioning techniques to teach chimpanzees a language that is closer to a written language than the gesturial language used by the Gardners.[6] His symbols are pieces of plastic which vary in shape and which can be arranged vertically on a metallic board. His chimp, Sarah, has learned approximately the same number of signs or symbols as the Gardner's chimp, but Sarah has apparently been able to learn more complex sentences such as "apple is red."

Rumbaugh and other researchers working at the Yerkes Primate Research Center are attempting to teach chimps a language called Yerkish which consists of fifty geometric symbols printed onto typewriter keys.[7] The typewriter panel is hooked up to a projector so that the chimpanzee and the researchers have a visual display of the symbols selected and their order. The chimp Lana has apparently learned to ask for such things as food, companionship, and toys. Perhaps most provocative of all is the evidence suggesting that Lana can distinguish correct from incorrect word orders. The ex-

6. David Premack, "Language in Chimpanzees?" *Science* 172 (May 1971): 808–22.

7. Duane Rumbaugh, Timothy Gill, and E. C. von Glassersfeld, "Reading and Sentence Completion by a Chimpanzee," *Science* 182 (November 1973): 731–33.

perimenters present her with the beginnings of a sentence which is sometimes semantically correct and sometimes semantically incorrect or not in the correct word order. The chimpanzee completes the semantically correct phrases and erases the semantically incorrect phrases with approximately 90 percent accuracy.

The research on chimpanzees is very provocative because it would, if valid, lead us to revise our belief that only human beings can acquire and use languages. Most scientists will, however, reserve judgment until much more research evidence is available. To accept the idea that chimpanzees can learn to communicate with *symbolic* languages in a process identical with that used by human beings would be premature. Some of the problems that would have to be faced in reaching such a conclusion are discussed in the section that follows.

THE NATURE AND SIGNIFICANCE OF HUMAN COMMUNICATION

As is the case among animals, human communication involves biological structure. Before given individuals can adequately learn the complex habit patterns involved in the use of language, they must have a neural structure that functions within the normal range. Similarly, insofar as the various senses and the musculature are involved in speaking, hearing, and seeing during the communicative act among human beings, it has biological components. These components serve as prerequisite conditions rather than causal factors. In addition, individual human beings must undergo a long period of learning before they develop habit patterns, which permit them to respond to particular gestures, verbal and other, as substitute signs that have as their referents objects and events in the world of reality. The human communicative act shares these characteristics with the communicative act as it exists among other animal forms capable of sign learning. It is at this point, however, that the similarity appears to end.

Unlike the animal, the human being is born into an ongoing and elaborate culture. An important feature of this culture is the set of conventions that exist concerning the relationship between signs and their referents. For any given language (set of signs), the connection between a particular word of the language and that for which the word is a substitute is both *arbitrary* and *conventional*. In the historical development of language, particular objects or events were signified by specific sound patterns. These assignments were at first arbitrary. For example, the word "hippie" did not exist in the English language prior to the 1960s when the formation of groups with particular characteristics occurred. No one is sure how this arbitrary assignment came about, but it was somehow established. Once established, however, this particular vocal gesture began to serve as a substitute stimulus, that is, a sign, for which the referent was an individual with a particular appearance and life style. As usage persisted, it became conventional. That is, there developed an institutionalized practice to respond to this particular noise by internally experiencing people of this type. The existence of an established set of conventions, concerning the referents of gestures which originally may have been arbitrarily assigned, gives the human being an enormous advantage over other animal forms. We may designate a sign or gesture that is both arbitrary and conventional in the sense outlined above as a *symbol*. Many kinds of symbols exist.

A list of examples would be extensive, ranging through military insignia, sorority emblems, Morse code, algebraic symbols, and hundreds more. The most common, of course, are language symbols, verbal or written. Like all symbols, these are signs (substitute stimuli) that have as their referents events, things, or other phenomena, for which the verbal noise or written mark is a convenient substitute. Once learned, these convenient substitutes arouse the "mean-

ing" responses in the individual that only the referent itself originally aroused. While many animals acquire the ability to respond to (have meanings for) signs, it still appears that
only human beings can use symbols in the fullest sense. In
the chimpanzee experiments, for example, it is the human
beings who select the arbitrary symbols and set the convention. The entire range of symbols (words and otherwise)
used by a given society constitutes its language. Until chimpanzees select their own symbols arbitrarily and establish
their own conventions, they are not using language in this
sense.

We have, to be sure, left unanswered important questions concerning the origins of language, the source of arbitrary assignments, conventions, and so forth. These are beyond the scope of the present analysis. We may take the
existence of language as given, recognizing that its slow
development over eons of time is as yet ill understood. The
important thing is that human beings are born into an existing learning environment where language is conspicuously present. This happy circumstance makes it possible for
them to acquire tools for communication that are considerably more complex than those of their nearest animal
neighbors.

As individuals slowly acquire, during infancy and child-
hood, the ability to respond in conventionalized ways to the
vocal and written symbols that constitute language, they are
developing a repertoire of *meanings* in much the same sense
as was implied by this term in earlier paragraphs of the present chapter. That is, "meaning" is a product of learning. A
person's meaning for a particular symbol is the set of responses (both internal and overt) that the individual learns
to make to it. At first, a person can have such an internal experience only to a referent object or to itself, as a baby
experiences painful heat when exposed to the stimulus of a
boiling teakettle, a match, an oven, and so on. Upon repeatedly undergoing this experience, however, following the

warning utterance of parents that the object is "hot," individuals soon learn to have much the same internal experience to the vocal noise "hot" as they did earlier to the original objects that aroused the painful experience itself. Once such a habit has been established, they can respond to that particular verbal symbol by undergoing the corresponding internal experience even in the absence of high-temperature objects. Nevertheless, only insofar as their habitual responses to the symbol more or less parallel those of others, and insofar as they understand that this is the case, can such a symbol be used in the human communicative act.

Once such a conventional "meaning" has become a part of the repertoire, people can learn to initiate this particular vocal gesture (symbol) themselves, and respond to it in much the same way as they did earlier when it was initiated by someone else. This ability to initiate symbols and to respond to them in conventionalized ways appears to be a uniquely human accomplishment. It is undoubtedly a product of two factors: the enormous learning capacity of the average human being, and the prior existence of the cultural conventions of language.

The ability the human being has to initiate particular verbal gestures (words), which have associated with them conventionalized referents and internal meaning responses, and to respond to these symbols in much the same ways that other individuals respond (who share the conventions), is of course the ability to engage in human thought! The internal manipulation of meaning—the mental functioning of human beings—then, is critically linked to their involvement in a conventionalized language process, as George Herbert Mead so aptly pointed out several decades ago.[8]

Not only does the participation of individuals in the language process provide them with the means to communicate

8. George Herbert Mead, *Mind, Self and Society* (Chicago: University of Chicago Press, 1934). This work is the principal source for the theoretical approach of the present chapter.

with themselves (think); but it also provides them with the ability to communicate with others through conventionalized meanings. If individuals have learned to initiate a symbol that they respond to in the same way that they know others will respond, they have acquired the technique of human communication. In fact, the communicative act at the level of the human being involves exactly these elements. Where in the case of animals in the wild, communication proceeded on the basis of coordinated but *unlike* internal meanings for natural signs, human communication takes place because of isomorphism, that is, a certain *identity* between the internal meaning responses that separate individuals have learned to make toward a given symbol. A symbol that arouses the same general set of internal responses (meanings) within the individual initiating the stimulus as are aroused within the individual who perceives the stimulus is called a *significant symbol*. It is through the significant symbol that human beings learn to manipulate meaning within themselves (thought) and in exchanges with others (interpersonal communication). Such symbolic interaction appears to separate human beings clearly from other animals as far as communication is concerned.

Much has been made of the symbolic interaction process. The nature and structure of the language and the symbolic habits and significant symbols of a given people provide important keys to their social organization. Individual personality formation is also in large part a product of the communicative exchanges that the individual has engaged in.[9]

It is no exaggeration to say that the human communicative act, proceeding on the basis of the significant symbol, is a prerequisite ability without which it would not be possible for humans to have developed such elaborate societies and cultures. In fact, it is not possible to imagine any form of human society that could exist without this facility. The com-

9. A statement on the importance of symbolic interaction theory in social psychology can be found in Arnold Rose, ed., *Human Nature and Social Processes* (Boston: Houghton Mifflin, 1962).

municative act is the means by which a group's norms are expressed, by means of which social control is exerted, roles are allocated, coordination of effort is achieved, expectations are made manifest, and the entire social process is carried on. Without such exchanges of influence human society would simply collapse.

It is equally true that the involvement of individuals in the community of language is the key to their psychological nature. Without learning to use symbols and their associated internal meanings, they would be unable to manipulate meanings, form beliefs about themselves, ponder a problem, have human emotions, grasp a principle, plan ahead, learn in retrospect from the lessons of the past, and perform other human acts. They would be about at the level of intelligent chickens or at best at the level of superapes. They would be able to acquire unique meaning responses to natural signs, and if these happened to interlock with different meanings that other individuals had acquired to the same signs, some limited coordination of behavior could take place. But their minds and self-conceptions and their society would remain at the animal level.

Thus, the arbitrary and conventionalized sign—the significant symbol—is the element which sharply distinguishes human beings from other forms of life.

HUMAN SYSTEMS FOR ACHIEVING ISOMORPHISM IN MEANING

But how does the human being use this unique facility to carry out the communicative act? We know that the significant symbol is the key element distinguishing humans fom other creatures; but how does this element operate in the communicative exchange that results in one individual understanding the initiated communication stimuli of another? To answer this question, we need to develop a theoretical construct, an abstract model of the system within which the communicative act takes place. If the construct is made sufficiently general, it can encompass *mass* communication as well as the more simple interpersonal communication.

The problem of communication is not actually a "transfer" of meaning. In the communicative act, there is no essence, spirit, or invisible "something" that leaves the central nervous system of one person and travels to that of another. Such a concept is unnecessary and muddies the water of legitimate inquiry into the nature of human communication with questions about "thought transference," "clairvoyance," "mind reading," and other such mystic ideas.

But if the communicative act is not a "transfer" of meaning, then how does communication occur? A convenient way of answering this question is that it takes place through the operation of a particular set of components in a theoretical system, the consequence of which is that there is *isomorphism* between the internal responses (meanings) to a given set of symbols on the part of both sender and receiver. Many attempts have been made to conceptualize the theoretical system that is basic to the communication process. The system analyzed in the paragraphs below makes no claim of being original. It is an extension of the ideas of a number of previous writers.[10] It does show, however, how the use of the significant symbol makes possible the achievement of a certain identity of meaning between communicators and the person or persons toward whom they address their messages.

Figure 6 presents in schematic form the basic components of a theoretical system for the achievement of isomorphism of meaning between individuals engaged in the communicative act, that is, for "getting the meaning correlated"

10. These include: Claude E. Shannon and Warren Weaver, *The Mathematical Theory of Communication* (Urbana: University of Illinois Press, 1949); George A. Miller, "The Idealized Communication System," in *Language and Communication* (New York: McGraw-Hill, 1951), pp. 6–8; Wilbur Schramm, "How Communication Works," in *The Process and Effects of Mass Communication* (Urbana: University of Illinois Press, 1954), pp. 3–26; plus many others. A review of relevant literature is contained in Melvin L. De Fleur and Otto N. Larsen, *The Flow of Information* (New York: Harper & Brothers, 1958).

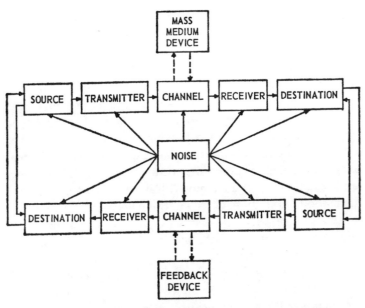

**FIGURE 6. THE COMPONENTS OF A GENERAL SYSTEM
FOR ACHIEVING ISOMORPHISM OF MEANING.**

between communicator and audience. The first general component of this system is a *source*. It is the function of the source to formulate "meaning" into "message." That is, to select appropriate significant symbols (message) with which to express the internal responses (meanings) the communicator wishes to present to the audience. The transformation of meaning to message makes the former externally available in the form of significant symbols. In the case of a two-person communication system, the source would be the individual person's cognitive processes, with which we experience the internal responses we have called meaning.[11] In the case of

11. The study of internal meaning responses has received far less attention from psychologists than the importance of the problem might suggest. The most important research in recent decades is that of Charles E. Osgood and associates. This outstanding and imaginative line of research is reported in Charles E. Osgood, George J. Suci, and Percy H. Tannenbaum, *The Measurement of Meaning* (Urbana: University of Illinois Press, 1957). It was from this source that a number of ideas were drawn for the present analysis of the communicative act.

mass communication, the source might be some organized group that has formulated its collective meanings into some message the group as a whole wishes to convey through a single spokesperson.

The second component is the abstract scheme is the *transmitter*. Its function is to encode—to transform the "message" into "information." Information will be defined as some type of event in the physical world which will permit movement over space. Electrical impulses traveling along a wire, electromagnetic radiations in the air, printed visual stimuli on paper, and agitations of the air molecules are all examples of "information." It is these events in the physical world that conquer distance between distinct individuals and not some mysterious movement of meaning from the mind of one person to that of another.

Generally speaking, source and transmitter are but different phases of the communicative act carried out by the originator of the communication. They are analytically separable functions of the single human being. When people talk, they select symbols to express their denotative and connotative meanings (formulate meaning into message) and then enunciate verbally or write these symbols (encodes messages to information) in such a way that they are converted into either auditory or visual events that can be perceived as stimuli by the audience.

A third component in this system is some form of *channel*. In the case of one person talking to another, this is simply the air through which information (agitations of the air molecules) moves. For techniques of communication other than verbal, e.g., written, telegraphic, etc., other types of channels would move the information across space. Mass communication requires more complex channels, which will be discussed below.

Linked with the channel in this system is the *receiver*. This component has the function of receiving the information and "decoding" it—transforming the physical events of the information back into a message (system of significant symbols). In the case of ordinary talking, this would be done by the auditory apparatus of the human being, receiving air vibrations and transforming them into neural impulses, so they can become recognizable verbal symbols. In the case of written communication, visual mechanisms would perform parallel functions.

Once the message (set of symbols) has been perceived, the final component, namely the *destination,* responds to these with the denotative and connotative internal experiences we are calling meaning. Thus, the function of the destination is to interpret "message" into "meaning."

After these components have functioned, if the meaning of the destination is isomorphic with the meaning of the source which originated the act, then communication can be said to have taken place. Thus, communication amounts to achieving a parallel in the structure of the internal meaning responses of both a source and a destination. The meanings remain in the behavioral systems (cognitive structures) of the respective parties, and it is their *similarity* that constitutes communication and not their "movement."

Obviously, the achievement of perfect correspondence between every element of the denotative and connotative meaning responses of both source and destination is seldom achieved because human communication is almost always in some degree less than perfect. There are a number of reasons for this, some psychological, some cultural, and some simply mechanical.[12] But whatever the source of this lack of isomorphism of meanings, the degree to which they are less than absolutely identical, element for element, can be called *noise.* This may be an undesirable feature of the communication system, but nonetheless it is almost always present. For this reason, *noise* must be recognized as an additional component of the theoretical system of the communicative act. Its function (consequence) is to reduce to some degree the correspondence between the pattern of response ele-

12. The sources of noise, its characteristics and consequences, are important research problems for several of the sciences.

ments constituting the meaning of the source and the counterpart meaning of the destination.

To this set of theoretical components, which function between source and destination, we need add another set functioning in the other direction. Nearly always, when individuals engage in a communicative act, there is some sort of perceptible feedback originating in communicatees which communicators use as data for modifying their messages. For example, if the communicatee winces, grins, raises an eyebrow, or just looks blank as the communicator enunciates words, this constitutes a kind of message returning to the communicator. The communicator may choose to illustrate further, use a less complex vocabulary, or otherwise alter the message because of this feedback. In short, during the communicative act, the destination also operates as a source of feedback and the source as destination for feedback messages. Whether this feedback is unwitting, in the form of culturally defined gestures, for example the raised eyebrow, or is given in carefully chosen significant symbols is unimportant for our theoretical analysis. It simply implies that the system we are developing does require a reverse set of components.

The reverse components are also affected by noise. Gestures can be misunderstood, facial expressions or other data can be misinterpreted just as words can be incorrectly understood. A classic example is the case of Abraham Lincoln, whose audience failed to cheer or applaud after his Gettysburg address. He concluded that it had been an inadequate speech, while his audience was actually so moved by it that they felt applause would have been inappropriate.

This two-way set of components operates as a system, then, with information moving first one way and then another, or both ways at the same time. It can operate with extreme rapidity in an ongoing conversation, or more slowly if the two parties are using written or other forms of communication.

To accommodate the mass communication process, this elementary theoretical system must be somewhat elaborated. Essentially, this is an elaboration of the *channel* in both the major and the feedback set of components. The channel conveys information to some mechanical device, such as a radio broadcasting transmitter, which is essentially a process for transforming one kind of information into another which is somewhat more effective in spanning distance. The speaker's voice causes air vibrations (information) that are transformed into another form of information (electric impulses) and are further transformed into electromagnetic waves. These in turn are picked up by the home radio set, transformed back into electrical impulses, and converted back into agitations of the air. Parallel accounts can easily be constructed for the words of newspaper reporters, who first place their message on the typewriter. These are then set into linotype, sent to the press, delivered to the home, etc., by an elaborate process that substantially multiplies the number of persons who can be exposed at a given time to the reporter's messages. These elaborations are additional complexities of detail, however, and do not alter the communicative act in principle. The reporter is still the source and transmitter that converts meanings to information. Any given reader is still a receiver and destination which decodes visual information to message and responds to the stimuli with meaning responses. The fact that the channel has become considerably elaborated does not change the fundamental characteristics of this communicative act. There also is a clear feedback set of components, although the details of these are likely to vary considerably from one mass medium to another. Letters to the editor are different in detail from the results of an audience rating system, where a sample of the audience can give its preference rankings for given television programs. In spite of these differences of technique, there are still the components of source, noise, destination, etc.

It is also true that mass communication is likely to involve large numbers of people in addition to complex mechanical or electronic elaborations of the channels. However, this is a difference of quantity rather than of principle. The relationship between a given mass communicator and a given member of the audience still takes place with significant symbols; the nature of meaning remains the same; and the communicative act still occurs throught the various components that have been outlined above.

While these differences between mass communication and simpler forms of interpersonal communication do not involve differences in fundamental principles, this does not mean that they are unimportant. The degree to which isomorphism of meaning or perhaps to which overt compliance to messages occurs when a given communication involves a mass medium as compared to direct face-to-face communication is a proper object of research. There is a voluminous literature which suggests that such differences do occur, and for this reason, mass communication can differ considerably in its *consequences*—its effect on conduct as compared to communication by other means. While the communicative act follows the same theoretical principles in all forms of human communication, the consequences of the act may differ substantially as different techniques for moving information are employed.

Having seen something of the underlying principles that occur in human communication, mass and otherwise, we need next to ask how the communicative act can have some impact upon the individuals who engage in it. In particular, how does mass communication influence the audiences of the media? As will be seen in the next chapter, the answer to this question involves some of the most complex theories of the social and behavioral sciences.

6

MASS SOCIETY and the MASS MEDIA

To try to explain the consequences of the mass media of communication for the audiences whose attentions are turned toward them, a wide variety of ideas, assumptions, theories, and hypotheses has been advanced over a considerable number of years. In their theoretical thinking about the impact of the mass media of communication, scholars, critics, and enthusiasts have all been influenced in greater or lesser degree by the conceptions of the fundamental nature of human beings and of society that have been current in their time. Such conceptions of the social order and of individual psychological organization have undergone considerable change during the century that saw the rise of the media. An increasingly pressing need rose to understand how they operate within that social order and the manner in which they influence individual members of society as well as the social process. Although the lines of influence between general behavioral science theory and conceptualizations of the mass communication process have by no means been perfectly clear, it is important to show some of the ways in which students of communication have been influenced by general theorists. This can clarify in part why media scholars, or others who have commented on the nature of the mass communication process, have come up with the particular notions that they have. Effective contributions to mass communication theory have been made by the various behavioral sciences. However, the present chapter will treat in somewhat greater detail those from some of the earlier sociological theories of the general nature of society. This is not to minimize other contributions; our purpose is to give a reasonably detailed account of the historical influence of sociologists on mass communication theory.

The task of showing these lines of influence involves two basic difficulties. First, theories of the nature of society have never been uniform at any given point in time. In fact, sociologists of different theoretical persuasions have seen the organization of societal processes and changing patterns in societal relations from very different perspectives all through the history of sociological thought. Theories of society in the nineteenth century were developed on the basis of complex organic models. Later, the rise of quantitative research procedures introduced new ideas that substantially influenced the analysis of the nature of society and brought additional schisms into sociological theory. More recently, the introduction of "functionalism" and the growth of interest in "social systems" has produced still further divisions, but it has tended to return the thinking of many theorists to organic-type conceptualizations. Second, on the other side

of the coin, there have really never been any rigorously articulated sets of theories concerning mass communication. As
we shall see even at the present time, there is no body of relatively consistent, agreed upon, and formalized assertions
that can truly be called "mass communication theory." To be
sure, there has been a great deal of speculation about the
way in which mass communication takes place; much energy
has been spent on charges and countercharges concerning
the manner in which the media may influence individuals
and groups; and from time to time various conceptual
schemes or even broad hypotheses have been widely discussed with respect to some phase of mass communication
or some aspect of the media. There has also been a substantial accumulation of empirical data that illuminates particular communication processes or specific effects. But, as yet,
even though we use the phrase "mass communication theory," the field has not been unified by the development of
a standard set of concepts, an interrelated body of hypotheses, or an overall explanatory framework. In fact, it is fair
to say that there is no real agreement in this interdisciplinary
area of study as to exactly what constitutes the subject matter of the field of "mass communication." By the late 1950s,
one writer even proclaimed the field to be dead.[1] About the
best one can do is to reconstruct in retrospect the types of
theoretical assumptions that seem to underlie the analyses of
problems associated with mass communication at particular
times.

Given the above-mentioned lack of coordination, the
task of tracing relationships between general thought concerning the nature of society and more specific interpretations of the nature and effects of mass communication may
seem hopeless. Yet, it is a necessary task; thinking about
mass communication has changed, and this change has not
been random. There has been something like a progressive
development and increasing sophistication of ideas concern-

1. Bernard Berelson, "The State of Communication Research," *Public
Opinion Quarterly* 23, no. 1 (Spring 1959): 1–17.

ing the media and their impact, in spite of the fact that this development has often been, and remains, halting and disorderly. Clearly, we now know more about mass communication than we did in 1920; we also know more about it than we did in 1940 or even 1970. But, we must account for the direction of this change and formulate some idea of where it has led us. Only when we understand clearly what have been the underlying postulates concerning the nature of societal processes in general can we begin to understand why hypotheses related to mass communication have been formulated in the way they have. The importance of establishing such linkages between general theory and mass communication theory is not so much that we may more clearly view in retrospect the factors that have influenced thinking about the media in the past, but that we may formulate more adequate theories in the future and fully understand their bases. With this perspective in mind, we turn to an overview of sociological thought insofar as it has influenced students of the mass media during the early part of the communication revolution.

THE RISE OF THE IMAGE OF THE MASS SOCIETY

Society is large and organized. It also seems to grow more complex. These two elementary observations were the foundations upon which the systems of thought of the founders of sociology were developed. Speculation about the nature of the social order—the manner in which it is changing or how it might be improved—had been the subject of philosophical writing since the beginning of recorded human experience. However, the founding of sociology as a systematic discipline devoted specifically to the study of societal processes did not take place until the first half of the nineteenth century, at about the same time that Benjamin Day started selling his newspaper on the streets of New York for a penny a copy.

Auguste Comte is usually credited with giving the new field its name, and he also advocated the application of the Positive (Scientific) Method to the study of society. Comte's major contributions to the task of studying social phenomena scientifically were more philosophical than substantive. However, he did include in his voluminous writings an *organic conception of society*, a theoretical model that was widely used by pioneer sociologists.

The concept of society as organism was not original with Comte, but he made it a fundamental postulate. The significance of this idea is that important consequences follow from it. In simple terms, society can be thought of as a particular type of organism, namely a *collective organism*. This did not mean for Comte that there is just a rough analogy between the organization of some individual biological organism, such as a particular plant or animal, and a human society. Comte assumed that society was an organism in its own right. He saw that it had structure, that specialized parts functioned together, that the whole was something more than the sum of its parts, and that it underwent evolutionary change. These characteristics were those of organisms in general, and so society could be properly classified as such, recognizing that it clearly differed from other specific varieties of organisms.

Comte marveled at the great diversity of tasks, goals, and functions that characterized a society and commented on how each individual and group can seem to be pursuing private ends and yet the overall result is that of a harmoniously functioning system. One of the basic principles of the organization of society (as organism) which accounts for this interested him greatly. That principle was *specialization*. The division of functions that people voluntarily assume, he felt, was the key not only to the continued stability of society, but also to its possible disorganization.

> The main cause of the superiority of the social to the individual organism is, according to an established law, the more marked specialty of the various functions fulfilled by organs more and more distinct,

but interconnected; so that the unity of aim is more and more combined with diversity of means. We cannot, of course, fully appreciate a phenomenon which is forever proceeding before our eyes, and in which we bear a part; but if we withdraw ourselves in thought from the social system, and contemplate it as from afar, can we conceive of a more marvellous spectacle, in the whole range of natural phenomena, than the regular and constant convergence of an innumerable multitude of human beings, each possessing a distinct and, in a certain degree, independent existence, and yet incessantly disposed, amidst all their discordance of talent and character, to concur in many ways in the same general development, without concert, and even consciousness on the part of most of them, who believe that they are merely following their personal impulses? ... This reconciliation of the individuality of labour with cooperation of endeavors, which becomes more remarkable as society grows more complex and extended, constitutes the radical character of human operations [at the societal level].[2]

Comte saw great harmony and stability, then, arising from the assumption of specialized functions by individuals. He felt that inevitably these specialized activities would all contribute to the general equilibrium of society in that "... all individual organizations, even the most vicious and imperfect (short of monstrosity), may finally be made use of for the general good."[3]

But Comte also saw danger in too much specialization. It should be added that this point is of considerable significance for the student of mass communication, because the same idea was used by later theorists to develop the concept of the *mass society*. The mass society concept was of central importance for early thinking about the media. The

---

2. Auguste Comte, *The Positive Philosophy,* trans. Harriet Martineau (London: George Bell and Sons, 1915), 2:289.
   3. Ibid., p. 292.

most important element of this idea was that ineffective social organization failed to provide adequate linkages between individuals to maintain an integrated and stable system of social control. This theme is clearly stated by Comte:

> Some economists have pointed out, but in a very inadequate way, the evils of an exaggerated division of material labour, and I have indicated, in regard to the more important field of scientific labour, the mischievous intellectual consequences of the spirit of specialty which at present prevails. It is necessary to estimate directly the principle of such an influence, in order to understand the object of the spontaneous system of requisites for the continuous preservation of society. In decomposing, we always disperse; and the distribution of human labours must occasion individual divergencies, both intellectual and moral, which require a permanent discipline to keep them within bounds. If the separation of the social functions develops a useful spirit of detail, on the one hand, it tends, on the other, to extinguish or restrict what we call the aggregate or general spirit.[4]

Comte went on to discuss extensively and critically the possible consquences of an overexpansion of the division of labor. He felt that the more individuals were unlike one another in their position in the social system, the greater would be their reduction of understanding of other people. He saw that people with the same specialty would develop ties with each other, but would become alienated from other such groupings. "Thus it is that the principle by which alone general society could be developed and extended, threatens, in another view, to decompose it into a multitude of unconnected corporations, which almost seem not to belong to the same species. . . ."[5]

As the societal organism evolves (according to this type

4. Ibid., p. 293.
5. Ibid.

of theory), it develops harmony and stability through its division of labor. At the same time, there is the possibility that overdevelopment can lead to disorganization and decline by disrupting the basis for effective communication between individual parts of the organism. Given the postulate of the organic nature of society, the concept of specialization of function follows by definition. But an increasing degree of such specialization leads to increased social differentiation. If such differentiation reaches the point where effective linkages between parts of the system are threatened, then the equilibrium and harmony of the organism is also threatened. This theme recurs in the writings of later theorists, and is one of the *basic beginning points for discussing "mass" society.* The relationship between this idea and "mass" communication will be made clear.

It should be recalled that Comte worked out his views of the nature of society during the 1830s. This was before the industrial revolution had achieved a wide impact on Europe. Comte felt somewhat threatened by the possibility of an increasing level of specialization in the society he saw before him. But social theorists who came later were confronted with the *reality* of a great increase in the division of labor which the new industrialization was bringing. It is little wonder they were deeply impressed with its implications.

Speculation about the organic nature of society and its consequences constituted only a minor part of the work of Comte. However, the second founder of modern sociology, Herbert Spencer, pursued the organic concept with great vigor and in great depth. Spencer, like Comte, was primarily a philosopher and was concerned about science as a means for obtaining valid knowledge. This concern led him to formulate what he thought were the most important principles that seemed to him to pervade all the sciences. His famous *laws of evolution* (from which Darwin drew inspiration) were given complete development in his work *First Principles*, published in 1863, more than twenty years after Comte had completed his *Positive Philosophy*.

Spencer applied his evolutionary concepts to the study of society and wrote *The Principles of Sociology* in four volumes between 1876 and 1896. There are many parallels between the two writers, but Spencer claims that his own ideas were worked out independently of those of Comte. In any case, the theory of society which Spencer elaborated in great detail was a purely organic one. After defining society as a functioning system, he discussed the social order at length in terms of its growth, structures, functions, systems of organs, etc., developing an extremely elaborate (outright) analogy between society and an individual organism.

The division of labor was a very important part of this analysis, and was regarded as the basic unifying factor which held the organism together:

> The division of labour, first dwelt upon by political economists as a social phenomenon, and thereupon recognized by biologists as a phenomenon of living bodies, which they called the "physiological division of labour," is that which in the society, as in the animal, makes it a living whole. Scarcely can I emphasize enough the truth that in respect of this fundamental trait, a social organism and an individual organism are entirely alike. . . .
>
> [Society] undergoes continuous growth. As it grows, its parts become unlike: it exhibits increase of structure. The unlike parts simultaneously assume activities of unlike kinds. These activities are not simply different, but their differences are so related as to make one another possible. The reciprocal aid thus given causes mutual dependence on the parts. And the mutually-dependent parts, living by and for one another, form an aggregate constituted on the same general principle as an individual organism.[6]

But Spencer did not go to the next step and contemplate the possible *difficulties* for society that might occur if speciali-

6. Herbert Spencer, *The Principles of Sociology* (New York: D. Appleton, 1898), pp. 452–62.

zation went too far. He was convinced that the most fundamental process of nature was evolution, and that evolution was natural and therefore good. The great changes that he observed in English society, as the industrial order came, he regarded as an unfolding of society according to natural evolutionary laws. To suggest that social changes brought by natural evolution might be undesirable was unthinkable. So deeply did he hold these views that he became convinced that any interference in the natural development of society was completely unwarranted and was bound to have disastrous consequences. He bitterly opposed legislation aimed at any form of social improvement on the grounds that nature meant the fittest to survive, and in the long run this would benefit society. While Comte advocated planned social change, Spencer argued vigorously for a policy of almost complete laissez faire.

Even so, it can be seen that the two major founders of sociology developed similar organic evolutionary models of the social order and both postulated a process leading to increasing social differentiation. The one had grave reservations as to the possible consequences of overspecialization, and the other had grave reservations over any attempt to interfere in what he regarded as the natural evolution of the society. Neither had any full appreciation of the fundamental changes in the structure of the social order that were to come with the twentieth century. Comte, writing on the eve of the industrial revolution, and Spencer, writing during its early phases, could not foresee that the very fabric of society would be changed by the upheaval in the economic institution that the factory system and the new economic order would bring. The same acceleration in science that brought the mass media of communication, and indeed that prompted these two philosophers to found a science of society, also fashioned the forces of society's new industrial organization. The impact of this new order was to be felt in every corner of the world.

Another theoretical formulation came from the province of Schleswig-Holstein in Germany. In 1887, a young man of that region by the name of Ferdinand Tönnies produced a theoretical sociological analysis entitled *Gemeinschaft und Gesellschaft*. In this work, he posed two contrasting theoretical types of societal organization—one preindustrial and the other largely a product of industrialization. In his analysis of the nature of society, Tónnies concentrated less upon organic analogies, or the possible consequences of specialization, but focused his attention upon the kinds of social bonds that exist between the members of societies and groups in two very distinct types of social organization.

Gemeinschaft does not translate easily into English. The word "community" is often offered as its equivalent, but the complexity of Tönnies' meaning is not well captured by such a simple translation. The idea of Gemeinschaft is best illustrated by suggesting some of the kinds of interpersonal ties that are included within it. The bonds and feelings that exist between the members of a normal family offer one example. But the idea goes beyond the bounds of family. The members of a particular village or even of a given small society can be said to be characterized by Gemeinschaft. This type of relationship can develop because people are related to each other by blood, and hold each other in mutual respect; it can be produced because people are tied by tradition to a particular place where they lead a deeply integrated life; there can even be a Gemeinschaft of the mind, as where members of a religious order share a deep commitment to a given set of beliefs that become a basis for a strong social organization. The Gemeinschaft type of organization, in short, is one where people are strongly bound to one another through tradition, through kinship, through friendship, or because of some other socially cohesive factor. Such a social organization places the individual within the nexus of exceedingly strong systems of informal social control. In short, Gemeinschaft refers to a "reciprocal, binding sentiment ... which keeps human beings together as members of a totality."[7] That totality may be a family, a clan, a village, a religious order, or even an entire society, but if so, it has as a basis for its common unity this particular kind of social relationship between its members.

It is clear that there probably have been few societies whose social fabric was characterized completely by such intense feeling of "community" in the sense of Gemeinschaft. However, even as an abstract construction, this "ideal type" can serve as a framework for discussing changes in social organization and new kinds of linkages between members that take place if the society evolves into some other form. For example, under the impact of industrialization, when the division of labor becomes vastly more complex through increasing specialization, is there a decline in Gemeinschaft? Tönnies saw his own homeland undergo a transition from a basically agrarian society to one that was increasingly urban and industrial. While he did not suggest that societal evolution was simply a movement from Gemeinschaft in social relations to some other form, it was clear to him that another constructed polar type was going to be increasingly important to describe adequately an entirely different system of social relationships between the members of the newer society. The second of his theoretical constructs was *Gesellschaft*.

The essential condition of the social relationship in the Gesellschaft is the contract. The contract in its broadest sense is a rationally agreed upon voluntary social relationship where the two parties involved promise to fulfill specific obligations to each other or to forfeit specific commodities if the contract is breached. The contract is a formal relationship (often written, and always backed by impersonal mechanisms of social control) whereas the social relationship of

---

7. Ferdinand Tönnies, *Community and Society (Gemeinschaft und Gesellschaft)*, trans. and ed. Charles P. Loomis (East Lansing: Michigan State University Press, 1957), p. 47.

the Gemeinschaft is informal. In the new society of complex credit, world markets, large formal associations, and a vast division of labor, the contractual type of relationship is widely found between members. The buyer and seller relate themselves in this way as do the employer and employee. In fact, throughout all the major social institutions, the economic order, the political structure, the educational system, religion, and even in some instances the family, the older Gemeinschaft bond, based upon "reciprocal, binding sentiment," is being replaced by relationships of the contractual type. In certain spheres of social exchange, it is almost the exclusive kind of relationship that can exist between two parties, for example, buying or renting a dwelling. In some spheres it may seldom be found (e.g., within the family).

While no society has been or probably ever will be exclusively Gesellschaft, it is clear that this type of social bond has become ubiquitous and pervasive. It is also clear that Gesellschaft implies a very different outlook for individuals as they contemplate societal members than is the case in the Gemeinschaft.

> In the Gesellschaft . . . everybody is by himself and isolated, and there exists a condition of tension against all others. Their spheres of activity are sharply separated, so that everybody refuses to everyone else contact with and admittance to his sphere; i.e., intrusions are regarded as hostile acts. Such a negative attitude toward one another becomes the normal and always underlying relation of those power-endowed individuals, and it characterizes the Gesellschaft in the condition of the rest; nobody wants to grant and produce anything for another individual, nor will he be inclined to give ungrudgingly to another individual, if it be not in exchange for a gift or labor equivalent that he considers at least equal to what he has given.[8]

8. Ibid., p. 65.

The Gesellschaft, then, places the individual within a social system that is impersonal and anonymous. It is a situation where individuals are not treated or valued for their personal qualities, but where they are appreciated to the degree that they can uphold their end of contractual obligations. The Gesellschaft is a system of competitive relationships, where individuals seek to maximize what they get from exchanges and minimize what they give, at the same time learning to be wary of others.

The reader will recognize that these two pictures of societal organization have been deliberately overdrawn for theoretical purposes. However, the Gemeinschaft and Gesellschaft polarity does provide a very useful framework for interpreting the impact of changing social conditions upon the citizen of the emerging industrial order. The Gemeinschaft could easily be idealized as psychologically comforting and supporting, while the Gesellschaft could easily be condemned as psychologically distressing and tension producing. Such interpretations abound in literature, in popular thought, and even in social science, where the simpler Gemeinschaft life of an earlier or more rural society is identified as "good," while the impersonal Gesellschaft of the urban area is defined as "evil." But while many have speculated in these directions, our present task is to extract from such nineteenth-century writers as Tönnies ideas that were to influence those who turned their attentions to assessing the impact of the new media of communication on society. Just as an accumulation of theories and inventions in the natural sciences led to the physical basis upon which the media themselves were developed, the accumulation of sociological thought concerning the nature of the contemporary social order provided the basis of ideas upon which interpretations of the media were first attempted when they became realities.

Before pulling together the various concepts which we have examined into some kind of composite theoretical image of society as it was viewed by the end of the nineteenth century, there is one additional writer whose ideas were of particular significance. Near the end of the period (1893) Emile Durkheim published *The Division of Labor in Society.* In this important work, he brought together the several related themes which we have noted above from the writings of Comte, Spencer, and Tönnies.[9]

The overall purpose of Durkheim's extended analysis was to show how the division of labor of a society was the principal source of *social solidarity* in that society, and that as the division of labor was altered (as for example through social evolution), the unifying forces of the society underwent corresponding change. Solidarity refers to the kinds of social psychological bonds that unite the members, and although Durkheim used a very different terminology, he was addressing himself roughly toward the same general problem as Tönnies. By division of labor, Durkheim meant more than simply the degree of specialization in the economic institution:

> [We must ask] if the division of labor . . in contemporary societies where it has developed as we know . . . would not have as its function the integration of the social body to assure unity. It is quite legitimate to suppose . . . that great political societies can maintain themselves in equilibrium only thanks to the specialization of tasks, that the division of labor is the source, if not unique, at least principal, of social solidarity. Comte took this point of view. Of all sociologists, to our knowledge, he is the first to have recognized in the division of labor something other than a purely economic phenomenon. He saw in it "the most essential condition of social life," provided that one conceives it "in all its rational extent; that is to say, the one applies it to the totality of all

9. Emile Durkheim, *The Division of Labor in Society,* trans. George Simpson (New York: Free Press of Glencoe, 1964).

our diverse operations of whatever kind, instead of attributing it, as is ordinarily done, to simple material usages."[10]

To show the social implications of the division of labor, Durkheim contrasted *mechanical* and *organic* solidarity. Mechanical solidarity is that which unites a people who are essentially alike. Through their common life, and in the presence of only a rudimentary division of labor, the members of a given population work out a set of beliefs, values, and other orientations to which they are deeply, commonly, and uniformly committed. To the extent that these orientations are truly characteristic of every member, there is little basis for the development of extensive individuality. Where there is little or no division of labor, people not only act in like ways, Durkheim suggested, but think and feel in like ways. In this kind of society, "solidarity can grow only in inverse ratio to personality," because personality is what distinguishes one person from another. "If we have a strong and lively desire to think and act for ourselves, we cannot be strongly inclined to think and act as others do."[11] In the extreme case, *all* individuality would be submerged, and the members of the society would be completely *homogeneous* in their personal psychic organization. In such an admittedly theoretical case, the members of the society would be completely uniform in their action.

> The social molecules which can be coherent in this way can act together only in the measure that they have no actions of their own, as the molecules of inorganic bodies. That is why we propose to call this type of solidarity mechanical. The term does not signify that it is produced by mechanical and artificial means. We call it that only by analogy to the cohesion which unites the elements of an inanimate body, as opposed to that which makes a unity out of the elements of a living body.[12]

10. Ibid., pp. 62–63.
11. Ibid., p. 129.
12. Ibid., p. 130.

It is perfectly obvious that no society was ever characterized completely by this kind of social organization. The idea of mechanical solidarity as a basis for binding members of a collectivity to the whole is posed in this way as an abstract construct rather than a description that is supposed to portray reality with complete accuracy. The same can be said of Durkheim's second major concept, organic solidarity. The two taken together, however, offer a third useful interpretive framework in understanding the emergence of modern society.

If mechanical solidarity is based upon *homogeneity,* then organic solidarity is based upon *heterogeneity.* In a society with a well-developed division of labor, each person performing a specialized task is dependent upon others whose activities are coordinated with theirs. Spencer had elaborated in extraordinary detail the parallels between organisms and society as unified systems of reciprocally functioning parts. Durkheim saw the mutual dependency that specialization produced, and he recognized this as a kind of social force that bound the members of a society together to form a more or less harmonious functioning whole. But the important factor is that the division of labor, which produces organic solidarity, also increases greatly the degree of individuality and *social differentiation* within the society:

> Whereas the previous type [of solidarity] implies that individuals resemble each other, this type presumes their difference. The first is possible only insofar as the individual personality is absorbed into the collective personality; the second is possible only if each one has a sphere of action which is peculiar to him; that is a personality. It is necessary, then, that the collective conscience leave open a part of the individual conscience in order that special functions may be established there, functions which it cannot regulate. The more this region is extended, the stronger is the cohesion which results from this solidarity.[13]

13. Ibid., p. 131.

Durkheim went on to show how the growth of the division of labor increases the dependence of each specialized person on the rest, but this does not mean that such increasing heterogeneity leads to consensus of thought. On the contrary: "Each individual is more and more acquiring his own way of thinking and acting, and submits less completely to the common corporate union."[14] Thus, while in one sense highly specialized persons are locked into a web of functional dependency upon others, they are at the same time isolated in a psychological sense as specializations lead them to develop greater and greater individuality.

Durkheim also noted that the evolution of society to a more complex form leads to an increase in social relationships of much the same type that Tönnies called Gesellschaft: "It is quite true that contractual relations, which were originally rare or completely absent, multiply as social labor becomes divided."[15] Thus, an increase in the division of labor has the result not only of increasing individual heterogeneity, but of introducing an increasing number of more formal and segmental relationships between people.

Finally, Durkheim saw that under some circumstances the division of labor could result in what he called "pathological forms." "Though normally," he said, "the division of labor produces social solidarity, it sometimes happens that it has different, and even contrary results."[16] If social functions, that is, parts of the organic structure, are not well articulated with each other, organic solidarity can break down. Commercial crises, depressions, strife between labor and management, civil upheavals, riots, demonstrations, and protests by subgroups offer various kinds of examples.

Thus, the very division of labor that produces harmony up to a point contains the seeds of social disharmony if pushed beyond a certain point. This, of course, was (as Durkheim noted) the thesis of Auguste Comte. Such a state of disharmony Durkheim called *anomie*. This is a kind of pathology

14. Ibid., p. 137.
15. Ibid., p. 206.
16. Ibid., p. 353.

of the social organism that results when the division of labor becomes elaborated to a point where individuals are not capable of effectively relating themselves to others.

> Functional diversity induces a moral diversity that nothing can prevent, and it is inevitable that one should grow as the other does. We know, moreover, why these two phenomena develop in parallel fashion. Collective sentiments become more and more impotent in holding together the centrifugal tendencies that the division of labor is said to engender, for these tendencies increase as labor is more divided, and, at the same time, collective sentiments are weakened.[17]

In short, as society becomes more and more complex— as the members of the society become more and more preoccupied with their own individual pursuits and development— they lose ability to identify with and feel themselves in community with others. Eventually, they become a collectivity of psychologically isolated individuals, interacting with one another but oriented inward, and bound together primarily through contractual ties.

As the nineteenth century came to a close, this was in general the image of society that had emerged. The developing and accumulating body of sociological theory, uncoordinated and even conflicting though it was, seemed in one way or another to stress these themes. Society was a large and complex system. It was also growing much more complex. To some this represented Progress via natural laws of evolution to a more desirable and ultimately more harmonious system than before. To others, it represented an insidious movement to a bleak and isolated existence for the individual, narrowly concerned with special pursuits, and incapable of intense identification with others. Great debates arose concerning the advisability of interfering with the evolution of society through legislation. Other arguments arose concerning the best possible strategy for pro-

17. Ibid., p. 361.

ceeding with the further development of theories about these vast changes. But in spite of these divergent points of view over strategies and consequences, it seemed clear to most students of the social order that the Western world was experiencing an increase in heterogeneity and individuality, a reduction in the degree to which society could effectively control its members through informal means, an increasing alienation of the individual from strong identification with the community as a whole, a growth of segmental, contractual social relationships, and a great increase in the psychological isolation of the human being.

These general social trends were said to be leading to the *mass society*. The idea of mass society is not equivalent to *massive society*, that is, to large numbers. There are many societies in the world, for example, India, that have astronomical numbers of people, but are still more or less traditional in their organization. Mass society refers to the relationship that exists between individuals and the social order around them. In mass society, as has been emphasized in the theories we have examined, individuals are presumed to be in a situation of psychological isolation from others, impersonality is said to prevail in their interactions with others, and they are said to be relatively free from the demands of binding social obligations. These ideas have been carried by some sociologists well into the twentieth century, and are still important considerations, along with a number of modifications and countertrends.[18] In discussing the organization of the urban industrial social order of the contemporary Western world, Broom and Selznick have summarized the principal outlines of the idea of mass society very succinctly in the following terms:

> Modern society is made up of masses in the sense that "there has emerged a vast mass of segregated,

18. See, for example, the well-known treatment of the "mass" by Herbert Blumer, which is still regarded as the classic modern statement of the concept: Herbert Blumer, "Elementary Collective Behavior," in *New Outline of the Principles of Sociology*, ed. Alfred McClung Lee (New York: Barnes and Noble, 1939), pp. 185–89.

isolated individuals, interdependent in all sorts of specialized ways yet lacking in any central unifying value or purpose." The weakening of traditional bonds, the growth of rationality, and the division of labor, have created societies made up of individuals who are only loosely bound together. In this sense the word "mass" suggests something closer to an aggregate than to a tightly knit social group.[19]

This view of the *social* nature of human beings was coupled with an equally developed general theory of their *psychological* nature. Briefly, human conduct was thought to be largely a product of genetic endowment. That is, the causes of behavior were sought within biological structure. This line of thought was to have important implications for the early interpretation of the new mass media. The nature of general psychological theory and its importance in interpreting the mass media will be made clear in later sections.

WORLD WAR I AND THE INSTINCTIVE S-R (STIMULUS-RESPONSE) THEORY

It was against this intellectual backdrop that the mass media of communication diffused through the major Western societies during their early years. To assess the influence that such general theories of the "nature of human" nature had upon some of the early thinking about the media, we need to look briefly to the period when mass communication was still a relatively new social phenomenon with which the world had to contend.

The first decade of the twentieth century had barely passed before Europe and later the United States were plunged into the Great War. The very division of labor and the resulting heterogeneity and individuality that had made

19. Leonard Broom and Philip Selznick, *Sociology* (2nd ed.; Evanston, Ill.. Row, Peterson, 1958), p. 38. The quotation within the passage is from Kimball Young, *Sociology* (New York: American Book, 1949), p. 24.

the new industrial societies possible now became a problem. World War I was really the first of the global struggles in which entire populations played active and coordinated roles in the effort against their enemies. In most previous wars, the opposing military forces carried on their struggles somewhat independently of civilian populations. Unless combat happened to take place in their immediate area, the people left at home were not deeply and personally involved. This had been particularly true of England, which had not been occupied by an enemy since the Norman invasion. It was also true of the United States, which had last known foreign soldiers on its shores during Revolutionary times, although the Civil War had brought great hardships in some areas.

But the new kind of war was, in effect, a pitting of the manufacturing capacity of one nation against that of the other, and the armies in the field were backed by and totally dependent upon vast industrial complexes at home. These huge industrial efforts required the wholehearted cooperation and enthusiasm of the civilian populations who served in them. Total war required total commitment of the entire resources of the nation. Material amenities had to be sacrificed; morale had to be maintained; people had to be persuaded away from their families and into the ranks; the work in the factories had to be done with unflagging vigor; and not the least important, money had to be obtained to finance the war.

But the diverse, heterogeneous, and differentiated populations of the industrial societies were not bound together by that "reciprocal, binding sentiment ... which keeps human beings together as members of a totality."[20] They were not Gemeinschaft societies, but were in fact more like mass societies, which lacked such effective bonds. Yet, it was just such bonds of sentiment that were needed to unite these people into effective solidarity behind their respective war efforts. As each country became politically committed to the war, there arose a most critical and urgent need to forge

20. Tönnies, *Community and Society*, p. 47.

stronger links between the individual and society. It became *essential* to mobilize sentiments and loyalties, to instill in citizens a hatred and fear of the enemy, to maintain their morale in the face of privation, and to capture their energies into an effective contribution to their nation.

The means for achieving these urgent goals was *propaganda*. Carefully designed propaganda messages engulfed the nation in news stories, pictures, films, phonograph records, speeches, books, sermons, posters, wireless signals, rumors, billboard advertisements, and handbills. Top-level policy makers decided the stakes were so high and the ends were so important that they justified almost any means. Citizens had to hate the enemy, love their country, and maximize commitment to the war effort. They could not be depended upon to do so on their own. The mass media of communication available at the time became the principal tools for persuading them to do so.

Following the war, a number of persons who had been importantly involved in the manufacturing of propaganda were ridden with guilt about the gross deceptions they had practiced. Outrageous lies were told by one side about the other, and when placed before the populations of the time via the mass media, they were often believed. Such large-scale persuasion of entire populations with the use of mass media had never been seen before, and it was conducted in a skillful and highly coordinated manner. Also, those were apparently more innocent times; even the word "propaganda" was not understood by the ordinary citizen. After the war, when former propagandists published a rash of sensational exposés about their wartime deceptions, the general public became more sophisticated.

But to illustrate briefly the kinds of material the propagandists found effective and the kinds of responses to their stimuli that they were seeking, the following is quoted from one widely read postwar exposé:

> The Atrocity Story was one big factor in English propaganda. Most . . . were greedily swallowed by an

unsuspecting public. They would have been less ready to accept the stories of German frightfulness if they had witnessed the birth of the most lugubrious atrocity story at the headquarters of the British Intelligence Department in the Spring of 1917.

Brigadier General J. V. Charteris . . . was comparing two pictures captured from the Germans. The first was a vivid reproduction of a harrowing scene, showing the dead bodies of German soldiers being hauled away for burial behind the lines. The second picture depicted dead horses on their way to the factory where German ingenuity extracted soap and oil from the carcasses. The inspiration to change the captions of the two pictures came to General Charteris like a flash.

. . . the General dexterously used the shears and pasted the inscription "German Cadavers on Their Way to the Soap Factory" under the dead German soldiers. Within twenty-four hours the picture was in the mail-pouch for Shanghai.

General Charteris dispatched the picture to China to revolt public opinion against the Germans. The reverence of the Chinese for the dead amounts to worship. The profanation of the dead ascribed to the Germans was one of the factors responsible for the Chinese declaration of war against the central powers.[21]

Whether this particular propagandist was correct in his assessment of the impact of this falsified newspaper picture need not concern us. The example and the claimed effect give a classic illustration of the kind of theory of mass communication upon which such propaganda efforts were premised. It was a relatively simple theory and it was consistent with the image of mass society that was the intellectual heritage from the nineteenth century. It assumed that cleverly designed stimuli would reach every individual member of the mass society via the media, that each person would perceive

21. George Sylvester Viereck, *Spreading Germs of Hate* (New York: Horace Liveright, 1930), pp. 153–54.

it in the same general manner, and that this would provoke a more or less uniform response from all.

In the aftermath of the war, there emerged a quite general belief in the great power of mass communication. The media were thought to be able to shape public opinion and to sway the masses toward almost any point of view desired by the communicator. An American political scientist who tried to analyze objectively the impact of wartime propaganda and the role of the media in the mass society came to these conclusions:

> But when all allowances have been made, and all extravagant estimates pared to the bone, the fact remains that propaganda is one of the most powerful instrumentalities in the modern world. It has arisen to its present eminence in response to a complex of changed circumstances which have altered the nature of society. Small primitive tribes can weld their heterogeneous members into a fighting whole by the beat of the tom-tom and the tempestuous rhythm of the dance. It is in orgies of physical exuberance that young men are brought to the boiling point of war, and that old and young, men and women, are caught in the suction of tribal purpose.
>
> In the Great Society it is no longer possible to fuse the waywardness of individuals in the furnace of the war dance; a newer and subtler instrument must weld thousands and even millions of human beings into one amalgamated mass of hate and will and hope. A new flame must burn out the canker of dissent and temper the steel of bellicose enthusiasm. The name of this new hammer and anvil of social solidarity is propaganda.[22]

The basic theory of mass communication that is implied by such conclusions is not quite as simple as it might appear. To be sure, it is relatively straightforward S-R theory, but it is also one that presumes a particular set of unspoken as-

22. Harold D. Lasswell, *Propaganda Technique in the World War* (New York: Alfred A. Knopf, 1927), pp. 220–21.

sumptions concerning not only the social organization of society, but the psychological structure of the human beings who are being stimulated and who are responding to the mass communicated message. It is important to understand the full range of these implicit assumptions because *it has been through their systematic replacement or modification* that more modern theories of the mass communication process have been developed. As new concepts concerning the nature of the human being as an individual and the nature of society became available, these were used to modify the basic theory of mass communication by introducing different sets of *intervening variables* between the stimulus side of the S-R equation and the response side.

We may refer to the first mass communication theory as the "instinctive S-R theory." It has been given other more colorful names such as "hypodermic needle theory," "transmission belt theory," etc., but these seem to overlook its more basic underlying assumptins. While it may appear to be unrealistic in view of today's more adequate perspectives, it is not true that it was simply a *direct* S-R theory. There was more to its structure than what such writers as Katz and Lazarsfeld have suggested, namely, ". . . the omnipotent media, on the one hand, sending forth the message, and the atomized masses, on the other, waiting to receive it—*and nothing in between* [italics added]."[23] There were very definite assumptions about what was going on in between. These assumptions may not have been explicitly formulated at the time, but they were drawn from fairly elaborate theories of human nature, as well as the nature of the social order (which we have already examined). It was these theories that guided the thinking of those who saw the media as powerful.

World War I was a period when *instinct* psychology was at its peak. It was not until the end of the 1920s that the facts of human individual modifiability and variability began to be demonstrable with the use of new mental tests and other research techniques. As a consequence, the image of *homo*

23. Elihu Katz and Paul Lazarsfeld, *Personal Influence* (Glencoe, Ill.: Free Press, 1954), p. 20.

sapiens represented by the writings of William MacDougal and his contemporaries was called into serious question. Prior to that time, it was assumed that a given individual's behavior was governed to a considerable extent by inherited biological mechanisms of some complexity that intervened between the stimuli and the responses. Because of this, basic human nature was thought to be fairly *uniform* from one human being to another. People inherited (according to the theories) more or less the same elaborate set of built-in biological mechanisms, which supplied them with motivations and energies to respond to given stimuli in given ways. Much was made of the nonrational or emotional nature of such mechanisms, particularly among theorists of psychoanalytic bent. But even these were, in the final analysis, inherited forces (e.g., libido), which each person received at birth in more or less uniform degrees. The psychology of individual differences had not progressed to the point where a consuming interest in learning would develop among academic psychologists as a means of accounting for such differences.

Given a view of a uniform basic human nature, with a stress upon nonrational processes, plus a view of the social order as mass society, the instinctive S-R theory of the media as powerful devices seemed entirely valid: it stated that powerful stimuli were uniformly brought to the attention of the individual members of the mass. These stimuli tapped inner urges, emotions, or other processes over which the individual had little voluntary control. Because of the inherited nature of these mechanisms, each person responded more or less uniformly. Furthermore, there were few strong social ties to disrupt the influence of these mechanisms because the individual was psychologically isolated from strong social ties and informal social control. The result was that the members of the mass could be swayed and influenced by those in possession of the media especially with the use of emotional appeals.

Such a theory was completely consistent with general theory in both sociology and psychology as it had been developed up to that time. In addition, there was the example of the tremendous impact of wartime propaganda. This *seemed* to offer valid proof that the media *were* powerful in precisely the manner so dramatically described by Lasswell when he concluded that they were the "new hammer and anvil of social solidarity."[24] There was also the seemingly indisputable facts from the mass advertising of the time that the media were capable of persuading people to buy goods in degrees and variety hitherto undreamed of. This added to the conviction of great power and it reinforced the seeming validity of the instinctive S-R theory.[25]

There is no doubt that World War I propaganda was effective. However, this does not mean that only one theory is capable of accounting for those effects. If scholars of the day had been in possession of the results of research and thought on mass communication which have accumulated since that time, they might have chosen very different explanations indeed to account for the fact that the population of the United States entered the war with enthusiasm, entertained a series of unrealistic beliefs about the enemy, etc., and that the media played a part in shaping their behavior and beliefs.

But theories of human nature, both in terms of social order and personal organization, did not remain static. In the United States, both psychology and sociology had become more firmly established and were increasingly escaping the domination of the thoughtways of their European origins. Both fields became heavily concerned with empirical research. As a result, their theories were forced to be more closely checked against reality. In consequence, many earlier ideas were abandoned and many new ideas were advanced. Inevitably, these new theoretical directions had their impact on those who were attempting to understand the ef-

24. Lasswell, *Propaganda Technique,* p. 221.
25. Katz and Lazarsfeld point out that both those who feared the media as potentially insidious devices if controlled by evil men and those who hailed them as beneficial means to improve democracy were assuming a similar great degree of media power. See Katz and Lazarsfeld, *Personal Influence,* pp. 15–17.

fects of mass communication. The instinctive S-R theory had been built upon assumptions that were no longer regarded as tenable by general theorists, and consequently the theory had to be rather reluctantly abandoned by students of the mass media. In the meantime, there was very little to take its place. However, even as newer general theories were being devised to describe human nature and the nature of the social order more adequately, the field of mass communication itself was acquiring an *empirical* base. During the 1930s scholars developed an interest in the media as objects of research, and were beginning to turn away from mere speculation about their efforts to systematic studies of the impact of particular communication content upon particular kinds of people. As an increasing variety of research tools became available to them, their ideas about mass communication could be more adequately checked against their findings. Thus, the field of mass communication began to accumulate a body of data from which concepts and propositions could be inductively formulated. Even so, the field continued to be greatly influenced by trends in more general behavioral science, as the following chapter attempts to show.

7
MASS MEDIA as SOCIAL SYSTEMS

Although the mass communication research and theory, both of the recent past and of the contemporary period, has stressed almost uniformly "effects" as the major object of explanation, the present volume has repeatedly suggested that there are other, and possibly equally important, aspects of the media that deserve theoretical and empirical attention. One of the most challenging of such issues is their ability to *survive* and for long periods of time provide their audiences with content that powerful elites have regularly condemned as being in bad taste or even downright dangerous. A continuous dialogue has been carried on between the representatives of the mass media and these self-appointed representatives of "high culture." This issue of "elite culture" vs. "mass culture" has on some occasions stirred debate in the highest political, educational, religious, and legal circles of the nation. A long series of court battles has been fought over books, magazines, and other forms of print that their publishers claim are "artistic" but public prosecutors maintain are "pornographic." The freedom of speech principle vs. statutory prohibitions of lewd, lascivious, or salacious portrayals provide ample grounds for lively discussion. In recent years, the Supreme Court's 1972 decision to allow local communities to determine their own standards of what is and is not pornographic has intensified this debate. Even more controversial for social scientists and others concerned with mass media effects was the 1971 Pornography Commission Report which suggested that there may be *more* desirable and *fewer* undesirable effects of "pornography" than is commonly believed.[1] This congressionally sponsored report was summarily rejected by President Nixon and many congressional and religious leaders despite its scientific documentation.

Long before the mass media were invented, Plato may have provided the opening round in the controversy over the social costs and benefits of mass culture. In his commentary on the training of the children who were to become the leaders of his ideal Republic, he saw the mass culture of his day as posing a threat to the minds of the young:

> Then shall we simply allow our children to listen to any stories that anyone happens to make up, and so receive into their minds ideas often the very opposite of those we shall think they ought to have when they are grown up?
>
> No, certainly not [replies Glaucon].
>
> It seems, then, our first business will be to supervise the making of fables and legends, rejecting all

1. Pornography Commission Report (Washington, D.C.: Government Printing Office, 1971).

which are unsatisfactory; and we shall induce nurses and mothers to tell their children only those which we have approved.... Most of the stories now in use must be discarded.[2]

This theme—popular entertainment is harmful to the minds of the young—has been a consistent one from the beginnings of mass communication. It has been claimed from time to time that such charges can be validated by scientific evidence, but repeatedly this evidence has turned out to be less than convincing.[3] Social scientists insist that any important conclusions about the effects of the media be supported by solid evidence. Because of such insistence upon data rather than emotion, they sometimes find themselves in the awkward position of seeming to defend the media when actually they are simply refusing to accept the inadequately supported claims of critics.

Nevertheless, the insistence that conclusions be based on adequate evidence has never deterred the literary critic from charging the media with a deep responsibility for society's problems. Most nineteenth-century American writers at some point in their careers took time to criticize and condemn the newspaper for superficiality and distortion. The following excerpts from the pens of well-known and influential literary figures are samples of the climate of opinion prevailing among the literati during the time when the mass newspaper was diffusing through the American society:

> *Henry David Thoreau* (written just prior to 1850):
> The penny-post is, commonly, an institution through which you seriously offer a man that penny for his thoughts which is so safely offered in jest.

2. *The Republic of Plato*, trans. Francis M. Cornford (London: Oxford University Press, 1954), pp. 68-69.

3. Examples of such claims are Herbert Blumer and Philip Hauser, *Movies, Delinquency and Crime* (New York: Macmillan, 1933), and more recently, Frederick C. Wertham, *Seduction of the Innocent* (New York: Rinehart, 1954). The latter is a bitter denunciation of comic books.

And I am sure that I have never read any memorable news in a newspaper. If we read of one man robbed, or murdered, or killed by accident, or one house burned, or one vessel wrecked, or one steamboat blown up, or one cow run over on the Western Railroad, or one mad dog killed, or one lot of grasshoppers in the winter—we never need read of another. If you are acquainted with the principle, what do you care for a myriad instances and applications? To a philosopher all news, as it is called, is gossip, and they who read it and edit it are old women over their tea.[4]

Samuel Clemens (written in 1873);

That awful power, the public opinion of this nation, is formed and molded by a horde of ignorant self-complacent simpletons who failed at ditching and shoemaking and fetched up in journalism on their way to the poorhouse.[5]

Stephen Crane (written about 1895):

A newspaper is a collection of half-injustices
Which, bawled by boys from mile to mile,
Spreads its curious opinion
To a million merciful and sneering men,
While families cuddle the joys of the fireside
When spurred by tale of lone agony.

A newspaper is a court
Where everyone is kindly and unfairly tried
By a squalor of honest men.

A newspaper is a market
Where wisdom sells it freedom
And melons are crowned by the crowd.

A newspaper is a game
Where his error scores the player victory,
While another's skill wins death.

4. Henry David Thoreau, *Walden, Or, Life in the Woods* (Boston and New York: Houghton Mifflin, 1854), 2:148–49.
5. Samuel Clemens, *Mark Twain's Speeches* (New York: Harper & Brothers, 1923), p. 47.

A newspaper is a symbol;
It is a feckless life's chronicle,
A collection of loud tales
Concentrating eternal stupidities,
That in remote ages lived unhaltered,
Roaming through a fenceless world.[6]

One remarkable aspect of these statements is that you could simply substitute the word "television" for "newspapers" and obtain a rather accurate facsimile of the hostility and attacks primarily directed at television by critics today.

The *tenacity* and *stability* of the mass media generally in the face of such a long history of criticism by powerful voices needs explanation. The problem at first seems deceptively simple: the media appeal to the masses and the masses want the kind of content they get and so the media continue to give it to them.

Many social scientists, such as Skornia,[7] have exposed the inadequacy of this explanation by noting the old chicken-and-egg problem. It is difficult at best to know if the public taste determines the media fare or if the media fare determines public taste. The answer probably lies somewhere in between with public taste being both a cause and effect of media fare. The relationship between public taste and media fare thus becomes a circular one which, in terms of the chicken-egg analogy, is an ongoing process of chickens producing eggs and eggs producing chickens.

A promising approach to understanding the relationship between mass media content and public taste, and for accounting in part for the remarkable continuity of the (low) cultural level of media content is provided by viewing the media as *social systems* that operate within a specific external

6. Quoted in Milton Ellis, Louise Pond, and George W. Spohn, *A College Book of American Literature* (New York: American Book, 1939), 1:704.
7. Harry J. Skornia, "Television and the News: A Critical Appraisal," in *Mass Media and Mass Man,* ed. Alan Casty (2nd ed.; New York: Holt, Rinehart & Winston, 1973), pp. 214–24.

system—the set of social and cultural conditions that is the American society itself. In certain respects, this rise of interest in the analysis of social phenomena as occurring within the boundaries of social systems represents a renewal of interest in the theoretical strategies of the past, such as those of Spencer, Tönnies, and Durkheim discussed in chapter 6.

The analysis of social systems concerns itself with the *patterns of action* exhibited by individuals or subgroups who relate themselves to one another within such systems. A social system is, for this reason, an *abstraction*—but one not too far removed from the observable and empirically verifiable behaviors of the persons who are doing the acting. The social system, then, is a complex of stable, repetitive, and patterned action that is in part a manifestation of the culture shared by the actors, and in part a manifestation of the psychological orientations of the actors (which are in turn derived from that culture). The *cultural system*, the *social system*, and the *personality systems* (of the individual actors), therefore, are different kinds of abstractions made from the same basic data, namely, the overt and symbolic behaviors of individual human beings. They are equally legitimate abstractions, each providing in its own right a basis for various kinds of explanations and predictions. Generally speaking, it may be difficult or nearly impossible to analyze or understand fully one such abstraction without some reference to the others.

But, granted that the term "social system" is a legitimate scientific abstraction, how does this general conceptual strategy help in understanding the mass media of communication? To answer this question, we need to understand in greater detail exactly what is meant by the term social system, and what type of analysis it provides. To aid in providing such understanding we turn briefly to several ideas that are important aspects of the study of social systems. One of the most important of these ideas is the concept of the "function" of some particular *repetitive phenomenon* (set of actions) within such a system. For it was with questions about a particular repetitive phenomenon (the continuous production and distribution of media content in "low" cultural taste) that the present chapter began. The fact that such content has long survived the jibes of influential critics was said to require explanation. One form of explanation will be provided by noting the "function" of such a repetitive phenomenon within some stable system of action. The term "function" in the present context means little more than "consequence." To illustrate briefly, we might hypothesize that the repetitive practice of wearing wedding rings on the part of a given married couple has the function (consequence) of reminding them as well as others that the two are bound together by the obligations and ties that matrimony implies. This practice thereby contributes indirectly to maintaining the permanence of the marriage—the stability of that particular social system. The practice is in a sense "explained" by noting its contribution to the context within which it occurs. A comparison of a number of such systems with and without this particular item (but in other respects matched) would test the assertion.

In the above example, the social system is a relatively simple one. There are only two "components," and each of these happens to be an individual. Their patterns of action are derived both from the individual psychological makeup of the partners and from the cultural norms concerning marriage prevailing in their community, social class, and society. It is a miniature system whose stability is dependent upon satisfaction of its "needs." For example, such a system requires that the partners perform roles that meet the expectations each has of the other and the expectations the community has of married couples. This can be thought of as a "need" for adequate role performance, without which the stability of the system would be endangered. Other "needs," related to economic matters and emotional satisfactions, could be cited.

More complex illustrations of social systems can easily be pointed to, where the "components" of the system are not individual persons but subsystems. A department store, for example, is a complex social system consisting of the actions of managerial personnel, buyers, salespersons, the clerical staff, customers, transportation workers, a janitorial team, and security employees. Each of these components is a smaller system of action within the broader system of the store itself, and it in turn is a complex system of action carried out within the context of the external social conditions of the community. In spite of the complexity, any given set of repetitive actions might be analyzed in terms of their contribution to maintaining or undermining the system's stability. Granting to employees the right to buy merchandise at cost could have the function (consequence) of maintaining their morale and loyalty, and thus would contribute fairly directly to the maintenance of the system. Rigid insistence on the observance of petty rules, such as docking the pay of an employee who on rare occasions was late for work, might be disruptive of morale and loyalty, and by contributing to labor turnover it could be *dysfunctional.* Instead of contributing to the maintenance of the system, it could cause disruptions and instability. Such inductively derived conclusions would be subject to testing for validity, of course, but the functional analysis would have generated the hypothesis to be tested (an important role of theory).

A "functional analysis," then, focuses upon some specific phenomenon occurring within a social system. It then attempts to show how this phenomenon has consequences that contribute to the stability and permanence of the system as a whole. The phenomenon may, of course, have a negative influence, and if so, it would be said to have "dysfunctions" rather than "functions." The analysis is a strategy for inducing or locating hypotheses that can be tested empirically by comparative studies or other appropriate research methods.

The analysis of social systems is extremely difficult. No infallible rules specify precisely how to locate and define the exact boundaries of a given social system, particularly if it is relatively complex. As yet, no completely agreed upon criteria exist for establishing linkages between the components of a system, and no standard formulas can uncover the precise contribution that a given repetitive form of action makes to the stability of a system. A functional analysis of the contribution of some item to the stability of a system, then, is a procedure that is somewhat less than rigorous. But in spite of this source of potential criticism, this strategy has proved useful in our attempts to understand complex social phenomena, such as the mass media.

How can this type of analysis be applied to the mass media? First, we can identify that portion of the content of the mass media that is in "low" cultural taste or provides gratifications to the mass audience in such a manner that it is widely held to be potentially debasing as the "relatively persistent trait or disposition"[8] of the mass media we seek to explain. It would be difficult in practice to construct a *set of categories* under which to analyze the content of the media so that material of "low" cultural taste can be identified readily. It would be difficult, but actually it would not be impossible. Excessive violence, the portrayal of criminal techniques, horror and monster themes, open pornography, suggestive music, and dreary formula melodramas are typical categories of content that arouse the ire of critics. Considerable disagreement would probably occur as to the exact content that should be included in any given category. There would also be debates over the number of categories used. Nevertheless, it is theoretically possible to identify the content of any given medium that is *most* objected to by the largest number of critics. We will assume that given sufficient time and resources, and using survey techniques, preference scales, attitude measuring instruments, and other research procedures now available that the content of any

---

8. Carl G. Hempel, "The Logic of Functional Analysis," in *Symposium on Sociological Theory*, ed. Llewellyn Gross (New York: Harper & Brothers, 1959), p. 280.

given medium could be divided roughly into something like the following three categories:

low-taste content: This would be media content widely distributed and attended to by the mass audience, but which has consistently aroused the ire of critics. Examples would be crime dramas on television that emphasize violence, openly pornographic motion pictures, daytime serials, confession magazines, crime comics, suggestive music, or other content that has been widely held to contribute to a lowering of taste, disruption of morals, or stimulation toward socially unacceptable conduct. (Whether or not such charges are true.)

nondebated content: This would be media content, widely distributed and attended to, about which media critics have said very little. It is not an issue in the debate over the impact of the media on the masses. Examples would be television weather reports, some news content, music that is neither symphonic nor popular, magazines devoted to specialized interests, motion pictures using "wholesome" themes, and many others. Such content is not believed either to elevate or lower tastes, and it is not seen as a threat to moral standards.

high-taste content: This would be media content sometimes wisely distributed but not necessarily widely attended to. It is content that media critics feel is in better taste, morally uplifting, educational, or in some way inspiring. Examples would be serious music, sophisticated drama, political discussions, art films, or magazines devoted to politial commentary. Such content is championed by critics as the opposite of the low-taste material, which they see as distinctly objectionable.

Of course, the *first* of the above categories is the one to which we wish to direct most of our attention. It is the repetitive phenomenon whose contribution to the media (as a social system) needs analysis. Nevertheless, it would also be possible to study the other two categories with some-what parallel perspectives, but this will receive relatively little attention in the present discussion.

We need now to begin to identify the boundaries of the social system within which low-taste content occurs, so that eventually the contribution it makes to the system can be inductively hypothesized.

Rather than developing a purely descriptive scheme that will apply only to a single medium, it will be more fruit-ful to attempt to develop a *general* conceptual scheme into which any or all media could be placed, with suitable minor modifications in details. Such a general scheme will empha-size the similarities between media, particularly in terms of relationships between the components in the system

The first major component of the social system of mass communication is the *audience*. This is an exceedingly com-plex component. The audience is stratified, differentiated, and interrelated in the many ways that social scientists have studied for years. Some of the major variables that play a part in determining how this component will operate within the system are the major needs and interests of audience members, the various social categories represented in an audience, and the nature of the social relationships between audience members. These variables point to behavioral mechanisms that determine the patterns of attention, inter-pretation, and response of an audience with respect to con-tent of a given type.

The rough typology of content suggested earlier in this chapter is in some degree related to the characteristics of this audience. Organizations devoted to *research*, to measur-ing the preferences of media audiences, or to various forms of market research provide information to those responsible for selecting the categories of content that will be distributed to the audience. There is a link, then, between the audience as a component in the system and the market research-rating service organizations as a second component. In purely theo-retical terms, both components are role systems themselves, and are thus actually subsystems. This is in a sense a one-way link. For very minor (or usually no) personal reward, audience members selected for study provide information about themselves to such an agency. Information flows from the audience component to the research component, but very little flows back. This linkage between components is by comparison relatively simple.

The content itself, of whatever type, flows from some *distributor* form to the audience. The role system of the distributor component varies in detail from one medium to another. In addition, several somewhat distinct subsystems exist within this general component. First, there are local outlets, which are likely to be in the most immediate contact with the audience. The local newspaper, the local theater, the local broadcasting station play the most immediate part in placing messages before their representative audiences. But inseparably tied to them are other subsystems of this general component. Newspaper syndicates, broadcasting networks, or chains of movie theaters pass content on to their local outlets. The link between these two subsystems is a two-way one. The local outlet provides money, and the larger distributor supplies content. Or, the linkage may be that the local outlet provides a service, and the distributor (who is paid elsewhere) provides money.

The relationship between audience and distributor seems at first to be mostly a one-way link. The distributor provides entertainment content (and often advertising), but the audience provides little back in a direct sense. However, it does provide its *attention*. In fact, it is precisely the attention of the audience that distributors are attempting to solicit. They sell this "commodity" directly to their financial backer or sponsor. In addition, the audience supplies information to the research component and this is indirectly supplied to distributors in the form of feedback so that they may gauge the amount of attention they are eliciting. The linkages between components grow more complex as we seek the boundaries of the system.

To the audience, the research, and the distributing components, we may add the role system of the *producer* of content. This component's primary link is with the *financial backer* (or *sponsor*) component and with the distributor, from whom money is obtained and for whom various forms of entertainment content are manufactured. A host of subsystems are included in this producer component, depending upon the particular medium. Examples are actors, directors, television producers, technicians, foreign correspondents, wire-service editors, film producers, labor-union leaders, publishers, copyeditors, clerical staff, and many, many more.

Linking the sponsor, distributor, producer, and research organization are the *advertising agencies.* Paid primarily by the sponsor, this component provides (in return) certain ideas and services. For the most part, it provides the distributor with advertising messages. It may have links with the research component as well.

Over this complex set of interrelated components, there are other subsystems that exert *control.* The legislative bodies, at both the state and national level, which enact regulative statutes concerning the media, constitute an important part of such a control component. Another important part of this role subsystem is the official regulative agencies, which implement the policies that have been legislated. The link between the legislative body (control component) and the audience is, of course, one of votes and public opinion, to which the component is presumably sensitive and dependent. Information lines between audience, legislative bodies, and regulatory agencies are more or less open.

To the regulatory components whose role definitions are found in legal statute can be added the private voluntary associations that develop "codes" and to some degree serve as a control over the distributors. Such distributors provide them with money, and they in turn provide surveillance and other services.

The regulatory subsystems draw definitions of permissi-

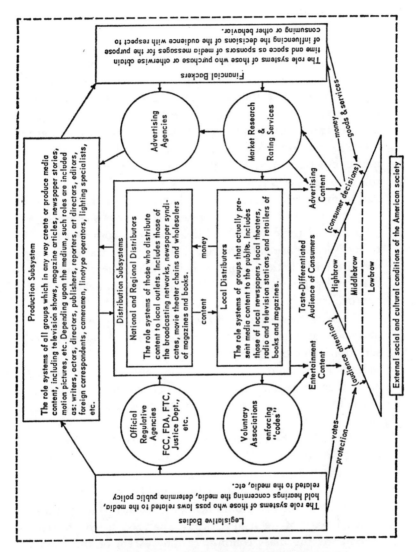

FIGURE 7. SCHEMATIC REPRESENTATION OF THE MASS MEDIA AS A SOCIAL SYSTEM.

ble and nonpermissible content from the general set of *external conditions* within which this extremely complicated system operates. Surrounding the entire structure as an external condition are our society's general norms concerning morality, and the expressions that these find in formal law. Similar, although less likely to be incorporated into law, are our general cultural norms and beliefs regarding what will be likely to entertain or otherwise gratify Americans. Thus, we seldom see traditional Chinese opera, but frequently see western horse opera. We seldom hear the strains of Hindu temple music, but frequently hear the "strains" and other noises of the latest singer whom teen-agers admire. If our interests run to more serious fare, we are likely to hear the music of a relatively small list of European or American composers who created their works within a span of about three centuries. Or, we are likely to view ballet, opera, drama, and so on, of a fairly limited number of artists whose products are defined by our society as classics or as innovative new approaches.

Each of the several media will fit into this general model of a social system in slightly different ways. A complete description of each of the media separately would be tedious. Indeed, each could well occupy the contents of an entire book. Opotowsky has attempted just such a detailed analysis of the television industry, although he does not use the social system concept.[9]

To add to the complexity of this conceptual scheme, it must be remembered that although each medium constitutes a somewhat separate social system in itself, the media are also related *to one another* in systematic ways. Thus, we may speak of the entire set of communication media, including those which have not been specifically analyzed in the present volume, as the mass communication system of the United States.

The structure of this mass communication system has

9. Stan Opotowsky, *T.V.: The Big Picture* (New York: Collier Books, 1962).

been heavily influenced by the general social, political, economic, and cultural conditions that were current during the period when our mass media were developing and remain as important sociocultural forces in the society within which they operate. Because of their importance for understanding our media as they are today, these conditions were analyzed in some detail in earlier chapters. Our free enterprise beliefs, our views of the legitimacy of the profit motive, the virtues of controlled capitalism, and our general values concerning freedom of speech constitute further *external conditions* (in addition to those related to moral limits and cultural tastes) within which the American mass communication system operates.

Within the system itself, the principal *internal condition* is, of course, a financial one. Most of the components in the system are occupational role structures, which motivate their incumbent personnel primarily through money. To obtain money, they are all ultimately dependent upon the most central component of all—the audience. Unless its decisions to give attention, to purchase, to vote, and the like, are made in favorable ways, the system would undergo severe strain and would eventually collapse.

Almost any dramatic change in the behavior of the audience would cause the most severe disruption in the system for any given medium. In an earlier chapter, the swift acquisition of television sets by the movie audience was plotted (figure 4). The consequence of attention loss to the motion-picture theater as a mass medium was shown to be severe (figure 2).

Such disruptions are infrequent, but they do occur. The key to heading off dramatic changes in audience behavior, of course, is to provide entertainment content of a type that will satisfy and motivate the largest possible number of audience members to carry out their roles in accord with the needs of the system. Such content will, in other words, *maintain the stability of the system.* The ideal, from the standpoint of the system, is content that will capture audience members' attention, persuade them to purchase goods, and at the same time be sufficiently within the bounds of moral norms and standards of taste so that unfavorable actions by the regulatory components are not provoked.

The type of entertainment content that seems most capable of eliciting the attention of the largest number of audience members is the more dramatic, low-taste content. Since the most central media system goal is economic profit, sex and violence or any other attention-getting and attention-maintaining content is functional in the sense that even though it may be of low-taste, it maximizes the size of the audience exposed to advertisements. In general, the larger the audience, the more the distributor and producer can charge for advertising. For example, ads in prime-time television periods cost more than those aired during relatively low-audience-size periods, such as early in the morning.

The assumption made by many media personnel and advertisers that low-taste content appeals primarily to the relatively uneducated, who still constitute a majority of the potential audience, may be false. Wilensky finds that educated people say that they prefer and expose themselves to high-taste content more often than do the relatively uneducated. But when observations are made of what the educated and uneducated actually do, there is little difference between their levels of exposure to low-taste media content.[10]

There is a great deal of evidence to show that the relatively uneducated spend more time than the educated being exposed to the mass media.[11] It may be misleading to conclude that they do so only because the uneducated relish low-taste content. The relatively uneducated majority also

10. Harold L. Wilensky, "Mass Society and Mass Culture: Interdependence or Independence?" *American Sociological Review* 29 (April 1964): 173–97.

11. See, for example, Bradley S. Greenberg, "The Content and Context of Violence in the Mass Media," in *Violence and the Media*, ed. Robert K. Baker and Sandra J. Ball (Washington, D.C.: Government Printing Office, 1969), pp. 423–49.

have relatively low incomes, which probably means they have less choice than their more educated and wealthier counterparts in how they spend their nonworking hours. The mass media may be more appealing to the relatively uneducated and poor in large part because the media are relatively inexpensive forms of leisure. Moreover, as Baker and Ball point out, it is probably superficial to think that the only reason people in general spend time with the media is because of the inherent appeal of their content.[12] Any number of functions, over and above entertainment or staying informed, are served by the media. Babysitting and companionship (even when it is electronic companionship) are examples of other functions that media fare may be serving for portions of their audience.

When all is said and done, however, it is still true that low-taste content sells—and sells big. This fact establishes it as the key element in the social system of the media. It keeps the entire complex together by maintaining the financial stability of the system. Critics who provoke public attention by denouncing media content or by proclaiming that a causal connection exists between media content and socially undesirable behavior may temporarily receive some recognition. They may also achieve some temporary disturbance in the system, or if they are persistent enough, they may ultimately even displace some specific form of low-taste content from a given medium altogether. Thus, if quiz shows are found to be "rigged," or if popular disc jockeys are discovered receiving "payola" (a fee for repeatedly playing a song to make it popular), the audience may be temporarily disaffected. However, low-taste content comes in such a variety of forms that the temporary or even permanent absence of one minor form does not alter the major picture. Critics have been complaining about newspaper concentration on crime news for a century, yet there has been no noticeable abatement in the reporting of such stories. Critics

12. Baker and Ball, *Violence and the Media*, pp. 330–33.

of the soap opera may have breathed a sigh of relief several years ago when these programs at last disappeared from radio. Their joy must have been short-lived when such day-time serials turned out to be quite popular with television viewers, so popular in fact that one soap opera even occupied a place in prime evening hours for several years. Analyses of the level of violent television content show that it goes down slightly after federal government investigations on the effects of television violence, only to return to even higher levels of violent content shortly after commission reports are published and the public outcry has subsided.[13]

When a formula is discovered for eliciting attention and influencing purchasing decisions from any large segment of the audience, it will be abandoned by the media only with great reluctance, if at all. The broadcast ballgame, the star comedian, the family situation comedy, the western thriller, the detective story, the adventures of the private investigator, the drama of the courtroom—all are beginning to rank with such time-honored formulas as the sob story, the funnies, the sex-murder account, the sports page, and disclosure of corruption in high places as attention-getting devices that can bring the eye or ear of the consumer nearer to the advertising message.

In short, the social system of the mass media in the United States is becoming more and more deeply established. Some future changes can be expected in the kind of content it will produce to maintain its own stability. At present, however, the function of what we have called low-taste content is to maintain the financial stability of *a deeply institutionalized social system that is tightly integrated with the whole of the American economic institution*. The probability that our system of mass communication in this respect can be drastically altered by the occasional outbursts of critics seems small indeed.

Far more likely than media system change brought about by periodic attacks on low-taste media content is media sys-

13. Ibid., pp. 151–59.

tem change brought about by the changes in the economic system such as the emergence of a "postindustrial" society. Because the media system is also a subsystem in the larger economic system, it will have to adapt to such changes if it is to survive. If Bell's forecast that systems which are in the business of producing, processing, and transmitting information will become increasingly involved in key economic sectors of our society is valid, then we would expect significant changes in the nature of the mass media system.[14] One change would surely be a marked increase in the knowledge and technical information functions of the mass media. We would thus hypothesize that the amount of "nondebated" media content will rise sharply with a corresponding decline in low-taste media content.

But as is usually the case when talking about changes in social systems, such future developments in the nature of the mass media are not likely to be that simple. Recall Durkheim's basic principle that as organisms or systems grow, they are likely to become more differentiated or complex.[15] Taking this assumption and combining it with the enormous technological advances in electronic communications' technology witnessed in recent years, it may be hypothesized that media systems will become more specialized. Some media organizations, for example, might specialize in low-taste content, others in knowledge and technical information, others in news content, and still others in high-taste content. Such technological developments as closed-circuit and cable television can make, and to some extent already are making, such specialization possible. In the next chapter, we turn our attention to a brief examination of such technological developments and how they, along with changes in the economic system, may bring about significant changes in the content and structure of mass media systems.

14. Daniel Bell, *The Coming of Post-Industrial Society* (New York: Basic Books, 1973).
15. Emile Durkheim, *The Division of Labor in Society*, trans. George Simpson (New York: Free Press of Glencoe, 1964).

8
EMERGING
MEDIA
SYSTEMS

In previous chapters we saw
how the emergence of new types of mass communication
have both reflected and affected the societies in which they
developed. The present chapter explores some major innovations which, if not themselves candidates for mass media
of the near future, most probably lay the technological
foundation for the emergence of new media systems. Our
discussion of another emerging communication revolution
begins with a brief description of its key technological
components—computers, cable television, and communication satellites. We then move to consider several sketches

of communication systems that may become mass media in the near future. We conclude with an examination of some potential effects of those technological developments on individuals and their societies.

COMPUTERS

The computer opened the door to the mass media of the future. Parker states: "It is already evident that the primary social significance of the computer is not as a calculator, or even as a basis for factory automation, but as a versatile device for storing, manipulating, and transmitting information, in other words, as a medium of communication."[1] Until recently, only corporations or agencies with a lot of space and money could use computers. As developments in electronics reduced the computer's size, improved its efficiency, and increased its storage capacity, a time-shared computer system emerged. Time-shared customers do not have to install a computer; rather, they install transmission and reception devices that link them to a computer. Such transmission and reception devices include touch-tone phones, teletypes, and visual display panels. Because customers share both time and cost, computers are economically available to many business, educational, governmental, and other organizations.

Travelers have frequent opportunities to witness such time-shared computer operations at work. When airline passengers make reservations, the ticket agent punches certain keys on a typewriterlike panel and sends a request to a central computer to sort through all the schedule information it has stored to see if there is space remaining on the desired flight. If the agent has transmitted the request properly, an

1. Edwin Parker, "Technological Change and the Mass Media," in *Handbook of Communication*, ed. Ithiel de Sola Pool et al. (Chicago: Rand McNally, 1973), pp. 619–45.

immediate reply is sent from the computer, which may be received on a visual display or teletype panel. Similar procedures are employed by many hotels to identify stolen credit cards, check a customer's credit, or make room reservations.

The time-shared computer system, while available to increasing numbers of organizations, is not yet a mass medium. Most people have neither the resources nor the skills necessary to have access to these systems. A mass communication system centered around the time-shared computer may, however, emerge as a result of the development of cable television.

CABLE TELEVISION

Community antenna television (CATV) was originally developed to serve geographically remote or small rural communities with limited over-the-air television reception capabilities. However, CATV soon became appealing to urban residents because it increased both picture fidelity and the number of channels they could receive. Channel capacity and picture fidelity are increased because cable transmissions are relatively unaffected by the airspace limitations and interference problems of conventional over-the-air television. Approximately 20 percent of American households now subscribe to CATV, a figure that is expected to more than double by 1980.[2]

Development of cable television is a relatively inexpensive and simple technological matter in countries equipped with an over-the-air television system. Very tall antennas with considerably greater reception range than conventional

2. Barry Schwartz, "The Anatomy of Cable Television," in *Human Connection and the New Media*, ed. Barry Schwartz (Englewood Cliffs, N.J.: Prentice-Hall, 1973), p. 84.

TV are installed on hills in relatively unpopulated areas. Transmissions are sent via coaxial cable to the subscriber. The initial cost of connecting households with the CATV antenna is made relatively modest by piggybacking coaxial-cable lines on existing telephone-pole routes, and by using the conventional TV set as the receiver. The subscription fees paid by cable TV customers substantially reduce cable companies' reliance on advertising revenue.

In addition to picking up over-the-air transmission, cable companies can also transmit their own local programs. Such programming was initially limited to a time, weather, and community-announcement station. Some cable companies have since expanded their production capacities to include community affairs, sports, theater, and other kinds of programs.

While the technological requirements of a mass cable television system have been resolved, legal, political, and economic problems continue to slow its growth. Independent cable television has not been allowed unchecked growth largely because of its economic threat to the broadcast television industry. Recently, however, broadcast corporation strategy seems to have changed from attempts to block CATV to one of incorporating CATV companies.[3] Such action raises antitrust and First Amendment issues.[4] Political issues raised by the prospect of centralized ownership of CATV in a few national corporations include the loss of a community-based and, thus, to some extent, community-controlled television system. To date, the Federal Communications Commission, which is supposed to regulate the electronic media ensuring that its development serves the public interest and protects a free marketplace of ideas, has not indicated the capacity to solve such basic issues.[5]

3. Nicholas Johnson, *How to Talk Back to Your Television Set* (New York: Little, Brown, 1970).

4. D. Gillmor and J. Barron, *Mass Communication Law: Cases and Comment* (St. Paul: West Publishing, 1969).

5. Johnson, *How to Talk Back to Your Television Set.*

COMMUNICATION SATELLITES AND OTHER COMMUNICATION INNOVATIONS

Technological advances in rocketry and electronics which propelled human beings into space also broke barriers to worldwide mass communication. A communication satellite system will soon be completed that will allow television audiences to receive international transmissions with a speed and fidelity equal to, or better, than present national transmissions. Airspace limitations which have kept the number of over-the-air channels small will be substantially reduced. Present limitations on transmission-reception range which prevent groups living in remote areas from having access to television will be virtually removed. The Canadian government, for example, is using its communication satellite system to bring television to its Northwest Territories.

The initial expense and resources required to install a communication satellite system are enormous relative to the costs of a cable television system. This fact has meant that only governments or large corporations can develop and own satellite communication systems. Moreover, control over the content of TV transmissions will most probably reside with a few wealthy industrialized nations that have the resources to build a communication satellite system. Such a system could have serious implications for processes of cultural invasion and diffusion. On the other hand, it could also provide an efficient vehicle for technical assistance to any community or nation equipped with a television receiver. The opportunities and dangers of a world television system will create the need for international agreements on communication policy.

Other by-products of advances in communication technology, such as the videophone and the video cassette,[6] may

6. Barry Schwartz, "Video Tape and the Communication Revolution," in Schwartz, *Human Connection*, pp. 66–79.

become products for mass consumption in the near future. Such developments may enrich communications by combining visual and audio dimensions. They may also affect the fortunes of some communication industries. The traditional movie industry, for example, already faced with severe competition from television, would be seriously undermined by the advent of inexpensive video cassettes. However, the addition of these communication gadgets would probably not produce basic changes in the process of mass communication or in the nature of mass media systems.

POTENTIAL MASS MEDIA FOR THE NEAR FUTURE

The emergence of time-shared computers, cable television, and communication satellites has led analysts such as Parker, Goldmark, Drucker, Schwartz, and Henderson to forecast the development of fundamentally new *modes* of mass communication.[7] They see the potential for basic alterations in the process of mass communicating and in the goals and functions of mass media systems. Such alterations could have far-reaching consequences upon our political, economic, and social life. We will limit our discussion to descriptions of two media systems which knowledgeable observers think could and should emerge—an "information utility" and two-way cablevision.

Parker describes an information utility in the following manner:

This new communication medium, which is coming to be called an information utility, will have one

7. Parker, "Technological Change"; Peter Goldmark, "Tomorrow We Will Communicate to Our Jobs," in Schwartz, *Human Connection*, pp. 172–79; Peter Drucker, *Landmarks of Tomorrow* (New York: Harper & Row, 1957); Schwartz, "The Anatomy of Cable Television"; Hazel Henderson, "Information and the New Movements for Citizen Participation," *Annals of the American Academy of Political and Social Science* 412 (March 1974): 34–43.

radical new property that previous mass media lack: what is transmitted over the communication channel can be controlled more directly by the receiver than by the sender of the message. It may look like a combination of a television set and a typewriter, function like a combination of a newspaper and a library, and permit a communication network that is something like a combination of a telephone and telegraph system.[8]

The telephone is the only mass medium in use today that permits customers to control the content of what is sent over the channel. All other mass media are essentially monological in form. The roles of communicator (source) and audience (destination) are fixed. Communicators control what messages are and are not sent over the channel. Thus, the prospect of equalizing or even transferring control over message to receivers portends a major change in the process of mass communicating.

Parker identifies five component parts of an information utility: (1) a time-shared computer system, (2) a storage medium, (3) a console or terminal device, (4) a communication link connecting the terminal with the system, and (5) a set of computer programs.[9] The time-shared computer system is the heart of an information utility. It is linked to the storage medium which contains vast amounts of information either in digital form, such as magnetic tape, or analogue form, such as microfilm. Persons wishing to retrieve or process a portion of the sorted information use terminal or console devices such as a teletype or touch-tone phone. Coaxial-cable and telephone lines are the most common communication links between the terminal and the system. The only remaining component required to set the information utility into motion is the set of computer programs which speak the computer's language. A request for information is trans-

8. Parker, "Technological Change," p. 621. Our discussion of information utilities is based upon Parker's discussion.
9. Ibid., p. 623.

lated into computer language, sent from the terminal over phone or cable lines to the computer, which retrieves and processes information from the storage medium and then transmits that information back for reception by the terminal device.

Like most innovations, information utilities became available first to those economic and political organizations that could afford to underwrite their development. The primary impetus for bearing the costs of developing information utilities is the increased speed and efficiency they provide in performance of information functions vital to the health of all complex organizations. An information utility, for example, increases the efficiency of information gathering, producing, processing, and communicating powers vital to production, evaluation, marketing, and development dimensions of economic activity. An information utility likewise increases the efficiency of social control, intelligence gathering, or forecasting and policy formation dimensions of political activity.

Various partial of full information utilities are already in operation or in the process of development.[10] Some medical facilities and universities and the Library of Congress are installing computerized libraries. Law-enforcement agencies are developing regional and national information utilities which greatly expand their recordkeeping and retrieval capabilities. In addition to the airlines and credit agencies mentioned earlier, banks, oil companies, and virtually every other large corporation make use of some kind of information utility. Telephone companies are increasingly dependent on information utilities for their functioning, as in the direct-dial system. But most information utilities are also dependent on telephone companies for their functioning, which is why an increasing portion of the telephone companies' revenue comes from their information as opposed to traditional communication services.

10. Ibid.

Access to efficient information systems is not only essential to the survival of powerful economic and political agencies, but is also necessary for effective public action. To date, the public has had sparse access to information utilities. A few groups, like the People's Computer Corporation, have tried to provide public access, but most citizens lack the resources and skills necessary to take full advantage of information utilities and the public services they could provide.[11] A few public information service organizations, such as Ralph Nader's or Common Cause, are gathering, processing, and disseminating information that may assist ordinary citizens to protect their health, or their political or economic interests. But there is really no adequate substitute for a mass information utility accessible to all persons regardless of their socioeconomic status, residential locale, or level of training in information technology.

It may be relatively economical to use the ordinary television set modified by coaxial-cable receiving and transmitting hookups between customers and time-shared computers as the basis for such a mass information utility. Let's say, for example, that information about available community, state, regional, and national services (e.g., legal, medical) was contained in retrievable form in a central storage medium, which in turn was connected to a time-shared computer. Cable television sets outfitted with transmission and reception devices would be linked to the time-shared computer. Through community educational programs or instructional manuals included as part of the CATV company service, people would learn how to talk to the time-shared computer. Whenever subscribers wanted assistance or how to go about coping with problems for which there were community, state, or other service programs, they could request and receive the desired information through the two-way cable time-shared computer information utility system without having to leave their homes.

11. Henderson, "Citizen Participation."

Mass information utilities, if developed, would probably replace some traditional media and force changes in others. For example, if most persons had a terminal hookup to a news information utility in their homes, newspapers and news magazines could become obsolete. People might be able to formulate their own newspapers by requesting the information content they desired and receiving it in their homes over a telephone, teletype, or cable television receiver. Rather than having wire services like the AP or UPI, news gatherers or reporters might send their stories directly to a central storage medium. Information utility customers could be their own editors. While information gathering and processing activities would still be necessary, decisions about what subjects were most important and how much of the available information deserved dissemination could be made by news consumers. This is one illustration of why Parker sees the shift in control over content away from transmitters to receivers as the most potentially revolutionary aspect of mass information utilities.

While two-way cablevision may serve as the receiving-transmitting arms of some future mass information-utility, a two-way cable system could also become a mass medium in its own right. The present one-way cable system could be modified by adding a parallel cable so that subscribers could transmit as well as receive messages. The key revolutionizing component of two-way cablevision is its capacity for mediated dialogue. The monological form of conventional television is broken. Participants in dialogue mediated by cablevision communication systems could break out of passive audience-receiver roles to become both communicator and communicatee, transmitters and receivers.

The numerous practical and legal problems that would have to be resolved make it difficult to determine how a two-way cablevision capacity would be transformed into a concrete media system. Nevertheless, one model for such a system is the two-way conversations between news commentators located at TV stations in different parts of the world which are broadcast periodically in news programs. The TV audience watches the conversation, but the news commentators are engaging in mediated dialogue in which they not only see and hear one another, but are also able to respond to or even interrupt each other. In this case, dialogue is mediated by an over-the-air and satellite media system.

Dialogue between everyday citizens could theoretically be carried out in much the same manner with the mediation of two-way cablevision. It might be possible, for example, to create an "electronic townhall." Citizens could through some agreed upon procedure receive time to debate a specific issue announced well enough in advance so that all interested parties would have an opportunity to participate in the debate. The nature of such mediated interchange could include some important aspects of face-to-face communication which heretofore have been absent from mass communication, such as immediate verbal and nonverbal feedback.

A few two-way cablevision systems are already in operation which could be utilized to establish "electronic townhalls." For example, in Tulsa, Oklahoma, twenty-six cable stations are linked together so that persons in each station can engage in dialogue with persons in the other stations.[12] Two-way cablevision could, of course, be adapted to serve almost infinite numbers of other political, educational, business, or even recreational functions. World chess or bridge tournaments, for example, could be held without the players or observers leaving their living rooms.

POTENTIAL SOCIAL IMPACT OF NEW MEDIA SYSTEMS

The information utility based on a time-shared computer and the two-way cablevision system, separately or together, open doors to new ways of living which have both optimistic

12. "Symposiums Examine Values," *Tulsa Daily World,* 12 May 1974.

and pessimistic implications.[13] Much of the public discussion has focused on the dehumanizing or otherwise pessimistic implications, such as invasion of privacy, "big brother" systems of surveillance, and centralization of power brought about by centralization and mechanizations of information systems. Our discussion focuses on a few optimistic implications, but does so in the context of identifying the forces that will ultimately determine whether future mass media undermine or improve democratic processes and the quality of life.

Innis's elementary premise—the nature of a society's communication systems has a limiting effect upon the nature of its social structure—is as applicable to these new communication-information systems as it was to analyses of the impact of former communication revolutions discussed in chapter 1.[14] The potency of these communication technologies derives primarily from the dynamic reciprocal relationship between information and power—economic power, political power, social power.

Information as a power resource and product is necessarily rooted in communication systems. Access and control are the key factors that will determine the consequences of new information-communication systems upon the distribution of freedom and equality in our society. Perhaps this can best be illustrated by referring to contemporary predicaments encountered by everyday citizens, members of Congress, minority groups, and credit applicants. The struggle of ordinary citizens to "fight city hall" usually means trying to get some person (rather than a computer) not only to talk to them, but also to give them the specific information they need to get a license, challenge a utility bill, or a thousand other things. Members of Congress have come to recognize that their outdated information systems have resulted in a considerable loss of power to the Executive, in large

13. See Parker "Technological Change," pp. 627–39, for a discussion of both the "optimistic" and "pessimistic" implications of two-way cable and information utilities.

14. Harold Innis, *Empire and Communication* (London: Clarendon Press, 1950).

part because Congress no longer has sufficient control or access to the information required to construct and oversee the national budget. Minority groups encounter frustration when excluded from informal communication networks because such exclusion means lack of access to and control of information which they may need to gain real, as opposed to token, equality. People who have been denied credit by a company or a bank can run around in circles trying to find out the reason for the denial. In one way or another, all these groups face problems of insufficient access to and control over information processes. Such inadequate access and control limits their power, thwarts their chances for equality, or restricts their freedom.

Some of the many factors that mitigate against increased public access to and control of present and future information-communication systems are lack of computer, videotaping, and other technical skills necessary to operate such systems; legal barriers, such as natural security classifications and FCC regulations; economic barriers, such as increasing corporate control over computer and cable systems as well as the sheer cost of the necessary hardware.

History may buttress pessimistic predictions that such information-communication systems as information utilities and two-way cablevision will be used primarily to increase the power of already powerful groups. Nevertheless, as Parker suggests, there may be some lead time that could be used to promote citizen participation in shaping the next communication revolution. Some specific efforts being made to enhance public access and control over media systems are: a proposed reinterpretation of First Amendment rights of free speech to include the right to be heard via rights of public access to the media;[15] legislative proposals to guarantee privacy and freedom of information; citizen action programs that teach the public how to use the new communication

15. Jerome Barron, "An Emerging First Amendment Right of Access to the Media," in Gillmor and Barron, *Mass Communication Law*, pp. 178–86.

technology and that increase public understanding of how information can be used as a political tool; and taking advantage of the FCC regulation that all towns of 10,000 persons or more with cable television must make at least one channel available for strictly public use.

It is tempting to ignore the fact that social, political, and economic forces largely determine how technological innovations are used. Like the powerful networks were able to slow the growth of cable television, other powerful groups, fearing a decline in their political power as a direct consequence of a new mass medium, probably have the resources to prevent its development.

The information-communication systems that are most likely to emerge from technological advances are those which alter economic, political, or social structure in ways that serve the interests of powerful groups. For example, new information-communication systems could dramatically alter how we work, alterations that could be profitable to economic organizations. Some forecasters expect the homes of the near future to resemble a communication center. If homes are equipped with a variety of information-communication devices including information utilities, video-phones and cassettes, and two-way cablevision, then all the hardware necessary for the performance of many work activities would be available in the home. Hundreds of jobs are based heavily upon information or communication activities that could be accomplished at appropriately outfitted residential communication centers. A few of these activities are research, diagnosis, advertising, marketing, policy formation, diplomacy, engineering, evaluation of programs or products, education, investment and trade, sales, record-keeping and retrieval, testing, and conferring. Some jobs would, of course, still require at least part-time on-the-spot presence of a worker. Surgeons, for example, could diagnose, test surgical procedures, and arrange for operations at home communication centers; but they would still have to travel to a "hospital" to conduct surgery.

Being able to perform some or all of one's work at home would have substantial consequences for the organization of economic activity, workers' life styles, family life, ecology, and the nature of urban and rural communities. A few of the advantages for employer and worker would be reduced costs of transportation and work facilities, savings in time required to commute from home to work, reduced need for day-care centers, more humanistic work atmosphere, and increased choice of place of residence.

Goldmark foresees the potential for development of new rural communities as a consequence of the reduced need for centralized urban work centers.[16] Many workers could choose to live in relatively unpopulated areas because they no longer needed to live close to their place of work. Such redistribution of the population may not only be advantageous to workers, but may also revitalize small towns or rural communities which have been deteriorating in recent years. Goldmark suggests that video cassettes and narrowband cable TV channels exclusively designed to carry cultural activities from anywhere in the world could provide rural residents with access to culture and arts now available only in large population centers.

It would take considerable energy to run such homework communication centers. These energy costs could be at least partially offset by reduction in energy requirements for travel to and from work, conferences, sales trips, speaking engagements, and the like. Moreover, decreased work-related travel would lessen traffic pressures and reduce air pollution. Highway construction funds might be freed for the development of efficient mass transit systems which, by the way, could also be run by computers and monitoring devices from residential communication centers.

The conventional electronic media have, for the most part, failed to provide communities with not only positive feedback, but also with any feedback of relevant informa-

16. Goldmark, "Tomorrow We Will Communicate."

tion. Schwartz has said "when a community or group gets feedback on itself, it changes."[17] Klapp notes that a communications system which allows groups to receive positive feedback about themselves is essential for development and maintenance of a strong collective identity.[18] Two-way cablevision has the potential for "socio-cybernetic" feedback which Weiner and Klapp might regard as necessary for community growth and strong community identity. In contrast with bio-feedback or psycho-cybernetics where individuals get feedback about their biological or psychological selves, socio-cybernetics refers to *groups* (e.g., families, communities, or even nations) getting feedback on themselves. Mediated dialogue provided via two-way cablevision could revitalize socio-cybernetic feedback processes vital to group identity, growth, and social cohesion.

Two-way cablevision could also enhance democratic processes of decision making. While the mediated dialogue of the "electronic townhall" might not completely recapture the rich interaction and debate of the New England town hall, it would provide more equal opportunity and freedom to participate in political processes. The quality and quantity of such public discourse would probably surpass that presently fostered by one-way information-communication systems. More direct public-opinion polling might also be feasible whereby viewers vote via the cable system. Many problems, such as establishing that a person is a bona fide voter, would have to be solved before the "electronic townhall" system could be used to conduct elections. But the obvious advantages of decreased election costs and ease of voting might encourage the development of cable voting devices.

With satellite communication, these processes of feedback and debate could extend beyond national borders to a townhall of the world. As the "hot line" telephone between Moscow and Washington, D.C., was hailed because it pro-

17. Schwartz, "The Anatomy of Cable Television," p. 84.
18. Orrin Klapp, *Currents of Unrest* (New York: Holt, Rinehart & Winston, 1972).

vided improved communication opportunities, worldwide cablevision could enhance the fidelity and scope of communication between nations. The effectiveness of the United Nations, for example, may be furthered by the opportunity for nations to engage in regular mediated dialogue.

If mass information-communication media of the future permit *mediated dialogue* and receiver *control over content*, then not only will the nature of mass communication have been radically changed, but so will the social functions of the media. The mass media of the future could serve such new or expanded functions as aiding individuals in their attempts to cope with social agencies and city hall; work-related functions; political functions, particularly in the area of public debate; conflict resolution functions; and community-integration functions.

It may seem necessary to conclude that if some version of the communication revolution forecast here is actualized, present mass media will become obsolete. We cannot now know what information-communication systems will, in fact, emerge. Therefore, attempts to predict exactly which media will survive, and what alterations in media systems will occur, are necessarily speculative. Economic and technical limits on the amount of information that can be stored, processed, or transmitted at any one time make it unlikely that new information-communication systems would entirely replace present mass media. But one thing seems clear: media capable of transformation into *mass information systems* have the best survival chances.

9

ENCOUNTERING
the
MEDIA

This chapter presents an overview of how thinking concerning the impact of the media on individuals and groups has undergone progressive change. We saw in chapter 6 that some mass society theorists attributed to the mass media the power to manipulate the minds and actions of the masses. Discovery of psychological and sociological mechanisms which limit the impact of media messages moved social science thinking away from this mass society perspective. At the center of this change in theoretical perspective was a fundamental redefinition of the nature of the encounter between media and individuals. The idea that people encounter the media as a mass of unconnected individuals was rejected. In its place emerged a conception of the media audience as a set of individuals who encounter the media as social beings connected to their social environments.

This change of perspective is somewhat analogous to the growth of understanding about the organizational and structural intricacies of mass media systems discussed in chapter 7. Developments in social science theory and research led to an increased understanding of the sometimes subtle ways in which audiences are structured and organized. As media structure and organization affects its approach to their audiences, the informal social organizational ties of audience members affect how they approach the media. As we shall see, the perspective which emerged and prevails today is that individual audience members encounter media messages as members of groups and that they do so with a constructed social reality which reflects their past and present social experiences.

Another perspective that posited enormous power to the mass media and that was subsequently rejected by most social scientists was Innis's technological determinism. Innis contended that the nature of the media technology prevailing in a society at a given point in time greatly influenced how the members of that society think and behave.[1] Books and other print media, for example, are said to promote cause-effect thinking in societies where print media dominate, because the technology of print forces a linear form of presentation either across or up or down a page. McLuhan, the contemporary reformulator of Innis's thesis, characterizes television as a "cool" medium because its capacity for rich configurations of audiovisual stimuli elicits high but passive audience presentation.[2] From the techno-

1. Harold A. Innis, *Empire and Communication* (London: Clarendon Press, 1950).
2. Marshall McLuhan, *Understanding Media* (New York: McGraw-Hill, 1964).

logical determinist's perspective, the most important characteristic of the audience-media encounter is the technological properties of the medium. Thus, McLuhan asserts that "the medium is the message."[3] While we saw in the previous chapter that some social scientists are attempting to understand the potential impact of the nature of new media technologies on audiences and society, few would accept the proposition that technology *alone* determines how people encounter and respond to the mass media. Most, for example, would reject McLuhan's claim that the *content* of media messages has no impact on audiences. Essentially, mass media theorists reject the extreme form of technological determinism put forth by McLuhan for two reasons. Social scientists generally reject the idea that any single factor (be it technology, the economy, or chromosomes) can be the single cause of social behavior. This distrust of single-factor theories was buttressed by theory and research developments that demonstrate the influence of both psychological and social factors on the individual's or group's encounter with the mass media. This is not to say that Innis's thesis was rejected out of hand; most media theorists would accept the proposition that the technological characteristics of a mass medium may be one of many factors that should be taken into account.[4]

We turn now to an examination of the three most important prevailing perspectives on how people encounter the media—the *individual differences* perspective, the *social categories* perspective, and the *social relations* perspective. We will attempt to show the progression of theory and research that led to each perspective's assumptions about the psychological and social variables which intervene in the audience's encounter with the mass media.

3. Ibid.
4. Couch has criticized sociologists for ignoring the form of audience-media relations that derive, in large part, from the nature of media technology. See Carl Couch, "Theoretical Notes of the Form and Consequences of Mass Communication" (Paper presented at the annual meeting of the American Sociological Association, August 1972).

THE INDIVIDUAL DIFFERENCES PERSPECTIVE

When psychological theorists seeking basic understanding of human conduct turned away from explanations of complex behavior based primarily on inherited mechanisms, they sought new explanations built upon very different principles. If nature failed to endow human beings with the automatic ability to guide their behavior, then they surely had to *acquire* it from their environment. Great interest was to develop among psychologists in the process of human learning. By the end of World War I, academic psychology was intellectually prepared for new directions. One new direction was provided by the concept of *conditioning*.

From English empiricism, psychologists had inherited a persistent interest in "association" and "habit" as important aspects of learning. As early as 1890, William James had suggested that habits formed through association may have a physiological basis.[5] John Watson introduced a further significant element to modern psychology with his emphasis on behaviorism.[6] But more than anything else, it was the classical conditioning experiments that fired the imagination of the psychologists of the late 1920s and the early 1930s.[7] Thus, there was a renewed interest in habit formation through learning, a new stress upon objective experiments as an aid in the development of theories of learning, and a broad new concept that promised to link the learning process to physiology. The result of these intellectual trends

5. William James, *Principles of Psychology* (New York: Henry Holt, 1890); see p. 566.

6. John B. Watson, *Behavior: An Introduction to Comparative Psychology* (New York: Henry Holt, 1914).

7. Although the basic idea of conditioning was understood before the turn of the century, physiologists such as Ivan Pavlov and Vladimir Bekhterev made it popular among American psychologists. An excellent discussion of this historical development is that of Ernest Hilgard and Donald Marquis, *Conditioning and Learning* (New York: Appleton-Century-Crofts, 1940), esp. pp. 1–50.

was a great expansion of interest in learning processes and a host of experiments with animal and human subjects. A number of competing theories of learning were formulated.

Along with this intellectual movement came an associated interest in "motivation." The study of incentives in laboratory experiments convinced psychologists that some motivational urges can be acquired through learning and that not all individuals can be motivated by precisely the same incentives. Adding to this trend in the increasing recognition of individual motivation and learning *differences* were the findings of students of human personality. Variations in personality traits became increasingly recognized, and the mental testers began to construct sophisticated devices to quantify those differences.[8]

New concepts were also formulated in social psychology to replace the idea of instinct. In particular, the term "attitude" grew in importance as a means of explaining differing directions of human preference and action. Introduced as a systematic concept in the writings of Thomas and Znaniecki at the end of World War I, this concept became the most basic and central theoretical tool of social psychology.[9] The invention of several rather elaborate and mathematically sophisticated techniques for attitude measurement added to its importance as a research tool and gave additional emphasis to the study of individual differences and their correlates.[10]

As these basic ideas concerning the psychological organization of the human individual were successfully clarified, certain fundamental postulates became rather widely

8. For an outstanding overview of development during this period of thought concerning human personality, see Gordon W. Allport, *Personality: A Psychological Interpretation* (New York: Henry Holt, 1937).

9. W. I. Thomas and Florian Znaniecki, *The Polish Peasant in Europe and America*, 5 vols. (Chicago: University of Chicago Press, 1918–21).

10. For a discussion of the history and present status of attitude and its measurement, see Melvin L. De Fleur and Frank R. Westie, "Attitude as a Scientific Concept," *Social Forces* 42 (October 1963): 17–31.

held. It was said that human beings *varied* greatly in their personal-psychological organization. These variations in part began with differential biological endowment, but they were due in greater measure to differential learning. Human beings raised under widely differing circumstances were exposed to widely differing points of view. From these learning environments they acquired a set of attitudes, values, and beliefs that constituted their personal-psychological makeup and set each person somewhat apart from others. Even twins of almost identical biological makeup became rather different in personality structure when raised in different social environments.

Added to this increasing recognition of human psychological modifiability and differentiation was the recognition that personality variables acquired from the social milieu provided a basis for individual differences in *perception*. The experimental study of human perception had revealed that values, needs, beliefs, and attitudes played an influential role in determining how stimuli are selected from the environment, and how meaning is attributed to those stimuli. Thus, one important product of human learning was the acquisition of stable predispositions or habits concerning the perception of events. Perception differed systematically from one person to another according to the nature of individual personality structure.

With these new theories in the background, students of mass communication had to alter their thinking about the media. It became clear that the audience of a given medium was not a monolithic collectivity whose members attended uniformly to whatever content was directed toward them. The *principle of selective attention and perception* was formulated as a fundamental proposition regarding the way ordinary persons confronted the content of the mass media. General psychological theory had established the concept of selective perception based upon individual differences in cognitive characteristics. It was not difficult to show that different types of people in an audience selected and interpreted mass communication content in widely varying ways.[11]

Although never specifically formulated as a theory, it can be suggested that selective attention and perception had become intervening psychological mechanisms that entered into the S–R schema of mass communication theory (pages 153–61). From a multiplicity of available content, individual members of the audience selectively attended to messages, particularly if they were related to their interests, consistent with their attitudes, congruent with their beliefs, and supportive of their values. Finally, response to such messages was also modified by psychological makeup. This general idea may be called the *individual differences perspective on the mass communication process*. Rather than being *uniform* among the mass audience, the manner in which audience members are exposed to media content could now be seen as *varying* from person to person because of individual differences in psychological structure. This in turn was said to lead to varying effects.

When communication "effects" are a focus of research attention, the assumption that the media are in some way "causes" of those effects is a natural one. Even if it is granted that intervening processes of some sort can modify this relationship, the underlying cause-effect conceptualization is not different, only more complicated. The individual differences perspective implies that media messages contain particular stimulus attributes that have differential interaction with personality characteristics of audience members. Since there are individual differences in personality characteristics among such members, it is natural to assume that there will be variations in effect which correspond to these individual differences. Thus, the logical structure of the individual differences theory is a "cause (intervening processes)-effect"

11. A major section in one of the first textbooks in mass communication consists of a series of reprinted research reports dealing with audience selectivity and its basis. See Wilbur Schramm, ed., *Mass Communications* (Urbana: University of Illinois Press, 1949), pp. 387–429.

structure, just as was the instinctual S–R theory before it. However, the intervening processes are the result of learning rather than inheritance.

THE SOCIAL CATEGORIES PERSPECTIVE

Sometimes overlapping the individual differences approach, but stemming from completely different disciplinary sources, is the *social categories perspective*. The latter assumes that there are broad collectivities, aggregates, or social categories, particularly in urban-industrial societies, whose behavior in the face of a given set of stimuli is more or less uniform. Such characteristics as age, sex, income level, educational attainment, rural-urban residence, or religious affiliation provide examples. In fact, knowledge of several simple variables— age, sex, and educational attainment—provides a reasonably accurate guide to the type of communication content a given individual will or will not select from available media. Comic books are read primarily by the young and less educated; *Ms., Playgirl,* and *The Ladies Home Journal* are read primarily by females; the readers of *Playboy, Field and Stream,* and *Mechanics Illustrated* are predominantly male.

An early research trend in mass media studies made such category membership a central focus. It sought to establish the ways in which such behaviors as newspaper reading, the selection of books, radio listening, and motion-picture attendance were related to a variety of simple characteristics by which people could be grouped into aggregates.[12]

The basic assumption of the social categories perspective

12. The following are representative examples of research reports guided by the social categories theory: Paul F. Lazarsfeld, "Communications Research," *Current Trends in Social Psychology* (Pittsburgh: University of Pittsburgh Press, 1949), pp. 233–48; Wilbur Schramm and David White, "Age, Education, and Economic Status as Factors in Newspaper Reading," in Schramm, *Mass Communications,* pp. 402–12; and H. M. Beville, Jr., "The A B C D's of Radio Audiences," in Schramm, *Mass Communications,* pp. 413–23.

is a sociological one, namely, that in spite of the heterogeneity of modern society, people with a similar location in the social structure will have similar folkways. These similar modes of orientation and behavior will relate them to such phenomena as the mass media in a fairly uniform manner. The members of a particular category will select more or less the same communication content and will respond to it in roughly equal ways. The social categories approach is a descriptive formula that can serve as a basis for rough prediction and as a guide for research.

Actually, it has a more complex theoretical basis than is apparent on the surface. It will be recalled that the sociological theorists of the nineteenth century stressed the increasing degree of *social differentiation* that was taking place in the developing industrial society. In the society with a rudimentary division of labor, Durkheim had suggested, people would be very much alike. But in a society with a complex division of labor, there would be much greater development of what he called "personality" (e.g., "individual differences"). However, people located at similar positions in this social structure would be similar in personality because of similarity of their immediate social environment. Thus, they would be attracted to one another and form categories that were somewhat homogeneous. Earlier, Comte had suggested that people who formed groupings on the basis of similar characteristics would become a "multitude of unconnected corporations, which almost seem not to belong to the same species"[13] (in modern terminology we would refer to "subcultures").

While the individual differences perspective presented a view of the communication process more consistent with findings in general psychology, the social categories perspective was consistent with, and seemingly derived from, general sociological theories of the nature of the urban-industrial society. Taken altogether, they brought contemporary mass

13. Auguste Comte, *The Positive Philosophy*, trans. Harriet Martineau (London: George Bell and Sons, 1915), vol. 2.

communication theory to a point where both the social differentiation of the early sociological theorists and the individual differences of the personality theorists were taken into account. Both approaches represent modifications of the original instinctual S–R theory, substituting on the one hand latent psychological processes and on the other uniformities within social categories as intervening variables between communication stimuli and responses. In 1948 Lasswell summed up precisely these two theoretical orientations, and the situational variables related to them, when he stated:

> A convenient way to describe an act of communication is to answer the following questions:
>> *Who*
>> *Says What*
>> *In Which Channel*
>> *To Whom*
>> *With What Effect?*[14]

While these two perspectives on mass communication remain useful and contemporary, there have been further additions to the set of variables intervening between media stimuli and audience response. One additional elaboration of the S–R formula represents a somewhat belated recognition of the importance of patterns of interaction *between* audience members.

THE SOCIAL RELATIONS PERSPECTIVE

Like many other significant discoveries in science, the role of group relationships in the mass communication process seems to have been discovered almost by accident. Also

14. Harold D. Lasswell, "The Structure and Function of Communication in Society," in *The Communication of Ideas,* ed. Lyman Bryson (New York: Harper & Brothers, 1948), pp. 37–51.

like many other important ideas, it appears to have been independently discovered at about the same time by more than one researcher. From the standpoint of mass communication research on how people encounter and respond to the media, one study stands out as the context within which the importance of group ties, as a complex of intervening variables between media and audience influence, was discovered. Early in 1940, before the adoption of television as a mass medium, Lazarsfeld, Berelson, and Gaudet developed an elaborate research design to study the impact upon voters of that year's mass-communicated presidential election campaign. At first, they were interested in how the members of given social categories selected material related to the election from the media, and how this material played a part in influencing their voting intentions.[15]

Erie County, Ohio, the site of the research, was a rather typical American area which had voted as the nation voted in every prior presidential election. Media campaign materials presented during the contest between Wendell Willkie and Franklin D. Roosevelt constituted the stimulus material. Several representative samples of residents of the area were the subjects. The study used an imaginative procedure that permitted repeated interviewing of a 600-member panel with suitable controls to check for possible effects of the seven independent monthly visits of the interviewers.

Some of the effects under study were: participating in the campaign (seeking information about the candidates and the issues), formulating voting decisions, and actually going to the polls. As it turned out, still other kinds of effects could be attributed to the campaign. Some respondents were *activated* by the mass-communicated material; that is, they had latent predispositions to vote in a given direction, but these predispositions needed to be crystallized to the point where they would become manifest. Others among the

15. Paul F. Lazarsfeld, Bernard Berelson, and Helen Gaudet, *The People's Choice* (New York: Duell, Sloan & Pearce, 1944).

electorate had pretty much made up their minds early in the campaign and these decisions were *reinforced* by a continuous and partisan selection of additional material from the media. Early vote intentions were reversed in only a small portion of cases. Thus, the campaign had only limited success in converting individuals from one party to another.

The influence of the social categories perspective as a guide to this research was clear. Age, sex, residence, economic status, and education were the key variables. These social category memberships determined "interest" and led to an early or late decision. Acting in concert, this complex of variables influenced not only people's degree and direction of exposure to the mass-communicated campaign material, but also the kinds of effects that such material would have upon them.

As suggested, designing the study around a search for the important intervening social categories was perfectly consistent with the mass society concepts that communication researchers had inherited from European sociological theorists. Little attention was given to the possible role of informal social relationships and such factors as primary group ties because these were presumed to be declining in the emerging *Gesellschaft* society. Elihu Katz has stated this argument cogently in the following terms:

> Until very recently, the image of society in the minds of most students of communication was of atomized individuals, connected with the mass media, but not with one another. Society—the "audience"—was conceived of as aggregates of age, sex, social class, and the like, but little thought was given to the relationships implied thereby to more informal relationships. The point is not that the student of mass communication was unaware that members of the audience have families and friends but that he did not believe that they might affect the outcome of a campaign; informal interpersonal relations, thus,

were considered irrelevant to the institutions of modern society.[16]

But when the interviewers talked with the people of Erie County, they kept getting somewhat unanticipated answers to one of their major lines of questioning:

> Whenever the respondents were asked to report on their recent exposures to campaign communications of all kinds, *political discussions* [italics added] were mentioned more frequently than exposure to radio or print.[17]

As a matter of fact, on the average day during the election campaign period, about 10 percent more people engaged in some sort of informal exchange of ideas with *other persons* than were exposed to campaign material directly from the mass media. About midway through the series of interviews, the researchers began to probe systematically into this kind of personal influence in an attempt to unravel the role of informal contacts with other people as an important set of variables in determining the effects of the media.

The end result of this somewhat unanticipated turn of events was the recognition that *informal social relationships* play a significant part in modifying the manner in which given individuals will act upon a message that comes to their attention via the mass media. In fact, it was discovered that there were many persons whose firsthand exposure to the media was quite limited. Such people obtained most of their information about the election campaign from other people who *had* gotten it firsthand. Thus, the research began to suggest a kind of movement of information through two basic stages. First, information moved from the media to relatively well informed individuals who frequently attended

16. Elihu Katz, "Communications Research and the Image of Society: Convergence of Two Research Traditions," *American Journal of Sociology* 65, no. 5 (1960): 436.
17. Lazarsfeld, Berelson, and Gaudet, *People's Choice*, p. 150.

to mass communications. Second, it moved from those persons through interpersonal channels to individuals who had less direct exposure to the media and who depended upon others for their information. This kind of communication process was termed the "two-step flow of communication."[18]

Those individuals who were more in contact with the media were called "opinion leaders" because it was soon discovered that they were playing an important role in helping to shape the voting intentions of those to whom they were passing on information. They were not only passing on information, of course, but they were also passing on their *interpretations* of communication content. This kind of "personal influence" became immediately recognized as an important intervening mechanism which operated between the mass communication message and the kind of responses made to that message.

Subsequent studies were aimed more directly at studying the mechanisms of interpersonal influence and the part played by social relationships in mediating the movement of information from the media to the masses. In fact, a rich literature has accumulated indicating that informal social relationships operate as important intervening variables between the stimulus and the response in the mass communication process.

It was suggested earlier that the role of informal social relationships in the communication process was independently discovered by more than one researcher at about the same time. Students of rural sociology had long recognized that informal social relationships among farmers played an important part in determining their propensity to adopt a given agricultural innovation. The rural society is one in which the farm family normally has strong social ties with its neighbors. When new ideas come from the outside, the

18. An excellent summary of this process is contained in Elihu Katz, "The Two-Step Flow of Communication: An Up-to-Date Report on an Hypothesis," *Public Opinion Quarterly* 21, no. 1 (Spring 1957): 61–78.

interpretations made by neighbors in such a setting can be of critical importance in determining the likelihood of adoption. The adoption of new farm technology is a process closely related to the mass communication process. New ideas are first presented to farm operators via communication media of one kind or another. These may be mass communication media, or they may be other formal channels of communication such as county agents or agricultural experiment station bulletins. The question is whether or not the individual farmer will respond to these communications in ways advocated by the communicators, namely, by adopting the recommended practice. Thus, conceptually speaking, a considerable similarity exists between the case of a farmer being advised to adopt a new form of weed spray via a radio program devoted to farm problems and the case of a person being advised to adopt a new household detergent via a radio commercial designed to sell soap. Both may adopt the innovation in accordance with the communicated suggestion, or they may resist it. The mechanisms that operate to mediate the decision to adopt or not to adopt may be quite similar in each case.[19]

The recognition of the convergence of theory between the students of mass communication and students of rural sociology who were studying the diffusion of farm technology stimulated a surge of interest in the diffusion and adoption process insofar as it was linked to mass communication. Intensive studies were undertaken concerning the nature of opinion leadership, the way it functioned in various contexts, and the part played by interpersonal relationships. In general it has been found that opinion leaders who are influential in the adoption process are in some respects very

19. For an excellent summary of research on farm adoption, see C. Paul Marsh and A. Lee Coleman, "Group Influences and Agricultural Innovations: Some Tentative Findings and Hypotheses," *American Journal of Sociology* 61, no. 6 (May 1956): 588–94. See also C. M. Coughenour, "The Functioning of Farmer's Characteristics in Relation to Contacts with Media and Practice Adoption," *Rural Sociology* 25 (September 1960): 263–97.

much like those whom they influence. They tend to conform closely to the norms of their groups, and they tend to be leaders in one area but not necessarily in others.[20] Opinion leadership does not seem to travel down the social structure, but is more likely to be horizontal. It appears to take place primarily between persons of somewhat similar status, although this is not always true. Katz and Lazarsfeld found that position in the "life cycle" was a key variable in determining who would influence whom in areas such as marketing, fashions, and public issues.[21] Young working women, in closer contact with fashion magazines and other media information about such issues, were sought by the less informed for advice about hairstyles, clothing, and the like. Married women with large families, who were well informed from appropriate media sources about household products, were sought as advisers on marketing, trying out new products, and so on. Thus, the age, marital status, and number of children (social categories) of traditional women predisposed them to acquire information about issues related to their traditional roles. These in turn were the criteria used by those needing advice on particular subjects when they turned to an opinion leader (social relationships) for information and influence.

De Fleur has suggested a number of conditions of social structure and of social functioning that will lead to the emergence and functioning of an opinion leader.[22] Further study is required, however, to identify the exact conditions under which a given person emerges as an opinion leader (individual differences). Moreover, the conditions that lead

20. For a review of literature on such issues, see Everett M. Rogers, *Diffusion of Innovations* (New York: Free Press of Glencoe, 1962), esp. pp. 208–47.

21. Elihu Katz and Paul F. Lazarsfeld, *Personal Influence* (Glencoe, Ill.: Free Press, 1954).

22. Melvin L. De Fleur, "The Emergence and Functioning of Opinion Leadership: Some Conditions of Informal Influence Transmission," in *Decisions, Values and Groups,* ed. Norman Washburne (New York: Macmillan, 1962), 2:257–78.

to the institutionalization—relatively permanent establishment—of an opinion leader also need additional research.[23]

THE FUTURE OF MASS COMMUNICATION THEORY

One of the most pressing problems in the interdisciplinary
study of mass communication is the strengthening of its
theoretical base. There has been an unfortunate tendency
among students of the media to equate the idea of "theory"
with relatively unsophisticated matters such as classification
schemes, the preparation of abstract diagrams that purport
to symbolize the communication process, or the mere listing
of factors that somehow will "make a difference" in the way
some communication effect takes place. Criteria of what constitutes a theory in more sophisticated fields are considerably more demanding. In a very real way, the three perspectives on mass communication that have been discussed in the
present chapter reflect these limitations. By any formal criteria, they are certainly not theories. They are conceptual
perspectives that have been given easy-to-remember names
for purposes of convenience. In reality, these conceptualizations did not emerge full-blown from research in precisely
the way they have been discussed. They have been pulled
together for the purposes of the present chapter and given
these names, although they have been implicit or explicit in
debates, writing, and research for years.

To some extent the lack of continued dedication to
fundamental theoretical problems related to the media
may be a product of the history of mass communication
as a field of research and study. Until recently, it has been

23. For a recent review of relevant research, see Walter Weiss, "Effects
of the Mass Media of Communication," in *Handbook of Social Psychology,* ed.
Gardner Lindzey and Elliot Aronson (2nd ed.; Reading, Mass.: Addison-
Wesley, 1969), 5: 77–195. Also see chaps. 5–11 in Ithiel de Sola Pool et al., eds.,
Handbook of Communication (Chicago: Rand McNally, 1973).

little more than a kind of intellectual way station—a kind of unclaimed territory where people from all kinds of disciplinary backgrounds have come in, picked up research problems, worked through them for a while, and then dropped them in favor of more pressing interests or pursued their implications back into the mainstream of their own discipline. Perhaps as communication continues to develop as a discipline in its own right, with its own research training, formal degree programs, increasing specialization, and a growing conceptual apparatus, it will be able to concentrate more fully on the systematic accumulation of theories of mass communication.

The three perspectives on the mass communication process discussed above need to be completely revamped and rewritten as systematic sets of propositions that show in straightforward terms just what is supposed to be related to what in terms of *independent* and *dependent* variables. To do this, some difficult definitional work will have to be undertaken so that the exact phenomena to which the concepts in the theories refer can be specified. Relationships between concepts within given propositions will have to be identified by means of some logical *calculus*—some set of recognized rules for reasoning—so that orders of dependency between propositions can be established. If this is done, such theories will yield *derived propositions* that can be tested empirically. Only then can their validity be adequately assessed.

This does not mean that all mass communication theory must be reduced to algebraic equations. The steps suggested above are possible without resorting to mathematics. Nevertheless, it is one thing to state propositions like this: "Ideas often flow from the media to opinion leaders and from them to less active populations." It is quite another thing to specify precisely what quantitative relationships are meant by such terms as "often" and "less," and to note exact empirical referents for other terms in such a statement, such as "ideas," "flow," "leaders," etc. In other words, we must specify more rigorously the conditions under which these events will occur, in what quantity or with what probability, and with what step-by-step theoretical implications for related media behavior.

This call for raising scientific standards in media theory construction indicates that students of mass communication have a great deal of homework to do before they can increase the sophistication of their theoretical formulations to the level of other disciplines. There is a serious gap between what we *think* we know about how people encounter and respond to the mass media and a rigorous set of theoretical formulations that specify how these events *actually* take place. In other words, there is a need to establish increased confidence that these basic perspectives are true (or else replace them) and thereby increase the degree to which we can discuss cause-effect sequences in mass communication in precise terms. Until the formulations identified in this chapter have been studied, restudied, reformulated, and restudied again, they will remain forever as "pre-theories"—interesting and seemingly plausible speculations that appear to be more or less consistent with our limited amount of media research but about which we really are not sure.

One obvious approach would be to *combine* the three perspectives discussed in this chapter. Such an *integrated* perspective would recognize that the effects of a given mass-communicated message sent over a given channel will depend upon a large number of psychological characteristics and social category similarities which audience members bring to their encounters with the media and will, moreover, depend upon the kind of social groups within which these people are acting and the relationships that they have with specific types of persons within them. Perhaps when it is possible to pin down some of these variables in specific detail, we can truly develop theories of mass communication.

10

TELEVISION and VIOLENCE

The perspectives discussed in the previous chapter on how people encounter media content selectively set the stage for an examination of social science theories of the *effects* of exposure to media messages. Despite the dominance of the effects question in discussions of the media's role in our society, social scientists have not formulated general theories of mass media effects. Rather, effects theories have been developed around rather specific scientific or public concerns, such as the effects of media messages on people's attitudes toward presidential candidates,[1] their feelings about the "enemy,"[2] their willingness to buy war bonds,[3] or their readiness to eat unconventional foods.[4]

We focus our attention in this chapter on specific theories of what has probably been the central effects question of recent decades—the impact of television portrayals of violence on audience behavior. We will outline the central assumptions of four specific theories that have generated most of the research on the effects of televised violence. These theories are called *catharsis, aggressive cues, observational learning,* and *reinforcement.* We will also illustrate how each of these theories has grown out of one or more of the perspectives previously discussed on how people encounter the media.

Attempts to understand and identify how television audiences are affected by violent television programming were intensified in the 1960s and early 1970s by a national sense of urgency concerning the causes of real-world violence. The 1960s will probably be remembered by social historians as a decade of violence—a time of urban riots, increasing rates of violent crime, and collective protests against such matters as the Vietnam war, institutionalized racism, and pollution. It was also a decade of assassinations of such major political figures as Martin Luther King, Jr., John Kennedy, and Robert Kennedy. Many concerned and politically powerful observers of the social scene could not resist making what seemed to be a logical connection between the incessant portrayals of violence on television on the one hand and the seemingly increasing rates of real-world violence on the

1. Paul F. Lazarsfeld, Bernard Berelson, and Hazel Gaudet, *The People's Choice* (New York: Columbia University Press, 1948).
2. For a view of such studies, see Carl I. Hovland, Irving L. Janis, and H. H. Kelley, *Communication and Persuasion* (New Haven: Yale University Press, 1953).
3. Robert K. Merton, *Mass Persuasion: The Social Psychology of a War Bond Drive* (New York: Harper & Brothers, 1946).
4. Hovland et al., *Communication and Persuasion.*

other.[5] The fact that youthful members of the first TV generation were the most visible participants in the violence of this era reinforced this line of thinking.

There are other reasons why television more than any other mass medium generates public concern. History reveals that public outcries against the harmful effects attributed to violent media content tend to focus on the newest mass medium. In the 1960s this was television. Television requires little in the way of reading or other skills. Thus, it is uniquely accessible to persons of all ages and education. Moreover, violence is a pervasive aspect of television programming. Gerbner and his associates in studies of typical weeks of TV content categorized 82 percent of prime-time television entertainment as violent programs.[6]

Government commissions asked social scientists to organize available theoretical and empirical work to see what tentative conclusions could be drawn about the effects of television violence. Social scientists also initiated research that might provide new insights into the relationship between television and real-world violence. The end products of these efforts are presented in the extensive reports of two national commissions dealing with the impact of TV violence. These were the Violence and the Media Task Force Report of the National Commission on the Causes and Prevention of Violence,[7] and the Surgeon General's Report on Television and Social Behavior.[8]

5. It is questionable that the level of violence in the 1960s was actually much higher than in prior periods of American history. See Hugh Graham and Ted Gurr, *Violence in America* (Washington, D.C.: Government Printing Office, 1969).

6. George Gerbner, M. Brouwer, C. Clark, K. Krippendorff, and M. Eleey, "Dimensions of Violence in Television Drama," in *Violence and the Media*, ed. R. K. Baker and S. J. Ball (Washington, D.C.: Government Printing Office, 1969), pp. 313–27.

7. Baker and Ball, *Violence and the Media*.

8. *Television and Growing Up: The Impact of Televised Violence*, Report to the Surgeon General, United States Public Health Service, from the Surgeon General's Scientific Advisory Committee on Television and Social Behavior (Washington, D.C.: Government Printing Office, 1972); *Television and Social Behavior, Reports and Papers*: vol. 1: *Media Content and Control*, ed. George A. Com-

While these documents provide detailed examination of the research revelant to this issue, our present aim is to summarize briefly the most prominent theories underlying such research. We will also try to show how these theories have grown out of more general perspectives on the ways people encounter and use the mass media. To a lesser extent, we will summarize what the research evidence can tell us about the validity of the catharsis, aggressive cues, observational learning, and reinforcement theories.

CATHARSIS THEORY

The central theme of catharsis[9] theory is that people in the normal course of daily life build up frustrations that eventually lead them to engage in aggression. Catharsis is the relief of such frustrations through vicarious participation in others' aggression. Aggressive tendencies, then, are effectively controlled by psychological and social mechanisms involved in vicarious experience. Seymour Feshbach is the most prominent proponent of the catharsis approach. For the catharsis theorist, viewing violent television content provides audiences with vicarious aggressive experiences. This serves as a harmless vehicle for relieving their feelings of hostility or frustration. For example, audience members watching TV characters cast in the role of "superspy" or "private eye" subjectively participate in the TV character's aggression. This lessens their own need to engage overtly in

stock and Eli A. Rubinstein; vol. 2: *Television and Social Learning*, ed. John P. Murray, Eli A. Rubinstein, and George A. Comstock; vol. 3: *Television and Adolescent Aggressiveness*; ed. George A. Comstock and Eli A. Rubinstein; vol. 4: *Television in Day-to-Day Life: Patterns of Use*, ed. Eli A. Rubinstein, George A. Comstock, and John P. Murray; vol. 5: *Television's Effects: Further Explorations*, ed. George A. Comstock, Eli A. Rubinstein, and John P. Murray.

9. Seymour Feshbach, "The Stimulating vs. Cathartic Effects of a Vicarious Aggressive Experience," *Journal of Abnormal and Social Psychology* 63 (1961): 381–85.

aggressive acts. The basic prediction made by catharsis theory, then, is that exposure to violent television content *decreases the probability of violent behavior* by TV viewers.

In a recent revision of the catharsis approach, Feshbach and Singer contend that televised violence may have a more important catharsis function for lower-class as opposed to middle-class audience members.[10] They reason that the family training or socialization given middle-class children equips them with a fairly good capacity to control their aggressive impulses. In contrast, the family training given lower-class children does not produce well-developed internal control mechanisms, thereby making them more dependent on the external control provided by cathartic TV violence.

Many differences between the catharsis theory and other specific theories of the effects of televised violence are due to their differing commitments to the assumptions of the more general formulations we have called the individual differences, social categories, and social relations perspectives on mass communication. In chapter 9 it was said that the individual differences perspective is the oldest of the three. Its central proposition is that differences in motivation, learning, personality, attitudes, etc., result in differences in the media content people select (selective attention). Differences in perception of media messages (selective perception) lead in turn to differences in how people interpret and respond to mass media stimuli. The social categories perspective, on the other hand, is based on the assumption that people who share a number of similar social characteristics (e.g., age, sex, race) also tend to share similar attitudes, norms, and values. These in turn lead them to respond to media messages in roughly similar ways. The central concern of the social relations perspective is the role of group relationships in influencing people's responses to media mes-

10. Seymour Feshbach and Robert Singer, *Television and Aggression* (San Francisco: Jossey-Bass, 1971).

sages. Interpersonal influence networks in the form of opinion leaders are said to act as conduits and interpreters of mass media messages for their followers (the two-step flow process of mass communication).

When we examine the relative impact of these perspectives on the orientation and assumptions of catharsis theory, we find that it is rooted in the individual differences perspective. The individual differences most central to catharsis theory are the level of accumulated frustration and hostility which individuals are experiencing prior to exposure to violent TV programs. The cathartic effect of televised violence should be greatest for these individuals with the strongest catharsis need, namely, individuals who have built up considerable frustration and hostility.

When Feshbach and Singer[11] incorporated the idea that lower-class persons may have greater catharsis needs than middle-class persons, they based their modification of catharsis theory on an important "social category." The proposition that the effects of violent TV programming will be similar for members of the same social class, but different across social classes, moves catharsis theory beyond a concern with individual differences. It becomes a special case of the social categories perspective. Thus, both perspectives provide a background of this specific formulation.

AGGRESSIVE CUES THEORY

Leonard Berkowitz has been the primary framer of the aggressive cues (also referred to as the stimulating effects) approach to the effects of television portrayals of violence.[12] Its major assumption is that exposure to aggressive stimuli will increase a person's level of physiological and emotional

11. Ibid.
12. Leonard Berkowitz, *Aggression: A Social Psychological Analysis* (New York: McGraw-Hill, 1962).

arousal which, in turn, will increase the *probability of aggressive behavior*. Seeing a violent boxing match, for example, should stimulate emotional arousal leading to aggressive behavior on the part of TV audience members. Violent encounters, weapons, or threats not only physiologically and emotionally arouse audience members, but also cue them into aggressive responses.

The stimulus-response relationship in aggressive cues theory is neither simple nor unconditional. An aggressive stimulus (e.g., a violent TV program) does not always elicit an aggressive response, nor will it be likely to elicit the same degree of aggressivity in all audience members. One factor that is said to heighten both the likelihood of an aggressive response and increase the degree of aggressivity of responses is frustration *at the time of exposure* to a violent TV program.

The way in which violence is portrayed in television programs is also said to affect the likelihood of audience members behaving aggressively. Most important in this regard is whether or not the violence of TV characters is portrayed as being justified. When such violence is presented as justified (e.g., on grounds of vengeance or self-defense), it increases the likelihood of aggressive responses. This is so because viewers can adopt such justifications for their own aggressive behavior.[13] Another factor, which according to Berkowitz and his associates can affect the nature of responses to televised violence, is the extent to which the television portrayal is similar to anger-provoking circumstances with which the audience member is presently trying to cope.[14] Similarity can be established by such simple things as a TV character having the same name or occupation as a person that is angering the viewer.

A factor that is said to lower the probability of an aggressive response is *inhibition* of aggressive tendencies. For

13. J. Hoyt, "Vengeance and Self-Defense as Justification for Filmed Aggression" (Master's thesis, University of Wisconsin, 1967).

14. Leonard Berkowitz and Russell Geen, "Stimulus Qualities of the Target of Aggression: A Further Study," *Journal of Personality and Social Psychology* 5, no. 3 (1967): 364–68.

example, a television portrayal of a violent interpersonal encounter can elicit a sense of guilt in viewers by directing the viewers' attention to the pain and suffering of the victim of the violent attack. This presumably inhibits their aggressivity by sensitizing them to the pain and suffering that their aggressive responses may cause others.[15]

Aggressive cues theory also has its primary theoretical origins in the individual differences perspective. Individual differences in level of frustration or arousal at the time of exposure are said to affect the probability of aggression following exposure to violent programs. The process of selective perception, so central to the individual differences perspective, may also account for some of the variability in audience members' responses to aggressive stimuli. When the camera focuses on the painful consequences of aggression, for example, it has the effect of guiding viewers' perceptions to emphasize selectively the victim's pain and suffering. As noted, such emphasis seems to inhibit most, but not all, viewers' aggression. An individual difference that might affect the degree of inhibition which different viewers feel is the extent of their prior exposure via television and personal experience to the pain and gore consequences of violence. Those having much prior exposure would probably not respond with the same degree of emotional arousal and inhibition as those with little prior experience.

OBSERVATIONAL LEARNING THEORY

This theory, as developed primarily by Bandura and Walters,[16] rests on the assumption that people can learn aggres-

15. For reviews of the relevant literature, see Russell Geen and Leonard Berkowitz, "Some Conditions Facilitating the Occurrence of Aggression After the Observation of Violence," *Journal of Personality* 35 (1967): 666–76; and Richard Goransen, "A Review of the Recent Literature," in Baker and Ball, *Violence and the Media,* pp. 395–413.

16. Albert Bandura and Richard Walters, *Social Learning and Personality Development* (New York: Holt, Rinehart, & Winston, 1963).

sive behavior by observing aggression in TV programs and, under certain conditions, model their behavior after aggressive TV characters. Televised violence, according to this approach, *increases the probability of audience aggression* not only by providing opportunities for audiences to learn aggression, but also by presenting violent characters who act as behavior models for viewers. The fundamental learning processes by which children come to learn all forms of new behavior are also said to operate when children are sitting in front of a television set watching violent programs. As they might acquire new patterns of conduct from observing their brother's or sister's activities, they can learn new forms of aggressive behavior from observing violent TV characters.

Observational learning theorists do not contend that audience members will automatically perform the aggressive acts they have learned. Learned violent acts, like a great deal of the behavior learned in classrooms, is not put into practice unless a situation arises which calls for performance of that learned behavior. The probability of audience members' exhibiting learned violent behavior is enhanced by such factors as an expectation of being rewarded by others for such behavior, similarity between the situation presented in the TV portrayal and the social situation encountered by viewers after exposure, and anticipation of social support from a co-viewer who praises the violent actions of TV characters.[17]

Observational learning theory is a special case of the individual differences perspective, but it also includes aspects of the social categories and social relations perspectives. For example, one form of social relationship considered by observational learning theorists is the extent to which viewers encounter real social situations that are similar to those presented in television programs. Encountering similar interactional situations increases the likelihood of performance of

17. David Hicks, "Effects of Co-observer Sanctions and Adult Presence on Imitative Aggression," *Child Development* 39 (1968): 303–9.

aggressive behavior learned from observation of violent TV characters. Viewers frequently involved in interpersonal conflict would probably see more similarity between TV stories and their own life situations than would people who rarely have to cope with conflict.[18]

The influence of the social categories perspective on observational learning theory can be illustrated by examining interpretations made of the finding that while girls learn as much aggressive behavior from observation of violent TV characters as do boys, they perform fewer acts of learned aggression. Rather than saying that these individual girls exhibit less aggressive behavior than these individual boys, the subjects are treated as representatives of social categories—male and females. The explanation given for less actual aggressive behavior by girls than boys is that the female sex role and subcultural norms against aggressive female behavior operate to reduce the likelihood of girls displaying the aggressive acts they have learned.[19]

REINFORCEMENT THEORY

The central assumption of this specific theory of effects is that television portrayals of violence *reinforce whatever established pattern of violent behavior that viewers bring with them to the TV situation.* Klapper,[20] the major proponent of reinforcement theory, contends that television violence usually does not produce significant increases or decreases in the probability of audience aggression.

Reinforcement theorists look to such factors as cultural norms and values, social roles, personality characteristics,

18. See Goranson, "Review of Recent Literature," for a review of relevant studies.
19. Ibid.
20. Joseph Klapper, *The Effects of Mass Communication* (New York: Free Press, 1960).

and family or peer influences as the primary determinants of violent behavior. These and other psychological and social factors are also said to determine the effects of violent TV programs. For example, viewers' norms and attitudes should guide their perceptions of violent television programs. Those who have developed into rather violent persons with norms and attitudes that support violence as a means to personal and social ends probably "selectively perceive" the violent actions of TV characters in ways that support (reinforce) their norms and attitudes. Relatively nonviolent viewers, on the other hand, would "selectively perceive" the messages of the program so that it conforms to their antiviolence norms and attitudes. Thus, the effect of televised violence would be to reinforce the established norms and attitudes of both the violent and nonviolent viewers, making them no more or no less likely to engage in violent behavior than they would have been if they had not watched television.

A major exception to this rule, according to reinforcement theorists, involves a small minority of viewers who lack personal and social stability. People, particularly young children and adolescents, who lack strong and stable relationships with family, friends, teachers, and so on, may not have developed clear guidelines for their participation in aggression. Moreover, they may not receive sufficent group control over their use of aggression. Violent television programming may fill a void in these people's lives to the extent that they refer to the beliefs and actions of violent TV characters as guides for their own behavior.[21] In such cases, the effect of violent TV programs would go past reinforcement to bring about significant increases in the probability of these viewers' level of aggressive behavior.

Reinforcement theory shares with the other theories of aggression effects deep roots in the individual differences perspective. For example, reinforcement theory explains how people with quite different characteristics can all

---

21. Joseph Klapper, *Statement before the National Commission on the Causes and Prevention of Violence* (Washington, D.C.: Government Printing Office, 1969).

be reinforced by the same violent TV program. This is done by incorporating the process of selective perception into their theorizing. But there are fundamental differences between reinforcement and the other aggression effects theories. Most of these differences reflect the more central roles of the social categories and the social relations perspectives in reinforcement theory.

While catharsis and observational learning theorists have generally included one or two social categories into their thinking, they still tend to deemphasize the ways in which individuals are tied to a multiplicity of social categories and groups. Reinforcement theorists, in comparison, tend to view individuals as representatives of social categories. Race, sex, socioeconomic status, and religion are examples of the kinds of social categories that reinforcement theorists usually take into account. Individuals belonging to the same social categories should share similar norms, attitudes, values, prior experiences, and many other social and personal characteristics. These, as noted, should operate to make them respond very similarly to violent television programs.

The social relations perspective lies at the heart of the reinforcement theorist's rationale for the claim that most viewers will not undergo significant change as a result of exposure to violent television programming. If people's social relationships at home, work, and play are stable and effective, then their aggressive behavior should be governed more by the role expectations and norms of their friends or family members than by the behavior of violent TV characters. According to reinforcement theory, violent television programming should have a significant effect upon the probability of aggressive behavior only when social relations are disrupted or are unstable.

This brief review suggests that psychology has had more impact than sociology on the way specific theories of the effects of televised violence have been conceptualized and studied. The dominance of psychological concerns and concepts is evidenced by the relatively heavy influence of the individual differences perspective. As noted in chapter 9, the concepts and assumptions of the individual differences perspective (e.g., variations in needs, interests, or feelings affect perception) reflect the traditional psychological emphasis on the individual. The traditional sociological view that individuals are tied into a complex web of categories and associations, which play a part in determining the effects of violent TV programs, is contained in the social categories and social relations perspectives. These perspectives have served, at best, as only secondary sources for the catharsis, aggressive cues, and observational learning theories. Reinforcement theory probably comes closest to being derived from a fairly even mixture of both traditional general psychological and sociological theory.

POLICY IMPLICATIONS AND RESEARCH CONCLUSIONS

Each of the four specific theories of the effects of television portrayals of violence has policy implications for either *how much* TV violence should be presented or *how* it should be presented. Catharsis theory has some very interesting implications. If catharsis theory is correct, television networks could argue that by including violent portrayals in their broadcasts, they are performing a public service. Logically, under this view, moves to reduce the amount of violent programming should be resisted on the grounds that this would limit opportunities for catharsis. This in turn would increase the probability of audience aggression.

The aggressive cues theorist, in contrast, regards televised violence as a source of aggressive stimuli that may *increase* aggressive behavior. In terms of policy implications, the aggressive cues theorist is led to recommend extreme care in the *way* violence is presented in TV programs. If this theory is correct, writers, producers, and directors should carefully design portrayals of violence so that factors which tend to reduce the probability of aggressive responses are incorporated into the script.[22] Such program design, theoretically, would reduce tendencies toward violence among susceptible members of the audience.

The observational learning theorist usually recommends still different policies. Violent TV programming should be based upon an informed understanding of how to reduce the probability of aggressive behavior. Controlling *how* violence is portrayed may reduce the chances of people exhibiting learned violent acts.

Finally, the major policy implication of reinforcement theory is that attempts to reduce the incidence of real-world violence by reducing the level of TV violence or changing the way it is presented are bound to fail. These theorists direct policy concern to the learning processes that occur in families or peer groups, regarding what takes place in the encounter with televised violence as a far less important source of real-world violence.

The steady increase in the proportion of violent TV programs noted by Gerbner and his associates[23] is probably a rather simple consequence of the profitability of such programming. One need not assume that it is a product of deliberation by media personnel about which effects theory is correct. In view of the considerable public concern over TV violence, however, it seems appropriate to conclude this chapter with an overview of what the research literature can and cannot tell us about the *validity* of the specific theories of the effects of televised violence. Policy implications, after all, are only as good as the theories on which they are based.

For the most part, research on the effects of violent television programming has yielded a literature of "short-term"

22. See Goranson, "Review of Recent Literature."
23. George Gerbner, "Violence in Television Drama: Trends and Symbolic Functions," in *Television and Social Behavior*, ed. George Comstock and Eli Rubinstein (Washington, D.C.: Government Printing Office, 1971), vol. 1.

effects.[24] Such research usually involves exposing subjects to anywhere from a few minutes to a few hours of TV programs followed by observations of the subjects' behavior for, at most, several hours after exposure. Most studies conducted to test catharsis, aggressive cues, or observational learning hypotheses have been carried out in research laboratories and have employed experimental research designs. In their simplest form, these experimental designs involve comparing two groups of subjects who are alike in all respects except one—the kind of programs they see. One group sees nonviolent programs and is called the "control" group. The other group sees violent programs and is called the "experimental" group. Because the only difference between the control and experimental groups is presumably the kind of programs they were exposed to, any differences in their behavior following exposure is said to be a result of differences in the kind of programs they saw. The type of program—violent or nonviolent—is called the "independent" variable because it should be the cause of any differences observed in the "dependent" variable—level of aggressive behavior after exposure. The kinds of aggressive acts used as dependent variables include such behaviors as verbal or written expressions of hostility, hitting a large inflatable doll called a "Bobo Doll," and administering electric shocks to other people.

Without going into further detail about how these various studies were conducted, we can briefly summarize the general conclusions that can be drawn from their findings. We will look first at how such research evidence bears upon the validity of catharsis theory. Actually, we find little support for its central prediction, namely, that subjects exposed to violent programming (experimental group) will be *less* aggressive than subjects exposed to nonviolent programs (control group). In most instances, the subjects exposed to violent

24. There are exceptions. See, for example, David Hicks, "Imitation and Retention of Film-mediated Aggressive Peer and Adult Models," *Journal of Personality and Social Psychology* 2, no. 1 (July 1965): 97–100.

programs were *more* aggressive following exposure than the subjects who saw nonviolent programs. In fact, this outcome is consistent with the prediction made in both aggressive cues and observational learning theories.

While such findings from laboratory research on the short-term effects of violent television programs provide general support for the aggressive cues and observational learning theories, they do not really establish their validity. Validity requires more than correct prediction. It also requires demonstrating that the process outlined in the theory is the *actual* chain of events set off by exposure to violent programs culminating in aggressive behavior on the part of subjects. A number of studies involving far more complex experimental procedures than those outlined above have been carried out by both observational learning and aggressive cues researchers. It would take a separate volume to give thorough examination to the details of such research and its findings.[25] For our purposes, suffice it to say that most of the data tend to support both the observation learning process and the aggressive cues process described in the first part of this chapter.

Proponents of reinforcement theory tend to downplay the importance of such laboratory research findings.[26] For example, they express doubt that laboratory research findings can be generalized to predict the effects of viewing actual violent TV programs in the natural setting of the home. The two primary bases for their misgivings are that the artificial laboratory setting may elicit artificial behavior, and that the kinds of aggressive behavior studied in the lab (e.g., electric shocks or hitting Bobo dolls) bear little relationship to real-life aggressive acts (e.g., murder and assault). There is no easy answer to these charges.

25. See Walter Weiss, "Effects of the Mass Media of Communication," in *The Handbook of Social Psychology,* ed. G. Lindzey and E. Aronson (2nd ed.; Reading, Mass.: Addison-Wesley, 1969), pp. 77–195.

26. See Ruth Hartley, *The Impact of Viewing Aggression: Studies and Problems of Extrapolation* (New York: Columbia Broadcasting System, 1964).

Reinforcement theorists are more likely to utilize field or survey research techniques in which selected samples of people respond to a researcher's questions by filling a questionnaire or by being interviewed.[27] One of the many ways in which these responses can be analyzed is to see if membership in relevant social categories is correlated with the way people respond to various questions. For example, researchers may ask questions designed to measure respondents' preferences for violent television programs. Then statistical tests are employed to see if differences in preferences are correlated with social category differences in age, sex, education, race, etc. Other types of questions frequently included in surveys are designed to measure social relations variables, such as stability of family life or degree of integration into the community. Still other common survey questions assess respondents' attitudes and norms about violence and their frequency of participation in violent behavior.

The reinforcement theorist is particularly interested in finding out if various social categories, social relations, or individual differences in attitudes, etc., show stronger correlations with differences in frequency of violent behavior than do differences in degree of exposure to violent TV programming. The survey research literature does not, however, contain conclusive evidence on this point. Some findings support, but others do not supprt, the hypothesis that violent TV programming reinforces preestablished patterns of violent behavior.[28]

There is a fundamental difficulty in utilizing correlational evidence obtained from a single survey to assess the validity of reinforcement or any other specific theory of effects. Put simply, the problem is that correlations do not really inform us about the underlying mechanisms of cause-

27. For illustrations of such studies, see G. A. Comstock and E. A. Rubenstein, eds., *Television and Social Behavior* (Washington, D.C.: Government Printing Office, 1971), vol. 3.

28. Ibid.

effect relationships. For example, suppose that researchers did find that the most violent people are also the most frequent viewers of TV violence. They would then face the familiar "chicken and egg" problem of not knowing which is the cause and which is the effect.

Questions of cause and effect become very complicated when trying to unravel the effects of the media. Their resolution is most likely to come from research that examines the long-term effects of exposure to violent television content. The problem of determining cause-effect relationships might be resolved by the kind of experimental procedures described earlier. But, the previously noted debate about whether or not findings obtained from research laboratories can be generalized to real-life conditions still undermines confidence in the broad applicability of emerging conclusions. Moreover, the experimental literature on short-term effects may not be very informative about the cumulative effects of years of exposure to violent TV programs. Both these problems are resolved when a long-term field experimental design is employed. Instead of observing subjects in artificial laboratory conditions, they are observed in their natural settings. The researcher makes arrangements with the subjects, their parents, or their supervisors to have some subjects view only violent programs (the experimental group) and other subjects view only nonviolent programs (the control group). Over a period of weeks or months, or even longer, trained observers record how much aggressive behavior is exhibited by each subject. Such procedures allow researchers to observe a wide variety of normal and realistic aggressive acts exhibited by their subjects without any prodding from the observer. When the field experiment terminates, researchers can determine if the experimental group's subjects participated in more, less, or about the same level of aggressive behavior as the control group's subjects. They can also compare the short-term effects of a day's exposure with the long-term effects of more extensive exposure.

While long-term field experiments are clearly desirable, they are extremely difficult to conduct. The major difficulty stems from the need to ensure that the only significant difference between the experiences and conditions which experimental subjects face and those encountered by the control group's subjects is the type of TV programs they view (e.g., violent or nonviolent). Another obvious difficulty is making sure that the observers are in a position to observe all the subjects and all their aggressive activity.

Despite these considerable difficulties, a few effects researchers have conducted field experiments in recent years.[29] For a number of reasons, including methodological problems, these studies have not provided incontrovertible evidence regarding the validity of catharsis, aggressive cues, observational learning, or reinforcement theory. There is reason to hope, however, that methodological problems will be resolved, and that future field experiments might provide the kind of evidence required to determine both the short-term and the long-term effects of viewing violent television programming. Until that time, debates about the validity of these specific theories of the effects of televised violence will continue.

29. For example, Feshbach and Singer, *Television and Aggression;* and Aletha Stein and Lynette Friedrich, "Television Content and Young Children's Behavior," in *Television and Social Behavior,* ed. J. P. Murray, E. A. Rubenstein, and G. A. Comstock (Washington, D.C.: Government Printing Office, 1971), vol. 2.

11

MASS COMMUNICATION and PERSUASION

In the previous chapter we saw how the general theoretical perspectives on mass communication underlie theories of the effects of televised violence. In this chapter we show how these same theoretical perspectives—individual differences, social categories, and social relationships—have affected the development of models for describing how persuasion effects are achieved via mass communication.

The development of theoretical perspectives on the way in which mass-communicated messages influence audiences have led to numerous attempts to capitalize on these conceptualizations for the purpose of *deliberately* manipulating people's actions. The mass efforts of the advertising world to influence purchasing are one obvious example. Perhaps equally obvious are public-service campaigns that attempt to persuade people to engage in a variety of socially approved behaviors. Again obvious is the case of political persuasion, where the voting act is the object of continuing efforts to manipulate behavior with mass communication content.

The relationship between contemporary perspectives on mass communication and conceptualizations of how persuasion can be achieved is not a straightforward one. Creating effective advertising has always been more of an art than an activity based upon scientifically formulated theories. The same is true of other forms of persuasion. Nevertheless, analyses of contemporary persuasion campaigns reveal certain regularities, certain significant similarities, in their *apparent underlying assumptions* about how the persuasion process works. These assumptions can be formalized into two rather broad "models" of the persuasion process that are described below.

In attempting to describe the nature of these formulations, two things will be quite clear. First, these models of the persuasion process (which is simply another way of talking about a "theory" of how it works) are *extensions* and *utilizations* of the theoretical perspectives on mass communication that were reviewed in chapter 9. Second, these models are *roughly formulated* at the present time.

THE PSYCHODYNAMIC MODEL

The first of these two conceptualizations can be called the *psychodynamic* model of the persuasion process. It is based almost exclusively upon what we have termed the "individual differences perspective" on mass communication. Although one of the earliest perspectives on mass communication to be recognized, the individual differences perspective continues to be widely used. This is revealed by the impact that it has had on the advertising and public relations world where it remains very popular. It has also provided the principal set of assumptions underlying such socio-psychological research on persuasion by behavioral scientists.

The essence of this application of the individual differences perspective is that an effective message is said to be one which has properties capable of *altering the psychological functioning* of individuals in such a way that they will respond overtly (toward the item that is the object of persuasion) with modes of behavior desired or suggested by the communicator. In other words, it has been assumed that the key to effective persuasion lies in modifying the internal psychological structure of the individual so that the psychodynamic relationship between latent internal processes (motivation, attitudes, etc.) and manifest overt behavior will lead to acts intended by the persuader.[1]

There have been many specific forms or variants of this general approach to persuasion, depending upon the particular psychological phenomenon under manipulation, and upon the presumed dynamic relationships thought to prevail between that psychological process and the overt behavior patterns it supposedly activates. For example, extensive use has been made of persuasive messages aimed at individual *attitudes* under the assumption that there is a close relationship between attitudinal structure and the way people behave in overt social situations.[2] A common example would

1. This was the central thesis of Vance Packard in his controversial book *The Hidden Persuaders*. He suggested that modern advertisers, using psychoanalytic mechanisms as intervening variables, were achieving powerful effects in persuading people to purchase consumer products. See Vance Packard, *The Hidden Persuaders* (New York: David McKay, 1957). It was also the guiding principle underlying the work of Carl Hovland and his students in the Yale Communication and Attitude Change Program which resulted in an impressive number of publications.

2. This assumption has been called into serious question in studies of the relationship between attitudes and action. See Melvin L. De Fleur and Frank R. Westie, "Verbal Attitudes and Overt Acts," *American Sociological Review* 23, no. 6 (December 1958): 667–73.

be the mass communication campaign aimed at reducing ethnic discrimination (overt behavior) by attempting to reduce ethnic prejudice (emotional attitude purported to lead to discrimination). Another example would be an attempt to promote the purchase of a patent medicine (overt action) by instilling a *fear* of poor health or continued suffering (psychological state or process). The general idea could be illustrated with examples ranging from blood-donation drives and charity appeals to antilitter campaigns and political oratory. Among the many other psychological concepts that have been used as intervening variables are sexual urges, status drives, desires for social approval, anxieties, opinions, vanity, and a host of others. In simple graphic terms, the *psychodynamic model* of the persuasion process would be as follows:

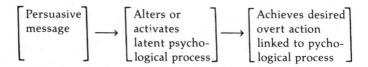

An extensive social-psychological literature has accumulated with respect to many variables thought to be potentially useful as modifiers of overt action.[3] Psychological theories of motivation, perception, learning, and even psychoanalysis have suggested ways in which attitudes, opinions, fears, self-conceptions, perceptions of source credibility, reinforcement, and many other variables are related to persuasion.

Some studies among the accumulated literature on such topics have been so widely quoted and reprinted that the rather tentative nature of the original conclusions is in danger of being forgotten. But wide quotation of reprinting is not equivalent to wide replication. Further evidence is needed to support the psychodynamic model of persuasion. Sys-

3. Carl Hovland, Irving Janis, and Harold Kelley, *Communication and Persuasion* (New Haven: Yale University Press, 1954).

tematic and valid assertions are needed as to precisely which variables under what exact circumstances can be used to manipulate what specific kinds of people toward what definite patterns of action when messages incorporating those variables are brought to their attention. Not only is the evidence as yet incomplete concerning the utility of this approach to persuasion, but those who employ this strategy sometimes make unrealistic assumptions. For example, some experimentalists have been willing to assume that if their communication was demonstrably able to change attitudes or opinions, then patterns of overt behavior would be correspondingly changed. Such as assumption is unwarranted. Festinger has reviewed relevant literature on this problem.[4]

But the fact that the validity of the psychodynamic model of the persuasion process has as yet not been fully verified does not mean that it is incorrect. It seems to work some of the time. For example, during an eclipse of the sun, the population of a midwestern town was repeatedly warned by local media to avoid viewing the eclipse directly or through dark glasses. Fear-threat appeals that described possible severe eye damage were used to persuade people to obtain a recommended viewing appartus or to avoid exposure altogether by viewing the event on television. A study conducted immediately following the eclipse indicated that there was a positive relationship between the amount of fear aroused and degree of overt compliance.[5]

In contrast, an earlier experimental study of somewhat parallel fear-threat messages regarding dental health among groups of high school students showed the reverse. Illustrated lectures showing damage to teeth as a result of improper dental hygiene were presented to several groups of subjects. An inverse relationship between fear-threat com-

4. Leon Festinger, "Behavioral Support for Opinion Change," *Public Opinion Quarterly* 28, no. 3 (Fall 1964): 404–17.
5. Sidney Kraus, Elaine El-Assal, and Melvin L. De Fleur, "Fear-Threat Appeals in Mass Communication: An Apparent Contradiction," *Speech Monographs* 33, no. 1 (March 1966): 23–29.

pliance was found. Those who received the strongest fear-threat showed the least compliance with the preventive program advocated by the communicator. Those experiencing the least fear-threat showed the most compliance. The results of this well-controlled and frequently quoted study were exactly the opposite of those from the study of the eclipse.[6] Such seemingly opposite findings in the case of two variants of a fear-threat health campaign indicate emphatically the need to sort out the conditions under which a given psychodynamic variable will lead to a particular type of action and when it will "boomerang" and suppress it.

The same can be said of the individual differences perspective in general. There are many kinds of "effects" that a message can touch off other than overt adoption of some action advocated in a persuasive communication. For example, the way in which children learn new ideas and practices from the media through a process of *observational* or *incidental learning* was discussed in the previous chapter.[7] This may be totally unrelated to the intent of communicators. People may take up new habits, adopt new fads, change their musical tastes, or bolster their loyalty to a political party without complying in any sense to a persuasive message deliberately designed to manipulate them. While the individual differences perspective suggests that variations in their personality structures will play an important part in determining the manner in which this happens, it would be incorrect to say that a fully articulated theory is now available explaining the role of such factors. At the same time, an impressive array of research findings shows how *some* individual characteristics do play *some* part in determining the kind of effect that a given message content will have on a particular type of person. These studies along with many others have been reviewed by Klapper.[8] He points up the need to consider many

6. Irving Janis and Seyman Feshback, "The Effects of Fear-Arousing Communications," *Journal of Abnormal and Social Psychology* 48 (1953): 78–132.

7. Wilbur Schramm et al., *Television in the Lives of Our Children* (Stanford, Calif.: Stanford University Press, 1961), p. 75.

8. Joseph T. Klapper, *The Effects of Mass Communication* (Glencoe, Ill.: Free Press, 1960).

other variables besides individual personality characteristics in developing theories of the effects of the media, and the dangers inherent in constructing simple cause-effect types of theory. This is a point of view with which we heartily agree. This chapter treats several theories in cause-effect terms because it is attempting to show the *development* of mass communication theory over time as well as its broad scope.

In 1948 Bernard Berelson attempted to summarize the status of the field of mass communication as it then existed. He noted that the older (S-R) theory of the all-powerful media had largely been abandoned, and he identified five central factors that seemed to be the focus of research at the time:

> Now, in the 1940's, a body of empirical research is accumulating which provides some refined knowledge on the effect of communication on public opinion and promises to provide a good deal more in the next years.
>
> But what has such research contributed to the problem? . . . The proper answer to the general question, the answer which constitutes a useful formulation for research purposes, is this: Some kind of *communication* on some kinds of *issues*, brought to the attention of some kinds of *people* under some kinds of *conditions*, have some kinds of *effects*.[9]

This set of propositions may have been far short of being a tightly formulated theory of mass communication, but it clearly rested upon the kinds of assumptions we have called the individual differences perspective. Faced with the need to predict the probable impact of a given type of communication on a given issue, and in cases where the "conditions" of communication (radio, print, etc.) are understood or controlled, the major variables not manipulatable by the communicator are the "kinds of people," i.e., individual differences among persons. In other words, communicators able

9. Bernard Berelson, "Communications and Public Opinions," in *Mass Communications*, ed. Wilbur Schramm (Urbana: University of Illinois Press, 1949), p. 500.

to select their message and issues, and by and large structure the conditions of communication as they wished, still had no direct control over their audiences' prejudices, predispositions, amount of prior information, etc. Thus, the independent variables (messages on a given issue presented under known conditions) are modified in their impact on the dependent variables (effects) by the action of intervening variables, i.e., individual differences in relevant psychological variables.

The Berelson formulation quoted above did extend somewhat the elementary form of the individual differences perspective by calling specific attention to the fact that variations in the *stimulus material* and variations in the *social setting* or other related conditions, as well as in the psychological structures of members of the audience, could be expected to have an impact upon the kinds of effects produced. In spite of its simplicity, it served as a guide for new directions in research. It was a kind of general statement of the salient categories of factors and variables which, along with individual differences, must be considered in trying to understand the communication process.

A far more specific psychodynamic formulation based on individual differences is Rokeach's theory of value change.[10] The value-change procedure is quite different from previous attempts to change people's attitudes. Rather than presenting information about the harmful or beneficial consequences of a particular activity or object, a technique of *comparative feedback* is used: Individuals take a value test and are given factual information about their own values as compared to the values of other kinds of people. Individuals who discover that they have ranked certain values in a manner that contradicts their conceptions of themselves as moral and competent persons will experience self-dissatisfaction. It is this dissatisfaction, not others' fear tactics or rational appeals, that sets the value-change process into motion and leads to modification of personal value hierarchies. For ex-

10. Milton Rokeach, *The Nature of Human Values* (New York: Free Press, 1973).

ample, when individuals' conceptions of themselves as people who are strong believers in equalitarian democratic ideals are contradicted by finding out after taking a values test that they actually place little importance on the value *Equality,* they are likely to experience self-dissatisfaction. One way to remove this self-dissatisfaction is to increase the importance of *Equality* in their personal value hierarchy. Thus, the feedback of comparative value information that causes self-dissatisfaction also points the way to regain a positive self-concept by appropriate value change.

In Rokeach's procedure, the internal psychological factor that is altered is the relative *importance* people place on a particular value. According to this theory, values underlie attitudes and behavior; therefore, change in a person's values should lead to changes in related attitudes and behavior. Rokeach has presented data indicating that this seems to occur.[11]

No research has yet been conducted to see if such value-change procedures are applicable to the case when the mass media act as the feedback channel for comparative information. There are, however, numerous instances in which the mass communicator's persuasion goal requires value change. Public-affairs programming intended to persuade audiences to increase the priority of ecological concerns, for example, clearly seeks to accomplish basic value change. Yet, basic research on values shows that value-change effects are extremely unlikely unless the communicator has a valid guide as to how to construct and present persuasion messages. The Rokeach procedure suggests that communicators seeking to increase something like an audience's priority for behavior in accord with ecological concerns should first provide its members with information leading them to conclusions about the amount of importance they personally place on values related to ecology (like *A World of Beauty*) as compared to specific categories of other people. For example, if a

11. Ibid.

communication shows that people who place relatively low importance on values related to ecology are litterers, water contaminators, and air polluters, some portion of the audience, on coming to believe that they personally have a *similar* hierarchy of values, may experience self-dissatisfaction. Those who want to entertain conceptions of themselves as ecologically responsible would, according to the theory, feel very dissatisfied with the fact that their value hierarchy paralleled those of ecologically irresponsible people. Those experiencing the self-dissatisfaction should then be significantly more likely to increase the importance of ecologically linked values within their own value hierarchy. Presumably, such value change would produce an increase in the frequency or likelihood of desired forms of behavior.

THE SOCIOCULTURAL MODEL

While the individual differences theory of mass media effects led to the formulation of the "psychodynamic model" of the persuasion process in attempts to use the theory for practical purposes, this model has by no means been the only one that has been tried. A somewhat more complicated alternative stems from a combination of the social categories and social relationships perspectives discussed in chapter 9. For the lack of a better term, we will refer to this as the *sociocultural model* of the persuasion process.

Little systematic theory has emerged from the experimental literature on persuasion regarding the use of sociocultural variables as a basis for appeals in persuasive communication. Social and cultural variables have been widely recognized by communication researchers and other social scientists as playing an important part in determining the way in which people adopt new ideas and things. But the way in which such variables can be deliberately incorporated into messages to facilitate persuasion has not received much attention. In fact, existing theories of persuasion, and of the adoption of innovation, see group, interaction, and cultural variables mainly in terms of *obstacles* to achieving persuasion or adoption.[12] The reason for this may have been the almost overwhelming preoccupation with the psychodynamic model that has already been discussed.[13]

Much basic research in behavioral science indicates that what we are terming "sociocultural variables" are important sources from which individuals gain definitions of appropriate behavior in a group context. They are, as we will indicate in greater detail, important sources from which the individual derives *interpretations of reality* as well as being significant forms of *social control*.[14] The body of basic research on such issues spans the social sciences from anthropology to sociology. In addition to numerous studies of culture, classic laboratory experiments such as those of Asch and Sherif show how even in the simplest and most artificial setting, the influence of *norms* plays a powerful role in guiding, defining, and modifying the behavior of individuals, somewhat independently of the state of their internal predispositions.[15] Sociological studies have supported this generalization. The work of Lohman and Reitzes,[16] Minard,[17] Newcomb,[18] De

12. An example of such analyses would be Herbert H. Hyman and Paul B. Sheatsley, "Some Reasons Why Information Campaigns Fail," *Public Opinion Quarterly* 11 (Fall 1947): 412–23.

13. To illustrate, one chapter of Hovland's widely read book on *Communication and Persuasion* is entitled "Group Membership and *Resistance* to Influence" (italics supplied).

14. See Kurt Lewin, "Group Decision and Social Change," *Readings in Social Psychology*, ed. Eleanor Maccoby et al. (New York: Henry Holt, 1958).

15. See Solomon E. Asch, "Effects of Group Pressure upon the Modification and Distortion of Judgments," in Maccoby et al., *Readings in Social Psychology*, pp. 174–83.

16. Joseph Lohman and Dietrich Reitzes, "Deliberately Organized Groups and Racial Behavior," *American Sociolgical Review* 19 (June 1954): 342–44.

17. R. D. Minard, "Race Relations in the Pocahontas Coal Fields," *Journal of Social Issues* 8, no. 1 (1952): 29–44.

18. Theodore M. Newcomb, "Attitude Development as a Function of Reference Groups: The Bennington Study," in Maccoby et al., *Readings in Social Psychology*, pp. 265–75.

Fleur and Westie,[19] Gorden,[20] Merton and Kitt,[21] and Mead[22] indicate the way in which such variables as *organizational membership, work roles, reference groups, cultural norms,* and *primary group norms* can play a part in shaping and channeling overt action in ways that are to some extent uninfluenced by internal psychological predispositions. At the least, it must be recognized that the behavior patterns of a given individual can seldom be accurately interpreted on the basis of individual psychological variables *alone.* Individuals almost always act within a social context that they take into account when making decisions about their behavior. To explain, predict, or manipulate such behavior, reference must be made to the social norms, role systems, social controls, and hierarchies of social ranking that surround action, in order that it can be effectively understood.

The sociocultural processes present in a given individual's situation of action, then, are important determiners of the directions that such action will take, or indeed, whether action will occur at all. These actions can even be contrary to individual predisposition, although certainly this is not the general case. The more frequently occurring situation would be one in which sociocultural variables modify the way that psychological processes give rise to overt action.

The sociocultural model of the persuasion process suggested from these considerations is based upon the assumption that mass-communicated messages can be used to provide individuals with new and seemingly group-supported interpretations—social constructions of reality—regarding some phenomenon toward which they are acting. By so do-

19. De Fleur and Westie, "Verbal Attitudes."

20. Raymond L. Gorden, "Interaction Between Attitude and the Definition of the Situation in the Expression of Opinions," *American Sociological Review* 17 (1952): 50–58.

21. Robert Merton and A. Kitt, "Contributions to the Theory of Reference Group Behavior," in *Continuities in Social Research: Studies in the Scope and Method of the American Soldier,* ed. Robert Merton and Paul Lazarsfeld (Glencoe, Ill.: Free Press, 1950).

22. Margaret Mead, "Public Opinion Mechanisms among Primitive People," *Public Opinion Quarterly* 1, no. 3 (July 1937): 5–16.

ing, it may be possible to mediate the conduct of individuals as they derive definitions of appropriate behavior and belief from suggested interpretations communicated to them. Even in cases where individual predispositions run contrary to the suggested action, it may be possible to obtain compliance by suggesting a set of social and cultural constraints to which they feel compelled to conform. An even simpler situation would be one in which individuals have not yet formulated strong psychological predispositions one way or the other toward the object of persuasion. In such a case, they would hold few group-derived definitions of appropriate action toward it. Under such conditions, suggested definitions would pose little social or psychological conflict in following the modes of action prescribed by the communicator. Represented schematically, such a model of the persuasion process looks something like this:

But what are the means by which groups provide the individual with "sanctioned" or "approved" modes of conduct toward objects, events, or issues that are brought to the individual's attention? This apparently takes place in many ways. Such concepts as *norms, roles, social control,* and *social ranking* are some of the elements in the "definitions of situations" that are culturally provided for individuals acting in social settings. These group-derived definitions of situations specify modes of orientation toward a wide variety of objects and events toward which responses must habitually be made. These modes of orientation constitute an important part of the institutionalized patterns of social organization of human groups. With respect to innovations, or new ideas, beliefs, or things of any kind, groups and societies vary widely in the degree to which stable, institutionalized rules exist "ready-made" for prescribing actions of the individual toward new phenomena. Margaret Mead has described societies having rigid and deeply institutionalized cultures that provide the individual with a ready-made "reality" against which to interpret *any* new phenomenon. Other societies are at the other extreme, where individuals are on their own to construct modes of reaction to new events on the basis of their own internal processes.[23] The American society apparently lies somewhere between these two extremes. Individuals are members of groups that are of significance to them, but at the same time the social organization patterns of such groups are sufficiently complex, contradictory, and heterogeneous so that modes of reaction to new issues are not uniformly prescribed.

We may suggest, then, that anthropological, psychiatric, social-psychological, and sociological evidence indicates clearly that one of the main functions of groups is to provide shared definitions for members by means of which they can interpret and act with respect to realities to which they as individuals have only limited direct access at best. Realities are defined and interpreted within social frameworks. This generalization has often been called the *reality principle,* and the interactional process by means of which such definitions are achieved has been referred to as *consensual validation.*

These two concepts have bearing on the present conceptualization in that it is suggested the *persuasive messages presented via the mass media may provide the appearance of consensus regarding orientation and action with respect to a given object or goal of persuasion.* That is, such messages can present definitions to audiences in such a way that listeners are led to believe that these are the socially sanctioned modes of orientation their groups hold toward given objects or situations. The communicator thus provides social constructions of reality,

23. Ibid.

shortcutting the process of consensual validation, particularly with respect to objects or practices concerning which groups do not yet have fully institutionalized cultural interpretations, or in the case where such interpretations are not contrary to the goals of the persuasion.

In specific terms it can be suggested that the communicator can stress the way in which a specific *role* is defined (so as to include the use of the object of persuasion). Such messages can demonstrate how adoption of the communicator's goal is *normative* in the group within which this role lies. The communicator can show how the nonadopter is a *deviant* and a *nonconformist* (in the negative sense). The way in which negative *social sanctions* are brought to bear upon such deviants and nonconformists may be clarified. The fact that only persons of *low rank* would behave otherwise can be explained. At the same time, the manner in which *social rewards* and *social approval* are given to the adopter of the communicator's goals may be stressed. Finally, the manner in which adoption achieves *group integration,* and how such behavior is consistent with *group-approved values,* can be brought out.

To illustrate in concrete terms the actual use of the sociocultural model as a strategy for persuasion, we may examine the tactics used by certain types of charity drives, commonly called "United Appeals," "Community Funds," and so forth. Such persuasive campaigns make use of both the psychodynamic and the sociocultural models of the persuasive process. As will be seen, they not only use mass communications as part of their tactics but other types of messages as well.

For the sake of emphasis, we will assume a hypothetical group of individuals who are not particularly sympathetic to this form of campaign, preferring to make their donations privately and specifically to their favorite charity. As we shall see, in spite of their contrary internal predisposition they have little chance of resisting. In other words, it is very likely that they will be persuaded to make a donation when the persuasive campaign reaches them.

The first step in the campaign of the typical "United Appeal" type of solicitation is an announcement (via the mass media) that the community has a specific quota which must be met by the drive. Thus, a group *goal* is defined with the suggestion that this has widespread approval in the community. This goal has been arbitrarily formulated by the organizers of the drive, of course; it does not necessarily flow from grass-roots sentiment on the part of the community members. Nevertheless, it is very likely to go unchallenged. Goals have a rather compelling quality in themselves if it is believed that they have group support (consensus). Such an impression can be created by getting socially eminent persons in the community to participate in the announcement of the quota. Such persons are eager to confirm their high rank publicly by participating. The mass media will always obligingly give full coverage to such an event and thereby confer status upon it.

Another significant step is to announce to the community that the "fair share" for citizens is some specified percent of their earnings. This concept will also be given ample coverage by the media. The idea of a "fair share" is sociologically meaningful. It is compelling to the individual because it seems to be an approved and shared *norm*. Who wants to be identified as "unfair," and thus *deviant* from approved values? If our imaginary individuals are led to believe that others are in fact giving according to this norm, they will at least feel some pressure toward conformity.

At the heart of the persuasion campaign is the task of creating *role systems* that are linked to the fund drive within work and neighborhood groups in the community. In stores, factories, schools, and as many other organizations as possible, a "chairperson" for the drive is appointed with attendant publicity. Leaders of such organizations feel compelled to cooperate in this because of the need to maintain appearances that the organization operates in the interest of the public. The chairperson usually appoints collectors for various divisions of the organization if it is at all large. The rank and file member of the group must play a *counter-role* to the roles of these collectors within their work setting. When asked personally by another worker, it is difficult to refuse a donation.

A tactic sometimes used in this sociocultural strategy is to prepare and distribute to members an IBM card with their name on it and with a place to mark how much they are "pledging" (to be collected later). Persons who choose not to pledge anything must sometimes signify their deviancy by signing the card to indicate refusal, or personally tell the group collector that they will not make a donation.

If our hapless individuals, who really wanted to give their funds to another worthy cause, have not been persuaded by these strategies, they will be confronted with an even more compelling situation when they get home. The organizers of the campaign appoint "volunteer collectors" who will call on residents in their immediate area and request a donation. Here we have the role of *neighbor* and that of *good citizen* (which includes charity) locked into a reciprocal system in miniature. It is socially embarrassing to refuse a neighbor a reasonable and socially approved request for a modest donation. Potential negative sanctions underlie such refusal, to say nothing of a degradation of status. Who wants to be known to neighbors as a tightwad who would refuse to donate a modest sum to an important charitable cause. Therefore, our friends at this point reach into their pockets for some folding money, and possibly grit their teeth a little while they smilingly conform. However, for capitulation to social pressure they will be given positive reinforcement. They will get a little button to wear in their lapels, or at least a card to place in their window, that will help indicate to others the nature of the approved norms.

With the skillful use of the media, therefore, plus the use of goals, social norms, roles, social controls, and ranking in real ways, such campaigns can be very successful. The variables utilized give potential donors an unmistakable "definition of the situation" and place them within a set of sociocultural constraints that are nearly impossible to ignore. While this rather complex illustration of sociocultural strategy does not use mass communications exclusively, they occupy a central place in the activities of the persuaders. In other adaptations of this strategy, the entire persuasive effort might behandled by the media alone. If there is any doubt that this strategy is widely used, the reader is invited to spend an evening before the TV set viewing commercials within the perspective of the sociocultural strategy. The smiling and happy people who act out their little dramas concerning beer, laxatives, deodorants, and denture paste are offering a most fascinating variety of "definitions of the situation." It is made abundantly clear that to be caught with the wrong beer, with detectable body odor, inactive bowels, or loose dentures place one far outside the pale of social respectability.

There are undoubtedly numerous other ways in which persuasion processes could be conceptualized. The psychodynamic and the sociocultural strategies, however, seem to capture two widely used models of persuasion via mass communication.

12

Toward an
INTEGRATED
THEORY
of
MASS MEDIA
EFFECTS

The foregoing chapters have presented a variety of theoretical issues and perspectives on mass communication. A number of these have pertained to the patterns of growth of the media and their functioning in society. Several have reviewed the way in which people are exposed to media messages. Others deal with the effects of those messages on behavior. The present chapter returns once again to the effects issue in an attempt to place it in a broader context.

We have seen that there are theories of specific effects, such as those dealing with the impact of televised violence.

We have also seen that there are theoretical formulations concerning media persuasion, such as the psychodynamic and sociocultural models outlined in chapter 11. What we lack is a *general* theory of the effects of mass communication on individuals and society. Such a theory should provide an explanatory framework for a broad range of media effects including audience cognitions, feelings, and overt behavior.

The present chapter sketches the outlines of an integrated theory. This includes identifying major factors and variables that must be part of such a theory as well as identifying many of the relationships that prevail between these components. While this effort requires presentation of some new material, much that has already been presented in previous chapters can now be pulled together.

At this point in time, our skeleton integrated theory must remain both rather tentative and vague in places because the underlying specific formulations from which it is drawn are in many cases themselves tentative and vague. Even so, its outlines can be perceived; and it is important to grope toward such a higher level of abstraction in order to understand where our research and analyses appear to be leading us.

SPECIFIC THEORIES AS STARTING POINTS

How does one start to develop an "integrated" theory? In any scientific field, efforts toward integration begin with specific formulations that deal with defined aspects of a process. These more specific theories are grouped together into some logical and empirically valid configuration. More abstract propositions and statements of relationship among components in the configuration are then induced.

Turning to mass communication, what are these more specific theories and what do they tell us? Starting with basics, we know from the discussion in chapter 5 that a prerequisite of effective mass communication is a *mode of message sending* that reduces noise to a minimum so that the message reaching the audience is pretty much the same as that intended and sent by the mass communicator. Moreover, the perspectives discussed in chapter 9 on how audiences *encounter the media* pull together a substantial body of theory and research to demonstrate the basic psychological and social mechanisms that prevent the media from having *arbitrary control* over their audiences. The theory and research discussed in chapter 9 also presents a strong challenge to the theoretical notions about *mass society* discussed earlier (chapter 6). Rather than assume the loose unconnectedness of people that would necessarily prevail in a mass society, it was shown that members of the media audience relate themselves to one another in groups and are engaged in stable *social relations*. These associations not only produce and maintain social realities that individuals share to varying degrees, but also operate to insulate individuals from easy media manipulation. These several theoretical issues must continue to be taken into account.

Chapter 7 showed that the media are *social systems* that operate according to specific goals, values, organizational style, and technological capabilities. Earlier, in chapters 1 through 4, our examination of the historical development of each of our contemporary American media illustrated how they emerged as systems with specific forms *shaped by their surrounding sociocultural context* and underwent progressive change as that sociocultural context changed. These earlier chapters also provide concrete illustrations of the fundamental sociological proposition that current media systems remain *linked to the larger society* in systemic ways.

In other words, the media do not exist in a vacuum. The behavior of a given medium is not only governed by the dictates of its own internal system, but is also affected and limited by the characteristics and context of the societal system within which it operates. Media content must be compatible with the sociocultural context as a whole in order for it to be comprehensible and desirable to an audience large enough for the medium to achieve its economic goals. Furthermore, media personnel are products of their society with learning experiences affecting every aspect of their communication behavior.

In as brief a form as possible we can now summarize what has been said up to this point in our overview of previous chapters:

> Mass media not only lack arbitrary influence powers, but their personnel lack the freedom to engage in arbitrary communication behavior. Both the media and their audiences are integral parts of their society. The surrounding sociocultural context provides mechanisms of constraint not only on the nature of media messages but also on the nature of their effects on audiences.

These broad propositions must be a part of any attempt to construct an integrated general perspective on mass media effects. For the most part, however, these propositions describe *limitations* on effects. As previous chapters have shown, the majority of scientific evidence gathered from laboratory and survey approaches to the study of media effects finds the media to have little *direct* influence on people, or only limited power under restricted circumstances.

On the other hand, theorists such as Harold Innis, Charles Cooley, and Daniel Lerner, plus a host of others from the past and the present, make a convincing case that the coming of new media to a society makes a tremendous difference in the lives of people and in the social process. Our discussion of media technology and social change in chapter 1 provided specific illustrations of this from the past.

We are caught, then, in a dilemma. A trustworthy method—science—says the media have few effects. Another trustworthy method—careful study by insightful historians and other analysts of the broader picture—say that they have sweeping effects. Is this a flat contradiction, or have these two approaches operated on different levels of abstraction? We feel the latter is the case. Most scientific work is conducted in the here and now, looking for immediate signs that specific persons have been altered by specific messages. Things probably do not work that way. Specific theories resulting from a scientific approach (individual differences, social relations, theories of response to violence, and the like) show many *limitations* on media power. Yet, here we are about to develop a theory that shows the media have a number of rather powerful effects on people. We are also saying that this theory can be obtained in part from the same specific theories that mainly pose limitations on effects.

To unravel this dilemma, we need first to return to some of the classical analyses that were formulated by sociologists observing the growth of urban-industrial society. These theoretical sources identify features of societies and their changing patterns that lead one logically to the assumption of broad patterns of media influence. These range from Durkheim's structural complexity theories[1] through Tönnies's Gemeinschaft-Gesellschaft typology[2] to Marx's dialectical mechanisms for change.[3] All these analyses of growing societal complexity lay the theoretical foundation for concluding that as mass media develop, they play a significant role in people's lives.

Essentially, these theories were developed before the media themselves were well developed. Furthermore, they did not actually address the problem of media. Nevertheless, a common theoretical theme that emerges from these writings is that as informal relationships characteristic of more traditional nonindustrial societies come into decline, unfulfilled needs for information rise accordingly. Extending this

1. Emile Durkheim, *The Division of Labor in Society*, trans. George Simpson (New York: Free Press of Glencoe, 1964).
2. Ferdinand Tönnies, *Community and Service*, trans. and ed. Charles Loomis (East Lansing, Mich.: State University Press, 1957).
3. Karl Marx, *Economic and Philosophic Manuscripts of 1844* (Moscow: Foreign Languages Publishing House, 1961).

reasoning, it follows that *people become dependent on media external to their groups when informal channels beyond their immediate groups begin to be disrupted*. As these informal channels become more difficult to maintain, as is the case in the shift from mechanical to organic solidarity, or from Gemeinschaft to Gesellschaft, or from communal to associative (bureaucratic) society—and as the structure becomes more complex, people have less and less contact with the social system *as a whole*. In other words, they begin to be less aware of what is going on in their society beyond their own position in the structure.

These propositions are easily derivable from the very heart of classical theories of societal change. They definitely do not represent a reversion to naive assumptions of a mass society lacking in meaningful group ties. The central derived proposition merely states that existing informal ties in societies of complex structure are not able to supply many needs people have for specific categories of information. This elementary fact of dependency on external media in increasingly complex structures provides the key to the development of an integrated perspective on the effects of the media.

What kinds of effects are we alluding to? They are the kinds of effects that are not easily detected in laboratory experiments, or in before-after studies of people who have been exposed to specific messages. We are referring to the enlargement of people's belief systems that new media bring; to the formation of attitudes toward a constant flow of new topics; to subtle shifts of individual and collective sentiment that may not be seen in the actions of individuals; and to a number of other kinds of society-wide changes. We believe that these changes come about mainly because mass media are present, and operating, in the society. In the section that follows, the basic assumptions of what we will now call a *dependency theory* of audience-media-society relations are set forth in an attempt to show that media effects *do* occur, even though most of our prior chapters have stressed limitations on such effects.

A DEPENDENCY THEORY OF AUDIENCE-MEDIA-SOCIETY RELATIONS

It is not necessary to subscribe to either the more naive assumptions of mass society theories or unsophisticated accusations of media conspiracies to conclude that the media influence many important aspects of our lives. Rather, we assume that the ultimate basis of media influence lies in the nature of the three-way relationship between the larger social system, the media's role in that system, and audience relationships to the media. This line of thinking is a departure from previous perspectives. It is at the same time more general and more abstract. It contrasts with approaches that focus solely on the nature of the individual or the nature of the society as the birthplace of media influence. We propose that the nature of the tripartite audience-media-society *relationship* most directly determines many of the effects that the media have on people and society.

While a number of aspects of audience-media-society relationships could be discussed, the one we focus upon first is the high level of *dependence* of audiences on mass media information resources in urban-industrial societies. The primary reason for this focus is that the degree of audience dependence on media information is a key variable in understanding when and why media messages alter audience beliefs, feelings, or behavior.

Dependency on media information is a ubiquitous condition in modern society. One finds it in settings ranging from the need to find the best buys at the supermarket to more general or pervasive needs such as obtaining information that will help maintain a sense of connectedness and familiarity with the social world outside one's neighborhood. There are numerous ways in which people are dependent on media to satisfy information needs. For example, one form of dependency is based on the need to *understand* one's social world; another type of dependency arises from the need to *act* meaningfully and effectively in that world; still a third type of dependency is based on the need for *fantasy-escape* from daily problems and tensions. The greater the need and consequently the stronger the dependency in such matters, the greater the likelihood that the information supplied will alter various forms of audience cognitions, feelings, and behavior.

As societies grow more complex, and as the quality of media technology improves, the media take on more and more *unique* information-delivery functions. In the American society, for example, the media are presumed to have several unique functions. They operate as a Fourth Estate delivering information about the actions of government; they serve as the primary signaling system in case of emergencies; they constitute the principal source of the ordinary citizen's conceptions of national and world events; they provide enormous amounts of entertainment information for fantasy-escape.

Some media information-delivery functions are more socially central than others: some are more essential than others for societal and individual well-being. Providing national sports coverage to residents of small towns is probably a less central function than providing them with information about national economic or political decisions that strongly affect their lives. It can be hypothesized that the greater the number and centrality of the specific information-delivery functions served by a medium, the greater the audience and societal dependency on that medium.

The second condition in which dependency is heightened occurs when a relatively high degree of change and conflict is present in a society. Forces operating to maintain the structural stability of a society always coexist with forces toward conflict and change. The relative distribution of forces for stability or for change varies over time and place. Societies undergoing modernization, for example, experience high levels of conflict leading to rapid change until societal adaptations are made which reduce conflict and promote structural stability. Social conflict and social change usually involve challenges to established institutions, beliefs, or practices. When such challenges are effective, established social arrangements become, to one degree or another, inadequate as frameworks within which members of a society can cope with the situation. People's dependence on media information resources is intensified during such periods. This is a joint consequence of the reduced adequacy of their established social arrangements and the media's capacity to acquire and transmit information that facilitates reconstruction of arrangements. We can hypothesize, therefore, in societies with developed media systems, that audience dependency on media information increases as the level of structural instability (societal conflict and change) increases.

These basic propositions of dependency theory can be summarized as follows: The potential for mass media messages to achieve a broad range of cognitive, affective, and behavioral effects will be increased when media systems serve many unique and central information-delivery functions. That potential will be further increased when there is a high degree of structural instability in the society due to conflict and change. We need to add, however, the idea that altering audience cognitive, affective, and behavioral conditions can feed back in turn to alter both society and the media. This is what was meant by a tripartite relationship between media, audience and society. The general relationships implied in these propositions are presented in diagrammatic form in figure 8.

We can now illustrate how dependency theory predicts certain types of effects. We will attempt to identify specific kinds of cognitive, affective, and behavioral changes in people that are regularly brought about by the mass media because of their information delivery functions in society.

Cognitive Effects The term cognitive has replaced what an older psychology or the ordinary person might call "mental" effects. These are effects on inner or psychic variables of the type discussed earlier in sections on psychodynamic persua-

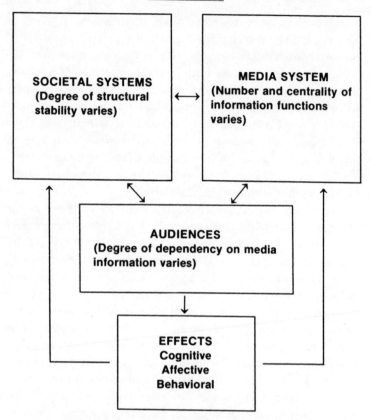

FIGURE 8. SOCIETY, MEDIA, AND AUDIENCE:
RECIPROCAL RELATIONSHIPS.

sion. Cognitive effects are distinct from effects on overt behavior, but the two may be functionally related. This section
makes reference to people's feelings of ambiguity, their attitudes, beliefs, and values.

The creation and resolution of *ambiguity* serves as the
first example of a cognitive alteration effect that is particularly likely to receive the attention of investigators working
from a dependency model.

Ambiguity is a problem of either insufficient or conflicting information.[4] Ambiguity can occur because people lack enough information to understand the meaning of an event, or because they lack adequate information to determine which of several possible interpretations of an event is the correct one. Research evidence shows that when unexpected events occur, such as natural disasters or the assassination of a political leader, many people first become aware of them through mass media information channels.[5] When the initial information gathered and delivered by the media is incomplete, feelings of ambiguity are created whereby audience members know that an event has occurred, but do not know what it means or how to interpret it. More information will probably be sought in attempts to resolve such ambiguity. In many instances, the only source for that information is the mass media. The ambiguity resulting from incomplete or conflicting media reports will probably be resolved by more complete information subsequently delivered by media to their audiences. In such cases, the media's role in ambiguity creation and resolution is relatively easy to see.

What is perhaps harder to see, but what may have more sociopolitical significance, is the extent to which people are dependent on the media for continuous or ongoing ambiguity resolution. People living in times of rapid social change, in settings marked by relative instability or social conflict, or confronted with specific situations in which something unexpected has occurred will often experience ambiguity. Such ambiguity is usually stressful. Ambiguity can be resolved in a matter of seconds where media information delivery is adequate, or it can persist for days, months, or even years in the absence of such media information.

4. S. J. Ball-Rokeach, "From Pervasive Ambiguity to a Definition of the Situation," *Sociometry* 36, no. 3 (September 1973): 378–89.
5. See, for example, Paul B. Sheatsley and Jacob J. Feldman, "The Assassination of President Kennedy," in R. Evans, *Readings in Collective Behavior* (Chicago: Rand-McNally, 1969), pp. 259–83.

Thus, *dependency* on the media for resolution of ambiguity is easy to understand. When people become heavily dependent upon the mass media for the information they need to resolve ambiguity, the defining or structuring effect of mass-mediated information is considerable. The media do not have the power to determine uniformly the exact content of the interpretations or "definitions of the situation" that every person constructs. But, by controlling what information is and is not delivered and how that information is presented, the media can play a large role in limiting the range of interpretations that audiences are able to make.

Examination of the essential roles played by the media in periods of modernization suggests that the media clearly have such a role in the reconstruction of social reality.[6] Persons living in societies undergoing change from traditional to industrial forms experience pervasive ambiguity. This ambiguity is particularly acute during the period between their psychological unhitching from traditional customs, values, and world views and their adoption of more modern versions. The utility of having relatively standardized information packaged and transmitted via media by those agencies seeking to promote and control the modernization process has long been recognized. Control over such media information delivery is essential precisely because of the need to control how people resolve ambiguity.

Another cognitive effect that can be particularly common when audiences rely heavily upon media information resources to keep up with their changing world is *attitude formation*. During any year or decade in recent history, numerous instances of media-initiated attitude formation can be found. Publics have formed new attitudes about such events as speed limits, environmental problems, energy crises, specific wars, and political corruption. New attitudes are continually being formed as various persons gain the public eye. Modern society presents a constant parade of new political

6. Daniel Lerner, *The Passing of Traditional Society* (New York: Free Press, 1959).

figures, religious leaders, sports personalities, scientists, and artists. There is also a seemingly endless variety of social movements toward which orientations must be worked out. Even physical objects become the focus of attitude formation. These can include new household gadgets, clothing, birth-control devices, car safety mechanisms, and innovations in communication technology. The media push a never-ending flow of such events, issues, objects, and persons into public attention. People work out their feelings toward them as they confront this flow.

The media are not monolithic in their influence on such attitudes. The selectivity processes emphasized in earlier perspectives undoubtedly play a role in the attitude formation process. Likewise, local community opinion leaders selectively channel people's atttention to events and influence the content or intensity of the attitude formed. Nevertheless, these psychological and social processes probably play more of a role in determining the *specific* content and intensity of the attitudes formed than they do in determining which events, people, or objects are likely to become candidates for attitude formation.

Another cognitive effect centers around the media's role in *agenda-setting*. Neither individuals nor their opinion leaders control the selection activities of the media that sort among potential topics for presentation or among available sets of information about those topics. Moreover, even though the media deliver information on a broad range of topics, people have neither the time nor the energy to form attitudes and beliefs about everything. They must select some more limited set of topics and issues about which to concern themselves. It is out of this set of necessities that the effect of agenda-setting takes place.[7] We need to understand two major features of this process. First, why is there a considerable similarity in the agenda of concern regarding certain

7. For a discussion of the various ways in which the term agenda-setting has been used, see Jack McLeod, Lee Becker, and James Byrnes," Another Look at the Agenda-Setting Function of the Press," *Communication Research* 1 (April 1974): 131–66.

types of topics among members of the media audience? Second, in spite of such instances of similarity, why do members of the public who attend to the media show numerous differences in their agendas of concern regarding media presented topics?

This seeming dilemma between tendencies toward both uniformity and differences in personal agendas can be resolved quite simply. Not all persons respond uniformly to media-presented information on a given topic; this has been understood by social scientists since the early formation of the individual differences perspective. People select material from the media in somewhat predictable ways that are related to their personality characteristics, problems, and needs. This does not mean that media audiences show no uniformities, however. We noted earlier that the social categories perspective permitted predictions to be made about differences in media habits because a given set of people were located at a similar point in the social structure (e.g., older, white, farmers in the Midwest vs. younger, black, industrial workers in urban areas).

From the individual differences and social categories perspectives come hypotheses concerning the agenda-setting effects of the media. To be certain, specific individuals will set their personal agendas in relation to their unique background of prior socialization, experience, and personality structure. However, the society produces broad strata of people with sufficient uniformity of social circumstances that they share many problems and concerns in greater or lesser degree in spite of individual differences. In our society, for example, many people are wage-earners with limited monetary resources to obtain their mass-produced necessities. In this sense they are *alike* regardless of their personality differences; they share a concern over such matters as rising prices, taxes, unemployment, and other economic matters that can quickly alter their standard of living. These override their individual differences. Thus, when the media present information of importance on economic matters, these topics can be expected to be placed high on their agendas of concern.

Where individual differences play an important role in agenda-setting is with respect to topics that are less tied to such social locations. Animal lovers of any social category will be likely to attend to and respond strongly to media-delivered stories of mistreatment of animals. People of all walks of life who enjoy fishing are likely to include in their agendas new policies of the Fish and Game Department.

Agenda-setting, in other words, is an interactional process. Topics are sorted by the media for presentation to the public. Information about those topics is selectively assembled and selectively disseminated. The public then sorts out their interest and concern with this information as a function of both their individual differences in personal makeup and their location in societal strata and categories. Out of this system of variables and factors emerges a list of topics to which varying numbers of people give differential assignments of importance. That list is the agenda of the media audience as a whole.

Still another cognitive effect that occurs in a media-dependent society is the expansion of people's systems of *beliefs*. Charles H. Cooley long ago used the term "enlargement" to refer to the idea that people's knowledge and belief systems expand because they learn about other people, places, and things from the mass media.[8] This idea can be more specifically explained by examining what Altman and Taylor call the "breadth" dimension of belief structure.[9] Beliefs are organized into categories. These categories, pertaining to religion, family, politics, etc., reflect the major areas of a person's social activity. The breadth dimension refers to the number of categories in a belief system and

8. Charles Cooley, *Social Organizations* (New York: Scribner's, 1909).
9. Irwin Altman and Dalmas A. Taylor, *Social Penetration* (New York: Holt, Rinehart & Winston, 1973), pp. 15–20.

how many beliefs are found in each category. Belief systems can be broadened (enlarged) by either increasing the number of categories or the number of beliefs in a given category. For example, the vast amount of new information about ecological matters disseminated by the media in recent years has surely fostered the enlargement of people's beliefs about everything from automobiles to "Baggies," from babies to compacters, and so on. These can be incorporated into existing opinions, attitudes, and values concerning free enterprise, recreation, work, religion, and the family. By their constant surveillance and presentation of aspects of the changing social and physical world we live in, the media broaden their audiences' belief categories and enlarge their belief systems.

The final cognitive effect that needs consideration is the media's impact on *values*. Values may be defined as very basic beliefs that people hold about either "desirable end states of existence" (e.g., salvation, equality, freedom) or "preferred modes of conduct" (e.g., honest, forgiving, capable).[10] Only under rare conditions would we expect mass media information to be able singlehandedly to alter such basic beliefs.[11] Mass-mediated information can, however, play an important part in creating the conditions for *value clarification*. One way that the media facilitate value clarification is by presenting information that precipitates *value conflict* within audience members. For example, the recent civil rights and ecology movements not only received broad media coverage, but also involved fundamental value conflicts. Civil rights movements posed a conflict between individual freedom (e.g., property rights) and equality (e.g., human rights). Ecology movements bring economic values into conflict with aesthetic and survival values.

Most people did not, however, have the interest, inclination, or information necessary to see these issues as value

10. Milton Rokeach, *The Nature of Human Values* (New York: Free Press, 1973).

11. Ibid.

conflicts. Mass-mediated information, in the form of reports of statements made by movement leaders or in the form of interpretations of the movement's motives and actions, usually includes identification of the underlying value conflicts. Once the value conflicts inherent in such movements are posed and clarified by the media, audience members are moved to articulate their own value positions. This articulation can be painful because it can force a choice between mutually incompatible goals and the means for obtaining them. For action to take place, however, choices must be made. In the process of trying to decide which is more important in a particular case, general value priorities become clarified. Thus, the media indirectly have had a cognitive impact on members of their audiences.

Affective Effects   Affective processes are those we generally refer to in terms of various categories of feelings and emotions. Human beings like and dislike; they fear, hate, love, and are amused by various features of their environment. In a society that has developed a considerable dependency on its media for information, affective change in people can be anticipated when the media deliver such information.

The impact of media messages on an audience's feelings and emotional responses is one of the least explored kinds of effects. Nevertheless, a limited body of writing on the matter makes some suggestions. It has been hypothesized that prolonged exposure to violent media content has a "numbing" or *desensitization* effect.[12] Such effects may promote insensitivity or the lack of a desire to help others when violent encounters are witnessed in real life. Along a similar line, Hyman has pointed out that social scientists have not paid attention to the effects of violent media content on audience *sentiments*.[13]

12. For example, see Frederich Wertham, *Seduction of the Innocent* (New York: Holt, Rinehart & Winston, 1954); and A. Rosenthal, *Thirty-eight Witnesses* (New York: McGraw-Hill, 1964).

13. Herbert Hyman, "Mass Communication and Socialization," *Public Opinion Quarterly* 37, no. 4 (Winter 1973): 524–40.

There is some evidence to suggest that the level of physiological arousal caused by exposure to audio-visual portrayals of violence does decline over time. But such evidence is no substitute for the kind of direct research on emotional responses that Hyman is calling for.

Fear, anxiety, and *trigger-happiness* are illustrations of affective effects that could be researched. For example, prolonged exposure to news messages or even TV dramas that portray cities as violence-ridden jungles may increase people's fear or anxiety about living in or even traveling to the city. In a state of anticipation of the worst, city residents or visitors may be emotionally triggered to respond violently to others' actions. These kinds of effects may be particularly likely for residents of nonmetropolitan areas who depend largely on the media for information about what's going on in the cities, and who have little firsthand experience with city life.

Actually, almost all media effects could be examined in terms of their affective dimension. For example, the affective element of attitude formation can have serious social consequences. In periods of intense social conflict the police may form a number of attitudes from media characterizations about groups with which they have to deal. If media-derived attitudes contain affective elements such as *anger, hostility,* and *frustration,* it may retard the ability of the police to keep their cool when the encounter actually comes. Exactly this pattern developed in 1968 in Chicago during the disruptions of the Democratic National Convention.

Morale and *alienation* serve as the final examples of the kinds of alterations in audience affect that can result from media messages. Klapp has proposed that in societies in which the mass media play central communication roles, the nature of media information has substantial effects on people's morale and level of alienation.[14] The reason why can be found in the pioneering writings of Emile Durkheim.[15]

14. Orrin Klapp, *Currents of Unrest* (New York: Holt, Rinehart & Winston, 1972).

15. Durkheim, *Division of Labor in Society.*

The sense of collective well-being and "we feeling" that promotes morale and combats alienation is a fragile product of successful social relations that cannot be developed or maintained without effective communication systems. A key element in that effective communication is the presence of regular and positive information about the groups and categories to which people belong, such as their society, community, profession, or ethnic group. People who rely on mass media systems as a primary source of information about their groups and categories can thus experience changes in morale and level of alienation when there are notable changes in the quantity or quality of the information delivered by the media about those collectives. According to this line of reasoning, any number of groups including women, blacks, Native Americans, or even Americans generally would be expected to undergo increased or decreased morale and changes in level of alienation as the nature of media messages about them underwent change.

Behavioral Effects Overt action is, of course, the kind of effect that interests most people. Changes in attitude, belief, and affective states are interesting as well, but it is the degree to which they influence overt action that makes them important. Of the numerous effects of media messages on behavior that could be considered, we have chosen to discuss *activation* and *deactivation*.[16] Activation refers to instances in which audience members do something that they would not otherwise have done as a consequence of receiving media messages.

As already suggested, activation may be the end product of elaborate cognitive or affective effects. For example, people may engage in *issue formation* or *issue resolution* as a consequence of attitudes they have formed and feelings they have developed. Take as an illustration, people whose primary contact with the contemporary women's movement

16. For an earlier discussion of activation effects, see Otto N. Larsen, "Social Effects of Mass Communication," in *Handbook of Modern Sociology*, ed. Robert E. L. Faris (Chicago: Rand McNally, 1964), p. 348.

is via the media. They may initially react to movement leaders' allegations of "sexism" with ambiguity, perhaps not even knowing what the term means. The problem of resolving ambiguity and the stress that accompanies it gain a high place on their cognitive agenda. Resolution of ambiguity leads to the formation of new attitudes and feelings about sexual equality and the women's movement. The culmination of this chain of effects is a felt need to act. Once established, the need to act is transformed into overt action by public expression of these new attitudes and feelings, thereby participating in issue formation. Subsequent media information, such as an announcement of a protest in support of a proposal made by a women's group, may further activate people to join the protest, while others may be activated to organize a counter-protest. These overt actions become part of the issue resolution process.

So much attention has been given to the undesirable behavioral consequences of television content that it might be well to mention briefly one socially desirable behavioral effect. Stein and Friedrich's recent research suggests that TV viewers may be activated to engage in both prosocial and antisocial behavior.[17] Subjects in their research who viewed a popular children's show ("Mr. Rogers") increased their level of cooperative activity over several weeks of exposure. Those subjects exposed to violent content, on the other hand, increased their level of aggressive activity. Thus the research showed that both *cooperation* and *aggression* may be activated, depending on the nature of the television message received.

Research conducted in the 1940s suggests that media messages may activate altruistic economic behavior. Merton examined how a radio marathon featuring a well-known singer of that era (Kate Smith) activated large numbers of

17. Aletha Stein and Lynette Friedrich, "Television Content and Young Children's Behavior," in *Television and Social Behavior* (Washington, D.C.: Government Printing Office, 1971), 2:202–317.

people to buy war bonds.[18] Processes by which media messages are used to activate charitable contributions were examined in chapter 11.

In many instances, such as voting and consumption, deactivation, or what people would have otherwise done but which they *don't* do as a consequence of media messages, can be as important as what they are activated to do. Yet deactivation effects have not received as much research attention. *Not* voting and *not* consuming provide two examples of deactivation effects that could be examined. Most people are heavily dependent on the media for information about state and national political contests and about the state of the economy. Political campaigns have not only become longer, but have also depended more and more on the media to communicate to voters. Such campaigns may not change many established attitudes toward the contestants. They might, however, elicit affective responses, such as overwhelming boredom, disgust, or cognitive assessments so that it makes no difference who wins. These inner states can culminate in nonvoting or the deactivation of people's intention to vote.

Likewise, when media messages help to create an affective state of fear about one's own and the nation's economic future or the belief that a depression is unavoidable, people may *not* buy stocks, new cars, certain foods, or a multitude of other products that they would have otherwise bought. This would actually have the effect of deepening a recession by too much deactivation of consumption behavior.

Having outlined the assumptions of the dependency theory of media-audience relations and some of the alteration effects it aids in understanding, we are now ready to address the problem of bringing this theory together with the previously discussed perspectives on factors that inhibit media influence.

18. Robert Merton, *Mass Persuasion: The Social Psychology of a War Bond Drive* (New York: Harper, 1946).

AN INTEGRATED MODEL OF MASS MEDIA EFFECTS

The basic elements of an integrated theory of mass media effects are presented in figure 9. This diagram presents an almost overwhelmingly complex set of factors and variables. Yet it is within such a complex system that mass communication effects are generated. We can summarize the relationships symbolized in the diagram in the following terms:

A flow of events emerges from a societal or sociocultural system. The societal system has its established culture consisting of material artifacts, symbolic processes, values, and regulative mechanisms. The dynamic processes of culture include forces toward stability, such as consensus and adaptation, as well as forces for conflict and change. The structure of the societal system includes informal and formal groups, with roles, norms, social control, and ranking procedures. Structure also includes various demographic categories.

This general societal system sets important limitations and boundaries on the media system and has considerable impact on its characteristics, information-delivery functions, and operating procedures. The societal system also has enormous impact upon persons; it gives rise to mechanisms that inhibit arbitrary media influence, such as individual differences, membership in social categories, and participation in social relations. The societal system also operates to create needs within persons that facilitate media alteration effects, namely, the needs to understand, act in, and escape in fantasy from one's world.

Media systems cover the flow of events emanating from the societal system and persons acting within that system. Operating procedures arise from the characteristics of the media system itself. These characteristics include its economic goals, values, technology, and organization. These in turn influence the number and the centrality of its information-delivery functions. The major product of media sur-

FIGURE 9. MASS MEDIA EFFECTS: AN INTEGRATED MODEL

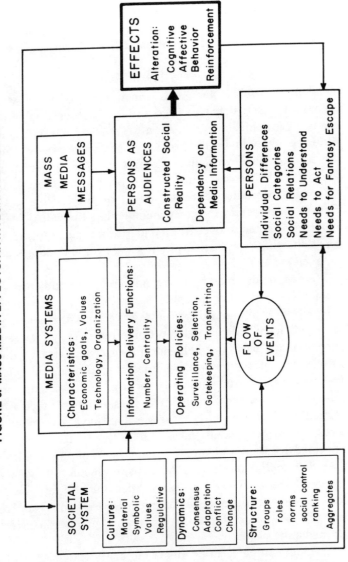

veillance of the flow of events, the sorting of those events, and the processing of information about those events through gatekeepers is the delivery of selected information pertaining to a limited range of topics. This constitutes media messages about the flow of events and the information available to the audience.

The key to this integrated framework is that persons as members of media audiences encounter media messages with both constructed social realities and considerable dependency on media information resources. The social realities people hold are the product of the processes by which the societal system enculturates and socializes persons and structures their social action. The dependencies people have on media information are a product of the nature of the sociocultural system, category membership, individual needs, and the number and centrality of the unique information functions that the media system serves for individuals and for society.

When media messages are not linked to audience dependencies and when people's social realities are entirely adequate before and during message reception, media messages will have little or no alteration effects. They may reinforce existing beliefs or behavioral forms. In contrast, when people do not have social realities that provide adequate frameworks for understanding, acting, and escaping, and when audiences are dependent in these ways on media information received, such messages will have a number of alteration effects. Media messages, in this instance, may be expected to alter audience behavior in terms of cognitive, affective, and/or overt activity. Thus, both the relative adequacy of the audience's social realities and the relative degree of audience dependency on media information resources must be taken into account to explain and predict the effects of media messages.

Finally, the effects of media messages flow back to influence people's needs or psychological and social characteristics. In some cases, they flow back to alter the nature of the societal system itself. Behavioral alteration effects, for example, in some rare instance may take the form of massive protest which not only gets people involved in producing a new series of events to be covered by the media, but may also increase the level of societal conflict, alter societal norms, or create new social groups. This series of events, in turn, can force changes in the nature of the relationships between the societal system and the media system, such as the passing of new laws designed to change the media's operating policies.

The rather complex model presented in figure 9, then, allows for a continuous process of interaction between the societal system, the media system, and the people who compose media audiences. It is also a feedback model in the sense that the effects of media messages on the audience about ongoing events may themselves set into motion another chain of events. Most important, this model avoids a seemingly untenable all-or-none position: the media have no significant impact on people and society, or the media have an unbounded capacity to manipulate people and society. It allows us to specify in a limited way when and why media messages will or will not have significant effects upon how audiences think, feel, and behave.

Other social scientists will undoubtedly wish to make additions to, revise, or even reject totally this integrated model of mass media effects. Nevertheless, we believe that it is a more theoretically sophisticated and sounder framework than has heretofore been available. There is little doubt that it is *very complicated*. For that we offer no apology! The process of mass communication is itself dreadfully complicated. Little wonder that numerous oversimplified approaches to describing it have failed to portray the effects it can have on people individually and collectively.

The present theory is obviously developed at a level of abstraction that would make a simple all-or-none test with empirical data impossible. This is a characteristic of every integrated theory. One must go to the specific theories for empirical testing and not to the abstract integrations induced from them.

The overall implications are that the study of mass communication—one of our newest academic disciplines—has already advanced to a point where such an integration can be attempted. The present formulation may prove hopelessly premature. Yet, if this model acts only to provoke others to denounce it and to formulate a better theory, the result will be advances in mass media theory and research. Under such circumstances, we will be satisfied. When all is said and done, the common purpose of social science examinations of the media and their relationship to people, whether of yesterday, today, or tomorrow, is ultimately to understand mass communication's impact on how we think, feel, and behave.

Index